PLACE AND PERSISTENCE IN THE LIVES OF
NEWFOUNDLAND WOMEN

PLACE AND PERSISTENCE IN THE LIVES OF
NEWFOUNDLAND WOMEN

For the women of Newfoundland

Place and Persistence in the Lives of Newfoundland Women

MARILYN PORTER

Department of Sociology
Memorial University of Newfoundland

Avebury

Aldershot · Brookfield USA · Hong Kong · Singapore · Sydney

Published by
Avebury
Ashgate Publishing Limited
Gower House
Croft Road
Aldershot
Hants GU11 3HR
England

Ashgate Publishing Company
Old Post Road
Brookfield
Vermont 05036
USA

British Library Cataloguing in Publication Data

Porter, Marilyn
    Place and Persistence in the Lives
    of Newfoundland Women
    I. Title
    305.4209718

ISBN 1 85628 444 1

Typeset by
Denise Porter
General Office, Science Building
Memorial University of Newfoundland
St. John's, Newfoundland, Canada
A1B 3X9

Printed and Bound in Great Britain by
Athenaeum Press Ltd, Newcastle upon Tyne.

Contents

Acknowledgements

This book covers a span of ten years work. It would be impossible to acknowledge all the many people who have given me different kinds of help, support and encouragement over that period. My colleagues in the Department of Sociology, and the closely associated Department of Anthropology and in the Women's Studies Programme have given me ideas, references and 'facts' in generous dosages, challenged my ideas and clarified my thinking. I would like to mention, in particular, Peter Sinclair, Bob Hill, Larry Felt, Raoul Andersen, Gordon Inglis, Barb Neis and Linda Kealey. Camelita McGrath, Sandy Pottle, Bev Brown and Elke Dettmar worked on the projects in Catalina, Grand Falls and South East Bight and made distinctive and valuable contributions. The women's community in St. John's was both supportive and inspirational. In particular the Women's Centre, the Provincial Advisory Council on the Status of Women and the Women's Policy Office offered me help, feedback and support. Many people wrestled with my handwriting and/or made me use a computer. For their endless patience, I thank Judi Smith, Annette Carter, Marilyn Hicks and her staff in the General Office, Larry Felt, Ellen Balka and Luke Porter. Central to the whole project are, of course, the many women in Newfoundland who let me talk to them, gather material from them and generally share their ideas and experiences with me. In particular the women of Aquaforte, Grand Bank, Catalina, Grand Falls and South East Bight were open and generous in every kind of way. Many other Newfoundland friends have been patient and accepting and gradually trained me to understand this place a little better. Finally my family, which has grown and changed over the last decade — Luke who wanted to grow up in Newfoundland and who knows about computers, Fenelia who lost interest in Barbie dolls and now keeps me abreast of the new generation of feminists and my mother, Nan Smith, who has been so resolute a feminist (by many names) and who always reads my work.

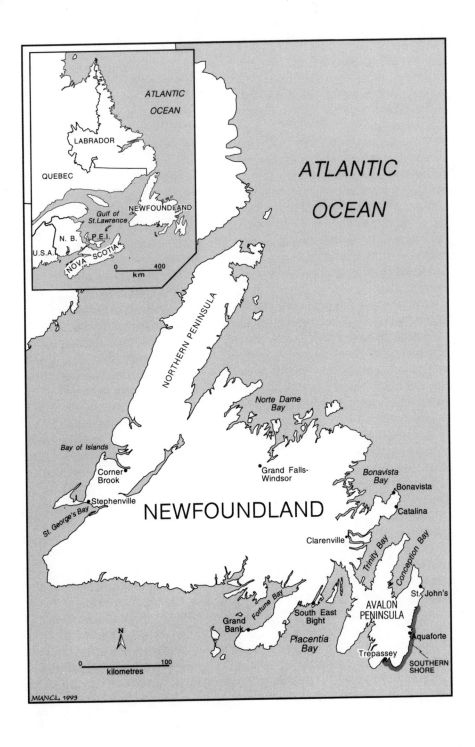

ATLANTIC OCEAN

LABRADOR

QUEBEC

ATLANTIC OCEAN

NEWFOUNDLAND

Gulf of St.Lawrence

N. B.   P.E.I.

U.S.A.

NOVA SCOTIA

0   400
km

NORTHERN PENINSULA

Norte Dame Bay

Bay of Islands

Corner Brook

Grand Falls-Windsor

Bonavista Bay

Bonavista

Stephenville

St. George's Bay

NEWFOUNDLAND

Catalina

Clarenville

Trinity Bay

Conception Bay

St. John's

Fortune Bay

South East Bight

AVALON PENINSULA

Grand Bank

Placentia Bay

Aquaforte

Trepassey

SOUTHERN SHORE

N

0   100
kilometres

MUNCL, 1993

1 Introduction

Introduction

I landed in Newfoundland in August 1980, an exile from the wave of cuts that had just begun to hit British Universities. As such, I was simply the latest in a long tradition of immigrants from England and Ireland, who, without work there, arrived in this unlikely spot because work was available here, albeit of a short term, marginal nature. Mine was a university sessional appointment: most of my predecessors, from the 16th century onwards, came to fish, and later to settle in predominantly fishing communities. Like many of my predecessors who wanted to settle here, I encountered resistance from a government distant from Newfoundland, but nevertheless exercising control over it. Like them, I eventually prevailed, settling here permanently in 1984.

This intersection of personal and community history illustrates some key factors in the composition of Newfoundland — its long, close and continuing connection with Britain; its history of poverty, and ideology of rugged self-sufficiency; its dependence on a few primary resources, notably fish; its political and economic subservience to, first of all Britain, and, since 1949, to the Federal Government of Canada, and the fierce loyalty and passionate attachment to place of people who choose to live in the wild landscape and unique culture of Newfoundland.

This book describes the growth of my intellectual and personal relationship with Newfoundland over the past 12 years. I came as a woman, and as a feminist nurtured in the hotbed of second wave feminism as it developed in Britain in the 1970s. Newfoundland women became, in a sense obviously, the main focus of my attempts to understand my new surroundings; and feminist theory provided my preferred tools. The series of essays that make up this book describe my gradually developing knowledge and understanding of the lives of the women of Newfoundland as well as respect for their

1

achievement in not only surviving in a harsh environment but doing it with a sense of dignity, worth and autonomy from which we can all learn.

The 1980s was a decade of ferment in the development of feminist theory. but I quickly realized that few, if any, of my existing concepts and theoretical tools were going to help me account for the very different reality that now confronted me. Newfoundland has never fitted easily into either the theoretical generalizations or the policy categories generated elsewhere, especially in mainland Canada. In any event, it became increasingly important for me that I should hear what Newfoundland women had to say about their lives and experiences and in my discussion of it, that I should preserve the dignity, courage and uniqueness with which they spoke. The essays here chart my attempts to do that, and thus they are also an account of feminism's changing concerns and priorities over the last decade.[1] Feminist theory has become infinitely more rich and complex in the period and this book is in no way a history of that development. It is, however, a demonstration of what happened when one feminist tried to understand the lives of the women around her, using and developing feminist theory. The result, therefore, is a complex interaction between changing realities, interpretations, priorities and theory. The reader will learn about some aspects of Newfoundland women's lives, but she will also learn how theory modifies and is modified by our experience of the world.

Newfoundland

The Province of Newfoundland and Labrador is the tenth and youngest province of Canada. This book focuses exclusively on the island portion of the province.[2] Lying in the mouth of the St. Lawrence Seaway, Newfoundland is skirted on both sides by the Labrador current, an influence that ensures that the waters remain very cold and that Newfoundland experiences a climate considerably more severe than other places on the same latitude. While the landscape is starkly beautiful, and the coast heavily indented with many good harbours, living in Newfoundland has never been easy. From the time of earliest settlement in the 16th century fish (especially cod) has provided the primary economic focus. Mines (including iron ore, zinc, asbestos) and forestry have also been important elements of the economy. But the population has always been small (currently about half a million); scattered in some 600 small, mostly coastal, communities dwarfed by the immense coastline of about 6000 miles. There are a few larger mining, timber-mill or administration centres, e.g., Grand Falls, Labrador City, Corner Brook, Gander, but no centre apart from St. John's has a population of more than 25,000. More than half the total population lives in St. John's or on the Avalon peninsula. Up until the 20th century communications were almost entirely by sea. In 1910 the railway across the island was built (finally dismantled in 1990) but it was not until 1968 that the Trans Canada Highway from Port-aux-Basques to St. John's made road transportation possible; and began to alter the focus for communication of the coastal communities from the bays on which they were located to spine roads down the peninsulas connecting them, via the TCH, to the rest of the island.

The fishery has not been the most valuable industry for many years, but it remained the major employer and the economic mainstay of the many small fishing communities.[3] Fishing communities in Newfoundland have always had a hard struggle to survive, and the fishery has been inexorably declining over the last few decades. However, the situation worsened rapidly during the 1980s, with rapidly declining fish stocks, until the summer of 1991, when the Federal government took the drastic step of closing the whole northern cod fishery, leaving 20,000 fishermen and many more plant workers without even the little work that still remained to them. The studies recorded in this book were framed in the context of a declining fishery, but they predate the current collapse. It is too early, yet, to say what the future of the fishery in Newfoundland will be, but this book attempts to shed light on how Newfoundland communities, and especially Newfoundland women will go about reconstructing their lives.

The earliest communities in Newfoundland were either established as part of relatively short-lived efforts at settlement, or were much more ad hoc arrangements as groups of fishermen 'wintered over' and gradually established small communities.[4] There was considerable resistance to such settlement by both the merchants who controlled the summer fishing effort and the British government. Most early settlement was thus without benefit of government, and was sometimes extra-legal. I describe this process, and especially the part women played in Chapter 3. Eventually the colony was established, although Newfoundland did not receive a colonial administration until 1832, finally achieving 'representative government' in 1855. These changes, however, scarcely affected the now numerous fishing communities outside St. John's. They continued to eke out a bare subsistence existence, hampered rather than helped by the St. John's based merchants.

After a period of relative prosperity (counterbalanced by an increasing population and exploitative merchants) the province began to decline after about 1910, until by 1934 it was declared bankrupt and government passed into the hands of a 'Commission of Government' (three drawn from Newfoundland and three from Britain). Direct rule was unable to alleviate some of the worst poverty in the province's history and this period marks the memory of many older people today. Despite continuing controversy about both the social and economic problems of the era and the official responses to them, noone denies the dire poverty that afflicted much of the island (Rowe, 1980; Overton, 1979; Noel, 1980; Alexander, 1983). However, the Second World War brought benefits and prosperity, especially in the form of US Air bases (at St. John's, Argentia, Stephenville, Gander and Goose Bay). This combination of memories of bitter poverty and a new confidence born of recent opportunity provided the background for the bitter fight over Newfoundland's political future. After a period of confused wrangling that divided the province, communities and families and still marks politics today, Joey Smallwood led Newfoundland into Confederation with Canada in 1949. Since then Newfoundland has inherited both the problems and the benefits of becoming part of a much larger entity. But it did not join Confederation on equal terms.

The Atlantic region is the poorest in Canada and Newfoundland lies on its very edge — marginal and peripheral to the mainland, economically, politically and culturally. There is, thus, a peculiar ambiguity in Newfoundland's 'Canadianness'. It is, of course, heavily dependent on transfer payments from the federal coffers. Newfoundlanders are well aware that most public resources — from transport and communications to health and education — only become possible as part of Canada's much greater economic resources. Estimates are that about half Newfoundlanders' income comes directly or indirectly from the federal government. But it comes at a price and, perhaps one sign of Newfoundlanders' resentment came in their enthusiastic support for Premier Clyde Well's stand against the Meech Lake Constitutional Accord, which led to the failure of that round of constitutional negotiations in 1990.

The historical context of poverty and neglect by central government opened the way for other influences. Churches and missionary societies have always played a particularly important role in Newfoundland. Much of their work was necessary and philanthropic. Rural Newfoundland would have had few education or health resources without their efforts. Again, there was a price, and the churches continue to exert a major influence on Newfoundland society today. One example is the unique denominational system of education, written into the terms of Confederation which leaves all grade school education in the control of denominational Boards of Education.

Some of the chapters in this book will develop this very sketchy background to Newfoundland. I want to turn now to a brief account of the research on which the book is based, and the theoretical context in which the original papers were developed.

Generating knowledge: a sequence of studies

The actual generation of both knowledge and the ideas we use to understand it is a much more patchy and hit and miss affair than often appears from finished products. So it was with this work. The actual research projects had a certain logic, as did the theoretical underpinnings, but they did not always fit together so neatly. And by the time one 'writes them up' both the theoretical priorities and the mode of analysis may have changed.

The first research carried out in Newfoundland was a small, ethnographic study in and around Aquaforte, 60 miles from St. John's on the Southern Shore, in 1981-82. My periods of residence there gave me a chance to give some substance to my reading and inquiry in St. John's. Above all, it gave me a chance to experience the very different life of the outports.

By this time it had become clear that while sociologists, anthropologists, economists and historians had established a solid body of empirical and theoretical work on Newfoundland it was concentrated exclusively on men and male activities and viewed the province from a male perspective. Of course, it was a maritime society, so it was not entirely unexpected that I should encounter assumptions in both the academic literature and in the society that made men more than usually visible and women and their contributions commensurately invisible.

Thus the first questions I asked had to do with the nature of maritime societies and the place of gender in their construction. The literature seemed to confirm some connection between maritime communities and rigid and extreme sexual divisions of labour. On the other hand the existing ethnographic work in rural Newfoundland communities described a surprisingly egalitarian and gentle culture. Furthermore, my own impressions were that it might also be characterized by strong and articulate women. The ethnographic and historical sources did not confirm or deny this. They simply made no mention of the place of women in Newfoundland society.

Scratching about in the material I could find, the few studies that did take gender seriously and theoretically came to have a special significance in shaping my perspective. Two studies in particular were formative - those of Ellen Antler (1977, 1982) and Hilda Murray (1979). Ellen Antler's work, xeroxed in the Centre for Newfoundland Studies or published in obscure journals, centred on an attempt to place an economic value on the work women did 'drying the fish' in the traditional family based fishery. Her work both spelt out the sexual division of labour in traditional fishing families and attempted to restore the explicit value of women's economic contribution. Hilda Murray's work, based on her Folklore MA thesis, was an account of women's work in a Newfoundland outport 1900-1950. Based on her own community (Elliston, TB), it was drawn from memories of her relatives and neighbours and her own childhood recollections. While it was anecdotal and untheorized, its value for me lay in its unswerving emphasis on what women do (or did) and how they understand what they do. Both Antler and Murray presented the reality of women's economic contribution to Newfoundland society and the degree to which it was recognized in their communities as 'more than 50%' — as the subtitle of Murray's book puts it. The dignity and self-worth of the women they described was in stark contrast to their omission or disparagement in the formal literature.

Meanwhile the prevailing paradigm of theoretical concepts that I brought with me from the UK was marxist-feminist. Our main focus had been an attempt to theorize women's economic contributions, especially their work outside the formal economy. The domestic labour debate had validated 'housework' as a legitimate area of concern. Concepts such as 'production' and 'reproduction', 'public' and, 'private' 'patriarchy' and 'domestic labour' and even 'work' were being refined and utilized. Inevitably, most of the work such marxist-feminists did assumed a context of urban, capitalist, western contexts. Aquaforte gave me one opportunity to explore the concepts in a rural, maritime situation. In any event, I was increasingly interested in both the concept of 'the sexual division of labour' as an organizing principle of societies and its apparently rigid and extreme reality in maritime communities.

The fruits of these first studies in Aquaforte appear here as Chapters 5 and 6. Chapter 5 focuses on the construction and consequences of the sexual division of labour in the changing economic context of Newfoundland. Chapter 6 approaches the separate worlds of women and men rather differently by re-working the concepts of 'politics' and 'culture' to show how the women had negotiated for themselves a place of security and power; a place that would be quite missed if it was 'read' using conventional accounts of the concepts.

The next stage of my work took me back into the libraries and their data collections. By this time it was clear that before we could understand women's position in Newfoundland, we first had to document it, and even to 'complete the record' from women's perspective was going to be a massive task. I began by mapping the existing data, both historical and contemporary.

The first stages in this exploration were historical; to discover how gender and household relations had been constructed in the changing context of Newfoundland society. I tried, quite simply, to write a history of the sexual division of labour in Newfoundland, and a shortened version of this attempt appears here as Chapter 3.

At much the same time I was becoming aware that the absence of data on women and studies that included women was not just an irritating lacunae to be filled in as convenient. It raised profound questions about the theories male — usually marxist — colleagues had been developing to account for economic and social relations in the Atlantic region. If such theories were invalid because they didn't take adequate account of one half of the experience they were supposedly theorizing, then maybe feminist concepts could be applied in such a way as to develop a truly useful understanding of the problems feminists and marxists clearly shared. It was at this point that I contributed the paper that opens this book (Chapter 1) to an audience of Atlantic region sociologists.

It was no accident that this entire debate took place within a Marxist framework. Throughout the history of the 'second wave' women's movement, Marxism had been the dominant theoretical influence. Within feminism, it was the marxist feminist 'current' that had been at the cutting edge of theoretical debate. I situated myself solidly in this tradition; benefitting enormously from a rich tradition and vibrant current debate. The priorities in my own work were, and continue to be clearly set by an agenda that focused on the economy as the key object of analysis.

But even at this point, in the mid-1980s, feminist theory had effectively challenged the narrow focus and interpretations of the Marxist tradition, opening up new sets of concerns and including and redefining areas of experience that had been ignored. Traditional categories such as 'politics' and 'culture' had been extended and soon race, sexuality, violence and much else had joined class and gender as organizing principles, which we ignored at our peril. At the same time feminists were also reevaluating both how we did research and its purpose in ways that went beyond the old quantitative versus qualitative debate. New ideas of participatory and emancipatory research were being developed and new standards of accountability were insisted on. While some of this lay in the future there was, none the less, a rapidly widening range from which I could select both my theories and my methods.

I chose to continue to work with the theories that had emerged from the previous research and pursue them in the framework of the ideas generated by the relatively new field of oral history. The project in Grand Bank enabled me to understand how women's work had changed, and how it had not changed, and how five generations of women understood their work and its contribution. It also taught me much about the power of oral history as a tool of feminist analysis. Aspects of this study appear as Chapter 4 in this book.

By now the 1980s were drawing to a close, and we still lacked solid baseline data on women's lives in Newfoundland. While the situation had improved marginally since I first arrived we were still very short of both quantitative data and specific studies, and the need for them was increasing daily. Other feminist researchers were entering the field, but as they explored new aspects of women's lives it seemed to increase the pressure to establish larger scale 'contextual' studies. Thus I embarked on a project that would, I hoped, become part of this new generation of studies. My focus was still economic life, although that formulation — rather than work, for example — is significant. I had, of course, been drawn into the debate generated by R. Pahl's (1984) study. Pahl had developed a much wider definition of 'work', pointing out that people, at least the working class, had always depended on a variety of forms of work and sources of labour. Furthermore, this activity centred not on individual paid jobs, but rather on the economic effort of the family. While feminists quickly pointed to the 'black box', untheorized nature of Pahl's household, the debate did open up interesting new ways of approaching the whole issue of gender and the economy.

In particular, I wanted to explore two theories — the different ways in which family structures gender, and the ways in which women's economic contribution is then mediated through the family.

The first step in the larger project was a small case study carried out in Catalina. In the course of documenting both the formal and informal labour of men and women and examining the role of the household two salient findings appeared. One was the sheer scale, variety and intensity of women's contributions to the household project, and the other was the structurally different ways in which women contributed to and were affected by household economic strategies. Chapter 7 describes this complex situation and begins the analysis.

The whole process became much more complicated when the main study began in 1988. The core of the project were comparative case studies of three representative Newfoundland communities — a traditional outport, a small fishing town and a much larger mill town and administrative centre. The sheer scale of the project forced a completely different methodology and style of work on me and my team. While we did, indeed, generate a large body of new material on women's economic lives two major problems haunted the project. One was the methodological one of whether, and if so, how, large scale feminist projects were possible. I eventually reached some conclusions about this that appear here as Chapter 9.

The other problem revolved around the primary focus on economic lives. I had selected one community, Grand Falls, partly because of a large regional hospital there. My initial interest was in the hospital as a major employer of women, in traditional female jobs. However, in the course of the project, our concept of health, health care and caring became much broader than the obvious and curative aspects of health care that go on in hospitals. Once we had recognized the limitations of the 'biomedical model' (Stacey, 1988) our eyes were opened to the vast range of other health giving and caring activities that occurred in the community, especially in the home and principally provided by women. In fact, it proved impossible to understand women's economic lives unless we took account of the implicit and explicit 'caring' work they also did. This goes far beyond child care. In Newfoundland, as elsewhere, women undertake an enormous amount of caring of all sorts for other members of their family and community, especially and increasingly for the elderly and infirm. Furthermore, the expectation and negotiation of such responsibilities is a key constraint on how women lead the rest of their lives, including their economic lives.

We were able to include some of these concerns in the main project, but, if nothing else, it alerted me to the inherent constraints and weakness of a focus on the economic, however broadly conceived. Chapter 8 does not represent the last word on women's work in Newfoundland, but it does, probably, mark the end of line of inquiry embedded in this series of essays. It is not that such work is invalid, but rather that the next steps open up whole new concerns and whole new areas of theory with which to address them.

We are now living in the 1990s. Much has changed in women's lives since I arrived in Newfoundland 12 years ago. Some of what you read about here has gone, probably forever. So far the decade has not been kind to Newfoundland. However, the women still remain, and they are equipped and ready, as ever, to survive. Quite how they will achieve that will be the subject of later studies.

Meanwhile, feminism has also changed. It has become more diverse, more responsive to a wider variety of experience; it is more flexible; more connected to a greater number of issues and it is certainly more complex. Feminist scholars today select different issues, approach them differently and analyze what they find differently. I too have changed. But to change is not necessarily to reject what went before. Indeed, we are learning to remember and recover both our previous experience and our previous work.

It is in this spirit that I have written this book. It is one strand in the story of women's lives in Newfoundland. It will be taken up and developed by other women working in other ways, but sharing the same concern to understand the lives of the women around us, and to use that knowledge to change the conditions under which women in Newfoundland lead their lives.

Notes

1. Feminist theory and research practice has moved steadily away from the assumption of absolute expertise on the part of the researcher and towards recognising a greater diversity of both expertise and knowledge. Above all, it has placed increasing emphasis on the responsibility of feminist research to enable women in different situations to 'tell their own stories' and set their own agendas. While this concern certainly became more pronounced in my own work, I part company from a vocal stand that resists any role for the researcher except facilitation. For a discussion of some of these issues see Stanley (1990); Kirby and McKenna (1989); Fonow and Cook (1991); Bannerji et al., 1991. It seems to me that intellectuals *do* have an equal responsibility to analyze what they find, honestly and vigorously. I take up some of these issues in Chapter 9.

2. I took a conscious decision to concentrate my research on the island of Newfoundland. Labrador is fascinating, but it required a wholly different set of skills and treatment. There are concentrations of white settlers along the south coast of Labrador and more recent immigrants to the mines of Labrador City, Wabush and the air base at Goose Bay. Otherwise Labrador society is dominated by settlements of the Innu and Inuit peoples. Anthropologists (especially from Memorial University) have studied these communities extensively, see A. Tanner, *Bringing Home Animals* (ISER, St. John's, 1979); M. Wadden, *Nitassinan* (Douglas and McIntyre, Toronto, 1991); G. Hendricksen, *Hunters in the Barrens* (ISER, St. John's, 1973). The white communities are much less observed, although the works of John Kennedy, *Holding the Line* (ISER, St. John's, 1982); and Evie Plaice, *The Native Game* (ISER, St. John's, 1990), are notable exceptions.

3. Peter Sinclair estimates that 35,000 people were directly employed in fishing (as distinct from processing) in 1985, i.e., just before the recent rapid decline. He has also estimated that about a quarter of the population lives in communities where the fishing industry is the only or core employment sector. (P. Sinclair, 1991, 1992).

4. Most settlers then and later came from Britain and Ireland, especially SE Ireland and SW England. With the exception of small pockets of Micmac Indians, the island of Newfoundland is, therefore, remarkably homogenous in ethnic origin. It is only very recently that small numbers of immigrants from other countries have established themselves, although since Confederation more Canadians from the

mainland have also immigrated, permanently or temporally, to the province.

2 Peripheral women: Towards a feminist analysis of the Atlantic Region

Introduction

In this first chapter[1] I am going to attempt to clear away some tangled ground, and with the terrain a little clearer to see whether a feminist perspective can introduce clarity to the competing theoretical understandings of Atlantic Canada. I am focusing on those perspectives directed at understanding the political economy of the region because this was the framework within which feminist analysis was first couched.[2]

The endeavours I find most interesting are those that have an explicitly political agenda directed at changing, as well as understanding the situation in which they find themselves, and in this chapter I want to argue that two of these endeavours would benefit from a closer alliance. These are the tradition that has used a political-economy approach to the region, which can be conveniently encapsulated under the label 'Maritime Marxist'[3] and the growing body of feminist research and discussion in and on Atlantic Canada.[4]

While there are obvious problems in collapsing all political-economic analysis into one 'tradition', there are even more problems with assuming that all feminists have the same project and approach. They do not — the divergences between the different perspectives within feminism are clear. An interesting aspect of the current vitality of feminist theoretical work is how far feminists subscribe to common agendas while continuing to develop quite different analyses. In the present case, many different 'kinds' of feminists are working towards an understanding of the position of women in Atlantic Canada, and developing a critique of current academic theories and methodologies. I shall draw on this broadly defined body of 'feminist' work to point out the weakness of male-biased work, and to indicate ways in which the feminist approach seems especially fruitful. Going beyond the usual plaint about the lack of significant consideration of gender in both government reports and academic discussions, I want to argue that certain theoretical weaknesses and/or mistakes inevitably arise from such an androcentric focus. However, in terms of making explicit suggestions about the contribution feminism can make to the political-economy approach, I shall be drawing on the work of Marxist-feminists. In particular, I shall try to suggest that we need to explore the usefulness and validity of concepts that are being refined in Marxist feminist discourse — concepts such as patriarchy, subordination, production and reproduction, and the sexual division of labour.

The argument, then, is rooted in the twin realities of both feminists (whether Marxists or not) and Marxists working in the particular context of Atlantic Canada in the 1980s. It is not another attempt to 'read off' theoretically correct political action from formulations rooted in alien historical, political and economic situations. It is, rather, a continuation of the project that Sacouman expressed in the context of developing a relevant political economy of and for the Maritimes:

> Our constituency, the real situation of urgency, and the plethora of stereotypes clouding our history have impelled Marxist intellectuals to take the materialist dictum of concrete analysis more seriously. In paying attention to this Marxist imperative, we have been able to ground our analyses of the regional problem in detailed empirical work which has in turn led to generalizations which call into question some of the emphases that are common in Canadian political economy (Sacouman, 1981:138).

Like Sacouman, feminists have found that Marxist theory cannot be 'applied' to their problems without discrimination. Many of the categories do not fit, the conclusions do not follow. While some have despaired and condemned the whole Marxist project as inherently gender-biased and useless for their purposes, a substantial number, including a growing number in Atlantic Canada, have directed their efforts in precisely the way that Sacouman has indicated — towards detailed, empirical, concrete studies of particular aspects of women's lives.

Sacouman's own work, like others in the same tradition, is rooted in a situation that is seen as predominantly male. As such, it neither locates itself firmly on issues of gender (or even notices them) nor does it use feminist perspectives to understand the situation it does see. My argument is that in thinking about the Atlantic region, there are two hitherto non-reciprocal concerns that should be brought into focus. These are: to examine theoretical questions that feminists have addressed in the context of the Atlantic region; and, to reexamine in the context of feminism, issues of the political economy of the periphery of an advanced capitalist society. In this chapter I shall pay attention principally to the second of these concerns, and within that I shall restrict myself to pointing out what kind of analysis could emerge if we take this approach seriously.

One of the difficulties in establishing such linkages is the lack of a common vocabulary. I, thus, sometimes stray onto the dangerous ground of 'applying' one vocabulary to the concerns of the other, which can lead to the errors of argument by analogy. One example of this is the notion of marginality, which has proved such a useful heuristic device both conceptually and politically. The experience of being marginalized is one shared by women and by the maritime communities of Atlantic Canada. Marginality, as conceived by theorists of Atlantic Canada, has derived partly from the region's obvious geographically peripheral position relative to centres of power and industry in Ontario and Quebec; and more importantly, from the concept that certain kinds of political and economic relations within capitalism are inherently weaker because of a structural imbalance between the centre and the periphery.[5] At first, feminist discussions of marginality focused on women's exclusion from mainstream male society, and tended towards a liberal analysis and politics that saw society as essentially androgynous (if biased) with the solution being the inclusion of women in existing structures. In slightly more radical formulations, there are similarities in the ways in which Maritime theorists and feminists have responded to the perceived inequities that Maritime Marxists describe as marginality, and which feminists embed in a number of related (and competing) concepts such as "oppression", "inequality" and "subordination".

A rather different approach to the concept of marginality was initiated by Simone de Beauvoir in her discussion of women as 'other', deriving from her interpretation of French existentialist thought.[6] More recently, feminists interested in the insights of Lacan, Foucault, Derrida and others have begun to develop a much more profound understanding of the construction and maintenance of female marginality in the deep structures of psychology, language and culture. Such discussions, of course, extend the concept far beyond the more conventional compass used by political economists. But if there is, in fact, a common agenda shared by feminists and Marxists in the Atlantic region, then one way of pursuing it would entail the sharing and extension of this kind of theoretical work.

The experience of marginality, however conceived, has generated strong and profound critiques of central or mainstream theory. It provided the political conviction that relevant answers have to be found for the particular experience of oppression that we work among and are involved in, both as woman and as workers in the Atlantic region. It also provides a useful example of the way in which concepts can be expanded, made more complex and flexible, by applying the focuses of the Maritime Marxists and feminists together.

Before I look at ways in which feminist concepts can be used to enrich analysis of the Atlantic region, it would be useful to examine the work feminists have already begun.

Another agenda: feminist studies of the Atlantic Region

To begin with, feminists working in the region came upon the stark neglect and omission of women. Often they had to generate quite basic data. Much of the necessary statistical data is still missing. The early studies are marked by considerable caution, and also by surprise that what they said had not been said before. As the body of studies has increased, so feminist analysis has grown more confident.

In Newfoundland, Ellen Antler's work stood almost alone for several years.[7] Her analysis concentrated on evaluating women's contributions in drying fish, and in the production of 'use values' necessary for the survival of the family (berry picking, pickling, growing vegetables, carding and knitting wool, etc.). She estimated that the process of drying fish added $2400 (1950 values) to the value of a season's catch in Labrador, and $1500-2000 (1969 values) in Conception Bay. In all, Antler suggested women contributed around 35% of the family income in direct, measurable economic values. The importance of this, of course, is less in the detailed figures than in making visible women's economic activity in rural families, which, in male analysis, had remained hidden behind the male headed 'household'.

By taking ethnographic evidence seriously, especially in a feminist context, we have been forced to analyze women's own understanding of their political and economic situation. In particular, many feminist observers have been struck by the active nature of women's participation, both in the social life of their communities and in the regulation of gender relations within their families. Discussions of this subject have focused both on political activity as such, and on the cultural construction of women's lives. Examples include my own study (Chapter 6), work on women's participation in formal political groups by L.Christiansen-Ruffman(1982), and the work of D. Davis, who focused on a South Coast community, Grey Rock Harbour (1982, 1983).

Pat and Hugh Armstrong, in an influential article, laid the ground plan and rationale for the construction of a 'feminist Marxism', rather than Marxist-feminism (Armstrong, 1985). There are good reasons for this. Most Marxist feminists have tried to think of the dualism as of equal weight, despite attacks from both wings. However the combination of language structure and an inherent deference towards the founding fathers has, in fact,

15

meant that Marxism has been accorded some kind of preeminence. To privilege the snippets of Marx and Engels on women, snippets which are partial, limited, and often plain wrong, is clearly ridiculous.[8] Yet, as the Armstrongs reminded us, what they wrote then is not the point: what is, is the method and approach we call historical materialism. In the course of their argument, the Armstrongs noted both the deficiencies of a feminism that does not take adequate account of class differences and structure, and of a Marxism that omits considerations of sex and, as they argue later, of bodies:

> How women have babies, and the conditions and consequences of childbearing, are relative to particular social formations. So is the sexual division of labour related to childrearing. But the fact that women, not men, have babies is not. To theorize production and reproduction at the highest level of abstraction involves a recognition of the differences in female and male reproductive capacities. Any other approach fails to comprehend the nature of production and reproduction (Armstrong, 1983:8). 161.

In the ensuing debate in *Studies in Political Economy* they established certain conditions under which Marxist-feminists work that do not consist simply of adding class to sex in various combinations, but "suggest ways to go forward in developing a political economy that comprehends the fundamental importance of sex divisions at all levels of analysis". Their conclusion that the sexual division of labour is essential to this mode of production, at the highest level of abstraction, is an exciting one, and one I will pursue later. Whether this approach will, in fact, lead to an even-handed 'feminist-Marxism', or whether it will lead to the pre-eminence of 'feminism' in place of 'Marxism' is still an open question. It will be answered in practice, as Marxist-feminists begin to tackle the problem of an analysis of the region, informed by both sets of concepts.

Connelly and MacDonald's work in Nova Scotia is one of those that begins the project of transcending the separate peripheries of feminists and Maritime Marxists. Like much other feminist research, their concern is to document and specify the material and historical nature of women's subordination in the region. They start from an understanding based both upon theory and their experience in Nova Scotia that "working class households here always required more than the male wage and that women here always contributed to the maintenance of the family household either by intensifying their domestic labour in the home, by earning money through an informal economy, or by participating in the labour force and earning a wage themselves" (Connelly and MacDonald, 1983:46). They go on to elaborate the point in the context of a dependent regional economy, especially in terms of the ability of families to combine wage labour and independent

16

commodity production of members (without giving priority to the husband) so that the wage earners are paid "less than their subsistence for their labour" and the primary producers receive less for their product than its cost of production (through relations of unequal exchange). So far we are no further on than Sacouman. However in their subsequent analysis of 'Big Harbour' (a fishing community) and 'Pleasant Bay' (based in forest work) and especially the way in which women's economic activities and family relations interacted with and affected the communities' ability to renegotiate with capital, they demonstrate conclusively that "women have always contributed an available cheap labour reserve", though not the only one, that women have consistently worked for less than their subsistence, and that their domestic labour has meant that total family wages have been less than the true cost of family subsistence. They conclude that "the allocation of women's work between the home and the labour force has occurred as a response by the family household to changes in the needs of the economy" (Connelly and MacDonald, 1983:68). This kind of detailed empirical work, carefully devoted to teasing out the implications and contradictions in the theories we rely on, is an essential prerequisite to developing a truly feminist-Marxist theoretical understanding. As yet, there is too little of it.[9]

All this work, albeit as yet of a preliminary nature, constitutes one part of the feminist agenda — the use of established frameworks and debates to explore and specify the particular situation of women. But my main interest at this point is to explore the other task, which is the use and relevance of specifically feminist concepts to our understanding of the political economy of the Atlantic region.

From missing to misconception: the documentation of omission

Elsewhere in this work I point out the overwhelming androcentric bias of the work emanating from the Institute of Social and Economic Research (ISER) in St. John's in the early 1970s, and also indicate possible reinterpretations of their data, based on taking women's points of view seriously. A similar point has been made by Linda Christiansen-Ruffman in her critique of the consequences of sexist methodology exemplified in R. Matthews' *There's No Better Place Than Here* (Christiansen-Ruffman, 1984). The point is one made generally in feminist work, that sexist bias, by omission or misinterpretation, does not merely affect the understanding of women but raises serious doubts about many of the conclusions that rely on the flawed argument. To illustrate this point, let us examine another important source of information about rural Newfoundland, the many studies done by or commissioned by the Government.

17

Let us take, for example, the Kirby Report, *Navigating Troubled Waters* (Kirby, 1982).[10] Nowhere in the Report is the issue of gender specifically addressed. Given that the terms of reference included the fishery, not merely fishing, and that both the terms of reference and the Report recognized that in Atlantic Canada the fishery has profound effects on rural communities, this omission of itself raises certain doubts about the competence of the findings. A look at particular demonstrations of the bias is not comforting. In the chapter on "the economic condition of fishermen, their household, communities and enterprises", we find reference to "the financial importance of non-fishing revenues brought in by other household members . . . their most frequent income-earning occupations are fish plant work, store clerking, construction, secretarial work, teaching, nursing and public service (including municipal) employment" (Kirby, 1982:27). In other words, the vast majority of these "other household members" are women — wives, one might hazard. Clearly then, wives' incomes are crucial to the survival of Atlantic fishing families, and by extension, to the hundreds of communities that are organized around, but cannot depend on, the fishery. One need not expect Kirby to consider what consequences this one fact might have for family relations, decision-making, or aspirations, or even the importance of female support for the inshore fishing to continue at all. However, you would expect him to evaluate the economic dependability and distribution of these other sources of income, especially fish plant work. Yet neither in this section, nor in his recommendations for the processing sector, does he appear to have taken in the importance of this aspect of the interdependence of harvesting and processing sectors.[11] The weakness of his approach becomes clear in his failure to address the possibility of manipulating the processing sector in such a way as to ensure the viability of the entire industry. One should not talk about closing or consolidating plants, and the "distribution of the population dependent on the fishery" without considering who is married to whom and what that means (Kirby, 1982:61).

Kirby shares many assumptions with other purely academic accounts. He treats workers as if they were gender free. He accepts that workers (male) live in families and family income is different to individual income, but he consistently only considers the position of the (male) head of household. He does not take into account the perspective of the "other household members", who may set very different agendas. By assuming the stereotypical, male-headed household, he is also doing violence to the reality of Newfoundland history, whose people have survived by subtle, varied and changing plural adaptations requiring the full economic participation of all members of the domestic unit. Indeed, there is a certain irony about the situation in much of the inshore fishery today, where the men continue to operate, both in technology and social organisation, in ways that are traditionally

18

characteristic of commodity production, while the women have transferred to the industrialized sector and become full-fledged wage earners in the fish plant, and in other auxiliary service jobs — a point I will discuss in more detail later.

In some ways the omission of gender from studies of fishing is simply part of a conventional wisdom and much anthropological evidence that associates maritime activities (and maritime communities) with an extreme and rigid sexual division of labour.[12] It is not after all a generic 'he' who goes down to the sea in ships, but usually and overwhelmingly, actual men. However, acceptance of this general pattern has led male observers to concentrate on the harvesting sector of the fishing industry, sometimes to the complete exclusion of the processing sector (in which, of course, many women are found). Newfoundland, for instance, has seen a stream of studies on different aspects of fishing,[13] but while Barb Neis and her collaborators have reversed the trend somewhat, there is still much less work on the processing sector.[14] In the more abstract studies, this is compounded by a failure to locate the male fishermen in families, or even in communities, thus ignoring much of the economic and social context of the male fisherman's work. One example of a study that exemplifies both these problems is Bryan Fairley's discussion of the capitalist nature of much of the contemporary Newfoundland fishery and the "bourgeois" nature of the Fishermen's Union (NFFAWU), (Fairley, 1985). At no point does Fairley consider gender at all. All the fishermen in whom Fairley is interested in are presumed (generally correctly) to be men. But when he discusses the different and contradictory interests of the three sections of the union, it makes less sense to presume that all the "processing employees" are also male. And what happens when a member of this "most developed segment of the working class" is married to the capitalist owner of a near-shore otter trawler? Are we merely referred abruptly to the debate on contradictory class locations and the problems inherent in that analysis, or has Fairley missed an important element in his analysis of the class position of the different fishing sectors?

Maritime Marxists and other theories of the region

I want to turn now from the problems arising from mere omission to the more interesting problems posed by a kind of omission arising from the partial, distorted or simply different use of concepts. A consequence of the seclusion in which feminists and Maritime Marxists have worked is the way in which certain concepts, which have also been developed in feminist theory, take on a different guise when we find them in studies of the political economy of the Atlantic region. Because those studies do not take adequate account of gender, they have developed and used concepts in ways that reflect that partiality.

The common theme of the Maritime Marxist 'school' has been to understand the region as a periphery of an advanced capitalist society. The region does not fit neatly into the category of a fully developed capitalist society with class relations based on wage labour and the process of expropriation, nor can it be described in terms of a traditional peasant society. Instead, we have something which is a variant on normal development, or else caught in a process of uneven development. It has been described in terms of an approximation, a case of arrested or slow development, a form of resistance or a process of progressive marginalization. It has been variously theorized as petty commodity production (Brym & Sacouman), domestic mode of commodity production (Sinclair), semi-proletarianisation (Sacouman), industrial reserve army (Veltmeyer) or dependent commodity production (Williams).

These ideas and characterizations depend, in turn, on particular preferences within the school of thought dominated by the work of André Gunder Frank and Immanuel Wallerstein. However, Maritime Marxists have taken particularly seriously the contribution of Leo Panitch in redirecting the attention of Canadian Marxists to a primary concern with class and class relations (Panitch, 1981). This focus and the working out of its implications informs the work of Brym and Sacouman, Sacouman, Williams, Barrett, Clow, Veltmeyer and Sinclair among others.[15] The case is surely convincing, but any alert feminist will recognize instantly that Marxist and neo-Marxist development of class theory depends (or has depended) primarily on the analysis of economic relations in terms of male, wage-earning, heads of households. It is an approach that fails to accommodate women's different place in the labour market, fails to specify the working out of class relations within the family and, above all, fails to specify the relationship between gender and class.[16]

Such an approach is inherently gender biased. One would expect analyses based on it to focus exclusively on male economic practices, only taking account of women in so far as they enter the labour market, and failing to spell out the connections between the family and the economy. In fact the writers above mostly do take account of the much greater importance of the family and/or household as an economic production unit in rural relations of production, but without recognizing the place of gender in such relations. To undertake that task would involve the exploration of the relationship between women and the family, and women and men in the complex circumstances of rural Atlantic communities. The main problem, for a Marxist-feminist analysis, then, is to explain the role of the 'non-capitalist'

20

household in the subordination of whole peripheral areas. But that is not enough: we need to explore what women do inside and outside the household, and how, and to what extent that constitutes a special subordination based on gender, on marriage, or on family relationship.

The core of the Maritime Marxists' case is an extended critique of the emphasis that dependency theory puts on market relations, to the exclusion of productive class relations. Veltmeyer clearly gives priority to class relations, especially in terms of the degradation of the Atlantic region's labour force into various categories of reserve army of labour (Veltmeyer, 1979). In passing, he notes Braverman's point that women contribute a key and increasing proportion of the 'latent' reserve army of labour. His case depends upon labour force participation rates, unemployment rates and other labour force data — an area of capitalist data collecting particularly prone to deforming the realities of working class life. Unemployment figures especially are well-known white washers.[17] But as women have discovered to their cost, all labour force statistics present a partial and sometimes misleading picture of both the amount of work that is done outside the view of statistics and the way that work relates to the visible work of the labour market, especially in terms of gender and family relationships. There is also mounting evidence demonstrating the way in which international data purporting to estimate the GNP of nation states falsifies by considerable factors the economic effort of societies by obscuring the contribution of women.[18] If we add the evidence suggesting that, for women, collective wealth is more important materially and ideologically than individual wealth, then we have reason to doubt the basis on which Veltmeyer rests his argument.[19] His line of enquiry would suggest that the labour force in the region will become progressively proletarianized. Indeed the development of theories of dependency in the Atlantic region centre upon this process. Hence the primacy of the important but controversial argument put forward by Sacouman and others that the essential description of class relations in the better part of the region is 'semi-proletarianisation'. I do not intend to embark here on a critique of this position as such, but simply to see where the argument relates to feminist issues.

Sacouman places his argument for the semi-proletarianisation of "domestic relations of petty primary production" squarely in what he calls the 'domestic mode of production' (Sacouman, 1980). Leaving aside the question of whether what he refers to actually fulfills the definition of a mode of production, its use in this context is confusing. Sacouman bases his argument on changes in the class composition of Maritime society — notably the persistence of petty production and multiple occupations, which are masked by census allocation of single 'occupations' and concentration on household heads. This would work against the proletarianisation thesis were it not for

21

what Sacouman identifies as "the truncation and yet maintenance of the domestic mode of production" with the wife being absorbed into wage labour (while retaining her work of reproduction and subsistence in the household) and the husband remaining as a petty farmer, fisherman or woodsman — but in conditions where the exchange relations transform his position into what Sacouman calls "semi-proletarianism" (Sacouman, 1980:233). This analysis succeeds in placing at the heart of the analysis the contradictory class locations of different family members and the complex way in which the family relates to the capitalist economy. But while it is clear that the petty producer is male and the 'other family members' are either wives or children (sometimes specified as such) the dimension of gender is neither explored nor related to the vast literature on the subject.

For instance in *The Main Enemy*, Christine Delphy develops her idea of a separate or subordinate domestic mode of production from a feminist point of view, through examining semi-peasant families in rural France (Delphy, 1977, 1984). Such families also exist within a society dominated by the capitalist mode of production. She identifies processes *within* the peasant household which she then claims are a universal description of gender relations within marriage. For Delphy, then, the 'domestic mode of production' specifies relations within the household, not between the household and the dominant capitalist mode of production. She goes on to argue that the work of family members is appropriated by the husband on the grounds that each family farm is assured of income equivalent to one wage (Delphy, 1977:7). The implication is that the wife's labour, which is incorporated into household production, does not merit a wage; or perhaps rather, that since the production of the wife is exchanged by the husband as his own, that her work belongs to him. Indeed, in France, the status of 'family aide' consecrates in law the unpaid nature of the work.

> Since 1907 a wife has legally had the use of her own wage, but in fact the custom in most marriages is such as to annul this concession, since all her earnings to into a common budget which the husband alone controls. Until 1965 a wife's entire labour power was appropriated: her husband could prevent her from working outside the home" (Delphy, 177:12).

The way in which Delphy decodes the artificiality of the distinctions between use and exchange values in the household, and points out that women's production only does *not* have exchange value in the framework of the family, is useful.

But in the context of Sacouman's argument, it is clear that Delphy's analysis fails to go back outside the family farm to relate it to the surrounding social relations of production.[20] There is no real sense, either in France or in Nova Scotia, in which the husband 'exploits' his wife, because he does not extract surplus value from her. Instead both husband and wife are exploited by capitalist relations of production. A more fruitful approach, and one which I will develop later, argues that women's surplus labour operates to reduce the value of both male and female labour power.

However, within Delphy's somewhat confused formulation, her discussion of the family mode (the Domestic Mode of Production) is relevant to Sacouman's ideas. She pinpoints the contradiction (also discussed by Deere) that as capitalist relations penetrate all economic relations, some commodities are transferred into full capitalist production. Capital now has to pay labour (admittedly at a low price) to produce commodities to sell to families, whose women previously produced those same commodities for free (bread, clothes, meals, etc.), leaving only the labour of transforming them back into use values for the housewife to perform in her (now) self-contained, fully proletarianized home.

Much of this correctly describes Atlantic Canada, and some of its consequences have been noted. Take, for instance, the almost universal adoption of "Pampers" in place of the daily wash of terry towelling diapers. This change is often seen by older women in the communities in cultural terms, usually in terms of a sense of symbolic loss. But its economic consequences are much more profound. There is the obvious freeing of mothers from many hours of labour, counterposed with the need for frequent and considerable expenditure that links the young family in a double yoke (as wage earners and consumers) to capitalist market relations in a way not experienced by their parents.

One distinctive feature of Atlantic Canada, noted by Sacouman and others, is that the usual accommodation is for the wife to earn wages while the husband remains essentially outside the capitalist mode of production. It is also less true that the husband (as a wage labourer) is dependent on a theoretically unlimited number of employers. Instead both men and women in rural communities in the Atlantic region depend on one market, one employer and, in fairly obvious ways, on the family unit. Combined with a less oppressive legal structure, this produces a renegotiated gender division of labour, which in quite critical respects is less oppressive than that described by Delphy. The a-historicism of an argument that depends on an analysis of the supply of unpaid labour within the framework of a universal and personal relationship (marriage) makes it hard to utilize even the recognized insights of her work. Nevertheless, there are common theses in Sacouman's and Delphy's work, highlighted by their common use of the concept of Domestic Mode of Production. Delphy, despite her claim to be a 'materialist', is highly critical of Marxism and of the way in which Marxist-feminists work. Marxist-feminists can take some of Delphy's

23

iconoclasm as useful criticism of established Marxist categories. But it then becomes necessary to work through those insights in the context of Sacouman's understanding of the class basis of economic oppression. This kind of reciprocal analysis can be developed in other contexts. Let us take the example of subsistence production.

There have been serious attempts to evaluate subsistence activities in rural (and urban) Atlantic Canada. But nowhere have I heard this related to the ongoing debate about what 'housework' is. In the context of rural fisheries, 'housework' may seem a trivial or meaningless category, but the debate was originally couched in terms of the relationship between productive and unproductive labour, the production and appropriation of surplus value, and the production and reproduction of labour power.[21] Phrased like this, it makes less sense to ignore such an approach to activities like hunting, house building and vegetable growing. In a paper that considers subsistence economy in relation to work and unemployment in Newfoundland, Hill lists the number of subsistence activities families undertake, and their estimated value (Hill, 1985). The paper uses this material to make a useful contribution to our understanding of how subsistence contributes to Newfoundland's economic survival: yet he fails to take the gender division into account. For instance, some subsistence activities may make an accounting loss because of the initial cost and depreciation of capital equipment — hunting and wood cutting are obvious examples. These are male activities. Berry picking, pickling, knitting and gardening require less capital equipment, or rather less specialized capital equipment, and thus may contribute a greater net amount to the family economy. These are female activities. It is also harder to draw the line between women's subsistence activities and their ordinary, and unrecognized, work of reproducing the household. Hill cites making clothes, for instance, as a subsistence activity. What about mending them? How are we to evaluate cooking, baking bread and cake making? A serious consideration of gender, and of feminist theory can contribute to our understanding of subsistence production.

Finally, let me return to the analysis of class relations, forearmed with a certain skepticism based on the known problems besetting the use of a gender-free concept of class. One would be particularly cautious in the context of Atlantic Canada, where the economy under analysis is based on the extraction of primary resources — lumber, mining, now oil and gas, but above all, fishing — all traditionally and actually male spheres. What can a feminist understanding of the concepts contribute to an approach based on the obvious and visible economy of fishing?

Let us take, for example, Peter Sinclair's study of the fishery of Northwest Newfoundland (Sinclair, 1985). His choice of topic makes him liable, with the best intentions, to fall into the same gendered characterizations as the ISER studies did 20 years before.[22] The analysis is gender-free to the extent that it is never specified that the fishermen of the Northwest coast are, indeed, all men. Sinclair's analysis embeds the economic activity of fishing within a household economy, without specifying how the relationship between the two (which is by implication and in fact a gender relationship) is negotiated and articulated. Critically, this leads him to develop a distinction between domestic commodity production and petty capitalism. In domestic commodity production, the owners of the means of production generate commodities by relying on their own labour and that of their household. This situation should, in theory, give way to full scale capitalist enterprises, but has, in fact, survived in such places as the Northwest coast of Newfoundland, despite the growth in numbers and in power of the inshore draggers, characterized as petty capitalists.

In the context of what he calls the differentiation or integrationist theories, Sinclair dwells upon the role of the state in perpetuating domestic capitalist production — which may very well be true. My quarrel is with a conceptualization of domestic commodity production that does not disaggregate the household. As the owners of the means of production are counterposed to "*their* household" (my emphasis), it is reasonable to suppose that the subject is the male fisherman. But how does 'he' release and control the household labour? How, and under what terms, is the value generated returned to the household? Most particularly, what happened with the shift to the ownership and operation of the capital intensive offshore draggers? Previous wifely contributions, such as the keeping of financial accounts and records, become less likely as the operation becomes more complex. A major difference between the traditional inshore fishery, conducted from open skiffs or motor boats or small longliners, and the near shore fishery, conducted from the offshore draggers, is the length of time spent away from the home port. The inshore fishermen rarely spends a night away from home, and is often visible from the kitchen window of his house. The offshore draggers, on the other hand, may go to another part of the island in search of fish, and be based there for weeks or even months, only returning home for occasional weekends. This effectively leaves the wife as single parent for the periods of her husband's absence, transforming her work and responsibilities for that time, but also causing repeated alteration in her situation during the periods of his return. Another aspect of this is the changes in the work of reproducing his labour power. 'Domestic' labour has either to be reallocated among crew members (for pay) or contracted out to laundries, restaurants, etc., or stored up for the wife to deal with upon his return home. All this has consequences for the economic division of labour and gender relations in the family, and reflects back on the conduct — and interpretations — of the fledgling capitalist enterprise.

25

As more money enters the household of the offshore dragger skipper, his wife's labour, transforming exchange value back into use value, also changes. Culturally the 'labour of ornamentation' may become not only a reality, but an expected adjunct. At the same time, the wives' appreciation of and escalating expectations for the 'suburban' lifestyle to accompany the new affluence may have consequences for the operation of the fledgling 'capitalist' enterprise, and certainly for the political understanding deriving from it. The gradual exclusion of the family from direct participation in the production process was one of the hallmarks of the development of capitalism in seventeenth century England and elsewhere.[23] Its particular manifestation in northwest Newfoundland is a critical aspect of Sinclair's argument. Yet he discusses both domestic commodity production and the petty capitalist form without even mentioning, much less exploring, the sexual division of labour implicit in them.

The work of the Maritime Marxist school has given us a real purchase on the economic situation of the region. To say that the analysis is not feminist then, sounds cavilling. Indeed, often, what is striking is that they share the same problems in terms of developing theory. In trying to develop an understanding of the region in terms of an analogy with the analysis of Latin American dependency put forward by Frank, Maritime Marxists encounter the same problems as feminists do in trying to work those ideas out without distorting the experience of the region. Like feminists, they have come to a painful and slow realization that simply to 'apply' concepts, however well developed in their own right, is to do violence to the subjective reality of experience.

Feminists have been well trained to become alarmed by falsely analogous arguments. We know that universal Marxist theory about class, or modes of production, or productive and unproductive labour encompass the particularity of gender. Quite right. But by the same token, we should cross-examine, for instance, the proliferation of 'modes of production' we find in Marxist Maritime literature.

The common concerns come closer in two respects. One is the difficulty of knowing when the central fabric of the original theory is damaged by being worked on a different matrix. Certain concepts, in being reworked, lose their original clarity and power. Productive and non-productive labour in the domestic labour debate is an obvious example — so is Delphy's use of the concept of Domestic Mode of Production. From this perspective, there are dangers that the Maritime Marxists may lose the original clarity of certain Marxist categories (such as Mode of Production) and the original energy of dependency theory.

Another direct contribution of feminism is made where the discussions of the Maritime Marxists depend upon renegotiating the distinctions between centre and periphery around the ambiguity of women's domestic and subsistence labour. This is one area that has been exhaustively examined in feminist theory, and at this stage we can claim with a certain confidence that we know what goes on in the home, and in the peasant household. It is less clear that the Maritime Marxists do.

The burden of this section is to argue that by combining the insights of feminist explanations of women's subordination — especially those merging from a Marxist-feminist perspective — with the Maritime Marxist explanation of dependency theory, we may produce both a more accurate understanding of the family and the economy in the Atlantic region, and a powerful extension of our understanding of the interaction of gender, class and other forms of domination in constituting the subordination of women.

To carry the argument a little further, I want to take a number of concepts that have been developed by Marxist-feminists, and indicate, albeit schematically, their possibilities for extending the political economic analysis of the Atlantic region.

Marxist-feminist starting points and the political economy of the Atlantic Region

To do this, I take a number of concepts — production and reproduction, domestic labour, patriarchy, the sexual division of labour — and examine them in the context of the problems that I have just raised.

Patriarchy

In Veronica Beechey's cogent formulation of the problem, "the concept of patriarchy has been adopted by Marxist feminists in an attempt to transform Marxist theory so that it can more adequately account for the subordination of women as well as for the focus of class exploitation" (Beechey, 1979:66). In her extensive analysis of the different uses and interpretations of patriarchy, she remains unconvinced about either its heuristic or theoretical value. She concludes by insisting that

a satisfactory theory of patriarchy should be historically specific and should explore the forms of patriarchy which exist within particular modes of production — for example the forms of patriarchal domination which existed when the domestic economy was the primary producing unit are different from the forms which emerge as capital seizes control over the production process" (Beechey, 1979:80).

In most feminist uses of the concept, there is an understanding that there are certain world-wide (though not necessarily universal) structures of domination and subordination that operate in particular ways in particular economic, historical and social situations. There has been concern that the concept of patriarchy blindly applied becomes a-historical and overgeneralized. Indeed, Sheila Rowbotham has argued that the very concept is a-historical. "'Patriarchy' implies a structure which is fixed, rather than the kaleidoscope of forms within which women and men have encountered one another".[24] Other Marxist-feminists have rejected the concept, either because of its ideological baggage, or because of its intrinsic weaknesses, but all continue to discuss historically specific forms of male domination.[25] For want of a more exact concept, I refer to this discussion as 'patriarchy'.

If we take the concept of patriarchy and merely impose it on maritime material, it will as Thompson says, "push too easily toward generality" (Thompson, 1983). But what if we stand firmly on our own specific, historical and material evidence, and interrogate the concept from that viewpoint? Is it useful? Does it help us to understand women in maritime communities? Without doubt, most maritime communities could be described as patriarchal. They are male-dominated, and that dominance is mediated through family forms. Newfoundland society especially, could be, and often is, described as classically patriarchal. But what about the ironic circumstance that leads to men involved in deep sea fishing, oil rig and other macho work being absent for considerable periods of time, and thus reducing male influence on the family? The first consequence of an application of patriarchy will be to break down the equation, patriarchy = oppression. For the testimony says that the picture is more complex. There are variations in the division of labour: there are countervailing strategies and locales of power; there is ceaseless negotiation between men and women; there are separations of spheres. Detailed accounts stress, above all, the ambiguity of the outcome and its transitional nature. We may, here, be looking at complex interaction between different modes of production (capitalist and domestic). On the other hand, we may have to reevaluate the relationship between ideology and economy. We may begin to specify different forms of patriarchy, and to assess resistance to them. We may even see ways in which women have co-opted patriarchal structures. This kind of enquiry provides us with a powerful comparative agenda for our specific work. At the same time, it forces us to refine the concept of patriarchy so that it becomes a useful tool in understanding our material. But, beyond that, it contributes substantially to the delineation of a theory of patriarchy, and thus to one of the crucial intellectual projects of feminism.

This debate arose initially out of Levi Strauss' work, which specified the "exchange of women by men" as one of the deep structures of social relations. It was combined with a longstanding concern to adapt Marxist analysis of productive relations to the condition of women, and has led to an extensive reexamination of the categories of production and reproduction, and of the conditions in which they are carried out. It has also included a reexamination of the relationship of family and household to capitalism, and to precapitalist societies, and it has been most telling in the examination of specific instances.[26] Again, maritime communities offer a context that allows us to examine specific communities in this framework. It also enables us to make some comparisons within the maritime context, which reflect back on the categories themselves. For instance, fishing communities are often characterized by a division between harvesting and processing sectors that correlates with the sexual division of labour. They are also often characterized by family enterprises. Absence of men for long periods, and women's control over marketing and distribution are also significant characteristics of some maritime communities. We have already noticed the way in which such cross-cutting divisions alter our understanding about the division of power between men and women. An examination of production and reproduction, or of family and household might help to elucidate the contradictions we have noticed — and it would add flesh and substance to the reified concepts.

Here the central issue has been whether women's work in the home affects the value of labour power directly or indirectly. Veronica Beechey's article, "Some notes on female wage labour" (Beechey, 1977), has some direct relevance to the situation in the Atlantic region. While her specific focus is on female wage labour in capitalist production, the argument she makes suggests that all women's labour is paid at below its value. In terms of the common circumstance in the rural Atlantic when women take waged jobs before men, this is a pertinent finding and helps to elaborate Deere's position (discussed below) that the low value of labour power is supported by the subsistence work of women in the household. Beechey, more specifically, argues that married women's waged work is advantageous to capital because the costs of production and reproduction of labour power are partly borne by the family.

Beechey accepts the argument about the semi-proletarianized and male worker in the third world, where the wife's subsistence work can contribute to his reproduction as well as hers. However, she goes further when she suggests that, like semi-proletarians, *all* married women can be paid at a price below the value of their labour power. In this case, it is the married women's dependence on an assumed male wage that enables capital to pass some of her costs onto her husband's wage.

But where does this leave us in terms of the family in the Atlantic region, where women do not necessarily have husbands with wages? Is their position analogous to the single women of Beechey's analysis, who simply get depressed into severe poverty or contribute doubly to their own subsistence? Capital can continue to super-exploit by feminising jobs for which it can pay lower wages even when the woman is the only wage earner, and this is clearly relevant both in terms of the relationship and relative strength of the harvesting versus the processing sector in the fishery, and in terms of the existence and possible growth of clerical work in the rural areas.

The development of this idea must await supporting empirical work. Meanwhile, we must consider Carmen Deere's influential essay on the analysis of rural women's contribution to capital accumulation (Deere, 1976). She argued that "the family structure and the attendant division of labour by sex are keys to the extraction of surplus from noncapitalist modes of production". Her argument relates to Africa, but it is germane to much of the experience in Atlantic Canada. She emphasizes the importance of the provision of goods and services necessary for the reproduction of labour power outside the capitalist mode of production. We are familiar with some of the ramifications of this position in the domestic labour debate. Her refinement is to point to certain processes at the "interface between modes of production within the periphery" (Deere, 1976:133). The unity of the family means that production and consumption of the means of subsistence are not divorced from one another, and that the division of labour by sex is immaterial where the capitalist can appropriate surplus labour time regardless of who generates it within the family. However, Deere differentiates rigorously between the domestic unit in advanced capitalism, and the peasant unit on the periphery, especially in conditions of semi-proletarianisation where subsistence production is a source of use values independent of the wage. As she expresses it,

> the essential difference between the two units in terms of the production and reproduction of labour power is that the domestic unit in advanced capitalist countries stretches the wage through the transformation of commodities into use values, thereby maintaining the workers' standard of living above what it would otherwise be; the peasant unit in the periphery produces the goods and services which are purchased with the wage in the centre" (Deere, 1976:141).

More importantly, she argues that in centre economies women are drawn into labour market, which has the dual consequence of decreasing the household production of use values, and increasing both the need and the

30

production (by female labour) of these same use values in the commodity market. Of course that also increases the labour of transforming them back into use values once they enter the home. In contrast, on the periphery, women continue to produce the means of subsistence within the household, as well as functioning as a low cost rural labour reserve. There are implications for this kind of argument in the context of the seasonal pattern of employment in Atlantic Canada, paradigmatically in fish plant work. Connelly and Macdonald's work is one indication of the way in which women move in and out of the labour market according to seasonal fluctuations, and how that is an element both in the exploitation of rural communities, and in their survival.

Finally, Deere argues that whereas the sexual division of labour is irrelevant in subsistence production, it is relevant, indeed crucial, in semi-proletarianism. The assumption Deere makes that it will always be men who are drawn into wage labour and women who remain in non-capitalist modes of production, relates to work done in third world countries by, for example, Boserup (1970) and Rogers (1980), but it is critically at odds with historical accounts of Europe, and particularly with the experience of Atlantic Canada. Sacouman (Sacouman, 1980:237) observes that "the typical commercial farm witnessed the wife, at least, engaging in wage work" (usually fish processing) while the husband maintained this status as an 'independent farmer', a scenario gradually changing in the direction of absorbing the husband, as well, into semi-proletarianisation. Equally, in many outport communities in Newfoundland, the men continue to fish inshore in family crews and sell their fish to the local plant in a relationship which is certainly not wage labour, while the women, no longer working on the household production of dried fish, take waged jobs when available — often in the same plants that process the fish caught by their husbands and sons.

To see how Deere's analysis can be applied to the apparently contradictory situation in Atlantic Canada involves considering the sexual division of labour as a fundamental organizing principle within both capitalist and non-capitalist modes of production.

The sexual division of labour

In Thompson's work on the relationship of gender, culture and economic success in four Scottish fishing communities, he stresses the need for specific comparative work through local studies of changes in sexual relationships over time, in relation to both economy and culture (Thompson, 1983). I will argue in Chapter 5 that the maritime context offers a paradigmatic 'case' of sexual divisions that is useful because of its supposed extremity and rigidity. Theory must work at this level. But to avoid the "static analysis in

31

anthropological work" and the "almost inherent . . . trans-historical use of patriarchy as a principal concept in analysis" we must also build theory from the bottom up (Thompson, 1983:22). The level of the enterprise is crucial. Detailed studies at the community level are vital, but we must be able to move on to talk generally about women in the Atlantic region. To do this we need to relate the findings vertically, as it were, to the level of the province, and then to the region. Analysis at this level has often been restricted to the examination of government documents, reports and legislation, provincial statistics, and the detailed interrogation of centrally based officials and 'leaders'. An approach grounded in the lived experience of the sexual division of labour is, at the least, less likely to slip into generality and the partial understanding of 'gender based' concepts.

In concluding their 1983 essay, Pat and Hugh Armstrong say "any theory of capitalism must be conscious of and provide explanation not only for the separation between home and work but also for that between women and men. It must put women and men back into their history at all levels of analysis (Armstrong, 1983:39). The argument for using the sexual division of labour as an organizing concept in developing our understanding of the Atlantic region is twofold. The first is that at all levels of analysis it guards against slippage into the partiality of 'gender free analysis'. If the sexual division of labour is present as an informing principle, it insists that gender is fundamental both in what is studied and how it is analyzed, no matter what the level of abstraction employed. Secondly, it will be clear from the preceding discussion how loaded with ideological baggage theoretical concepts become. The term 'sexual division of labour' is not a concept. It is a description, a reminder of the centrality of both gender and materiality. It can thus be adapted to the particularity of our situation, without sinking into argument by analogy, or importing unnecessary ideological overtones.

Conclusion

This chapter began with an awareness of the inadequacy of both the existing feminist and Marxist conceptual wardrobe for the analysis of the unique and complex situation of working women and men in the region. It began also with an appreciation of the radical impetus of both active feminist and active Marxists in the development of an accurate and opposite politics, based on the lived experience of ordinary people.

The possibility that Maritime Marxist analysis and Marxist-feminism are essentially related was the burden of my argument. This is not to say that two such different traditions and projects should be collapsed into one, but that neither will develop as it should without a real consideration of the other.

In this respect, the original paper was another small contribution to what the Armstrongs have called "the ambitious reworking project" toward a "political economy that is sex conscious as well as class conscious — towards a feminism that is class conscious as well as sex conscious" (Armstrong, 1983:7).

I have argued, firstly, that the political economic perspective developed by male Marxists is seriously defective in the light of feminist insights and concerns; and secondly, that the Atlantic region provides an appropriate context for developing, refining and making politically relevant certain feminist concepts. The vantage point of a position as a Marxist-feminist working in the Atlantic region produces an acute awareness of the urgency of an analysis of our own situation — an analysis that cannot ignore the contributions of male Maritime Marxists or of feminists if we are to transcend our separate peripheries and emerge onto the main stage of political action.

The argument is, finally, about possibility: about a combined vision that could unlock some of our most obdurate problems, about a combined energy that could make their solution a real possibility, and about the development of a genuinely feminist-Marxist analysis. As such, it establishes the theme that I will explore in the next few chapters in this book.

Notes

1. An earlier version of this chapter first appeared in *Studies in Political Economy*, Number 23, Summer 1987. While some of the concerns I express here now seem particular to the period of the mid-eighties, the discussion introduces the reader to the wide range of literature on the Atlantic fisheries and women in maritime cultures.

2. There are problems with collapsing the historical, cultural and economic differences between the Maritime Provinces (Nova Scotia, New Brunswick and Prince Edward Island) and Newfoundland, which is one reason why writers based in the Maritimes prefer to restrict their compass (see R. James Sacouman, "Semi-proletarianisation and Rural Underdevelopment in the Maritimes." *Canadian Review of Sociology and Anthropology* 17:3 (1980), R. James Sacouman, "The 'peripheral' Maritimes and Canada-wide Marxist political economy," *Studies in Political Economy* 6 (Autumn, 1981). For those based in Newfoundland, however, this would compound our actual distance with a theoretical isolation. In any case, the view from the Rock emphasizes similarities with the other Atlantic Provinces, see Bryant Fairley, "The Struggle for Capitalism in the fishing industry in Newfoundland," *Studies in Political Economy* 17 (Summer, 1985), p. 35. For these reasons, I refer throughout this book to the Atlantic region, mindful that this formulation glosses over important variations.

3. This tradition has been labelled 'Maritime Marxism' by, for example, B. Fairley, "The struggle for capitalism", (see n. 2, above); R.H. Hill. "The political economy of fishing in the context of regional underdevelopment", (paper presented to AASA, Halifax, 1983). The central proponents do have a geographical, political and theoretical identity. I use it here as a heuristic device, but in its inclusive rather than exclusive variant. Thus I use it to include other writers who are outside the central group but who share some of the same concerns and approaches, and more widely, to indicate opponents who have some of the same interest in refining an adequate political economy of Atlantic Canada.

4. The body of work on which I drew to formulate this argument included, E. Antler (1977, 1982); D. Davis, (1979, 1980, 1983a, 1983b, 1984); L. Christiansen-Ruffman, (1982, 1985b); Barbara Neis, (1984, 1988); P. Connelly and M. MacDonald, (1983, 1985), together with my own work on the Southern Shore. While the argument I make in this paper depends on this early generation of feminist work, it is

also apposite today, when the scope and variety of feminist work on the region has much increased.

5. Canadian Marxists, especially in the Maritimes, had long been interested in ideas which can be broadly subsumed under the head of 'dependency theory', e.g., A.G. Frank's work on Latin America, (New York, 1967) and I. Wallerstein's extension of related ideas into a 'world system', e.g., *The Origins of the Modern World System* (New York, 1974), and the debates extending their concepts have been especially influential. Two good discussions can be found in H. Veltmeyer, "A central issue in dependency theory", and G. Barrett, "Perspectives on dependency and underdevelopment in the Atlantic Region", both in *Canadian Review of Sociology and Anthropology* 17:3 (1980). More recent perspectives on the same issue can be found in B. Fairley, et al. (1990).

6. Simone de Beavoir, *The Second Sex* (1953).

7. Ellen Antler, "Maritime mode of production", and, "Fisherman, Fisherwoman and Proletariat", see n. 4.

8. As Sheila Rowbotham put it, the work "of a couple of bourgeois men in the nineteenth century", *Women, Resistance and Revolution* (London, 1972).

9. For related but rather differently oriented work on Nova Scotia, see the work of A. Miles, (1984); also, L. Christiansen-Ruffman, (1982); P.J. and G. Macnab de Vries, (1983); S. Ilcan, (1985).

10. The Kirby Report, which led to the restructuring of the Atlantic fishery had just been published when I wrote this.

11. This is not entirely fair. Page 117 does contain some recognition when he says "the closure of a processing plant can well mean the closing of an entire community because fishing incomes alone are often not sufficient to support a family", but he does not spell out the family relationships involved, nor integrate the consequences into his recommendations.

12. See J. Tunstall, (1962); J. Faris, (1972); M.K. Orbach, (1977). For more subtle comments, see *North Atlantic Fishermen*, eds. R. Andersen and C. Wadel (1972); J.M. Acheson, "The anthropology of fishing", *Annual Review of Anthropology* 10 (1981). Many assumptions,

especially by anthropologists, depend on Murdoch's seminal but doubtful observations, G. Murdoch, "Comparative data on the division of labour by sex", *Social Forces* 15:4 (1937). For a feminist evaluation of the field see J. Nadel and D. Davis, *To Work and Weep*, (1988)

13. See for example, O. Brox, (1972); Andersen and Wadel, (1972); G. Wright, (1984); P. Sinclair, (1985). Since the mid 1980s the crisis in the cod stocks have precipitated a number of studies including D. MacInnes, S. Jentoft and A. Davis (eds) (1991); P. Sinclair (1990, 1992).

14. See B. Neis, *The Social Impact of Technological Change in Newfoundland's Deepsea Fishery* (St. John's, 1986); *Occupational Stress and Repetition Strain Injuries* (with S. Williams) (St. John's, 1993); *Effect of Crisis in the Newfoundland Fishery on Women who Work in the Industry* (with A. Rowe and S. Williams) (St. John's, 1991).

15. See the pioneering collection *Underdevelopment and Social Movements in Atlantic Canada*, eds. Brym and Sacouman (Toronto, 1979) especially articles by Williams, Clow and Veltmeyer; R.J. Sacouman, "Semi-proletarianisation", and, "The 'peripheral' Maritimes,": H. Veltmeyer, "Dependency and underdevelopment: some questions and problems", *Canadian Journal of political and Social Theory* 2:2 (1978), For the recent, much revised, views of many of these authors see B. Fairley, C. Leys and J. Sacouman (Toronto, 1990).

16. See J. West, "Women, sex and class" in *Feminism and Materialism*. eds. A. Kuhn and A.M. Wolpe (1978) for a now dated but particularly clear commentary on the problems of gender and class analysis.

17. For a demonstration of this in Newfoundland, see R.H. Hill, *The Meaning of Work and the Reality of Unemployment* (St. John's, 1983).

18. See C. Bell, "GNP: Meaning behind figures", *Christian Science Monitor* 15 April 1976; C. von Werlhof, "The Proletarian is dead, long live the housewife?"; M.D. Evers et al., "Subsistence reproduction: a framework for analysis", in *Households and the World-Economy*, eds. J. Smith et al., (Beverly Hills, 1984). M. Waring, *If Women Counted* (1988).

19. For evidence and an interesting discussion of this point, see L. Christiansen-Ruffman, "Wealth re-examined".

20. Delphy's main weakness is that unlike Sacouman, who, rooted in the modes of production debate (A. Foster-Carter, "The modes of production controversy", *New Left Review* 107 (1978)), is careful to specify the subordinate nature of his domestic mode of production, Delphy argues that it is quite analogous, and within its own sphere of gender relations, as dominant as the capitalist mode of production (Delphy, 1977:4).

21. For the best condensed summaries of this whole now rather dated debate, see E. Kaluzynska, "Wiping the floor with theory", *Feminist Review* 6 (1980); M. Molyneux, "Beyond the housework debate", *New Left Review* 116 (1979); Introduction to *The Politics of Housework*, ed. E. Malos (London, 1980).

22. Partly as a result of these and other comments, Sinclair's more recent work on the Northern Peninsula does make real inroads in taking gender as a serious and central part of his analysis. See P. Sinclair and L. Felt, 'Home Sweet Home: Dimensions and Determinants of Life Satisfaction in a Marginal Region', *Canadian Journal of Sociology*, 16 (1), 1991; 'Separate Worlds: gender and domestics labour in an isolated fishing region', *Canadian Review of Sociology and Anthropology*, Vol. 29, pp. 55-71.

23. See A. Clark, *Working Life of Women in the Seventeenth Century* (London, 1919); C. Hall, "The history of the housewife" in *The Politics of Housework*, ed. E. Malos.

24. S. Rowbotham, "The trouble with 'patriarchy'", *New Statesman* (21/28 December, 1979). For the opposing position, see S. Alexander and B. Taylor, "in defence of Patriarchy", *New Statesman* (1 February, 1980).

25. For an extended and cogent discussion of this issue, see M. Barrett, *Women's Oppression Today* (London, 1980).

26. Key contributions to that complex debate include C. Meillassoux, *Maidens, Meal and Money* (Cambridge, 1975); M. Mackintosh, "Reproduction and Patriarchy", *Capital and Class* 2 (Summer, 1977); B. O'Laughlan, "Production and Reproduction", *Critique of Anthropology* 2:8 (1977); G. Rubin in *Toward an Anthropology of*

Women, ed. R. Reiter, (New York, 1975); R. McDonough and R. Harrison, "Patriarchy and relations of production" in *Feminism and Materialism*, eds. Kuhn and Wolpe, 1978).

3 'Skipper of the shore crew': The history of women in Newfoundland

Introduction

In this chapter, the first of two dealing with the historical origins of women in Newfoundland, I shall present an overview of our existing knowledge, based on secondary sources. Our current inadequate knowledge of the generation and maintenance of the sexual division of labour has generally limited the discussion either to broad generalizations or to extrapolation based on highly specific examples.[1] What we do know suggests that there is a tension between the remarkable consistency of the general lines of the sexual division of labour and the degree of variation that prevents the establishment of "universal" rules. Within the broad patriarchal relations of dominance and subordination, there is an almost infinite variation in both gender relations and the sexual division of labour. Nor is the pattern fixed in any single society. Sexual divisions are constructed, negotiated, and endlessly challenged. Work by anthropologists and sociologists tends to focus on ways in which patriarchal relations operate through the institutions of marriage and the family and in relation to capitalist productive relations. Historians have contributed a growing body of detailed studies that show subordination mediated through family patterns, economic and technological organisation, religious and political ideology, and many other factors.[2] My interest in the historical origins of Newfoundland women's experience grew out of the theoretical concerns I explored in Chapter 1. But there was another trigger, which was the apparent disjuncture between what the literature told me I *ought* to find among women in communities dominated by maritime activities and what I actually did find in the course of ethnographic fieldwork.

Newfoundland rural outports are maritime communities. Even today, the traditionally rigid sexual division of labour is unbreached. In addition, physical conditions in the outports are tough, and "male" activities such as hunting and woodcutting still play a large part in the rural economy. In short, the ethos of "fishermen" is a rugged male identity, and it is clamped firmly over the image of outport life.

This association of maritime communities with a rigid and extreme sexual division of labour is a commonplace of anthropological literature,[3] and rigid and extreme sexual divisions have been traditionally interpreted as giving rise to oppressive male dominance. J. Tunstall (1982) gave a classic account of the negative consequences of seafaring domestic relations among the Hull fishermen and similar tendencies have been reported from Aberdeen and San Diego.[4] J. Zulaika (1981), writing about Portuguese fishermen, describes similar manifestations, but makes some interesting and sensitive comments on the relationship between the demands of a tough seaman identity and its expression in sexual relations. Male anthropologists working in Newfoundland with this implicit understanding have stressed women's heavy work load, male authority in the family, male-biased inheritance rules, and the practice of exogamy.[5]

Yet it is not quite like that. My own observations and other feminist studies found outport women to be relatively independent, politically and economically, and moreover, to be in possession of a vibrant and positive women's culture.[6] Among possible countervailing forces, women's considerable economic leverage deriving from their continued share in the fishery seemed to me the most salient. However, it was also noticeable that all of the studies of male oppression associated with maritime activities had been based on communities where men were at sea for considerable periods of time. This was not true of most Newfoundland fishermen, and was certainly not true of the traditional inshore cod fishery. P. Thompson (1983), working in Scotland, had argued forcibly that the considerable variations in gender and family relations between Scottish communities are associated with different patterns of childrearing practices and economic adaptations.

In this chapter, I take a different approach, by examining the existing historical material, to see how current gender relations and sexual divisions of labour originated. But before I begin, I must enter a number of caveats about the material and my use of them.

There is a considerable quantity of material on the early history of Newfoundland (from the sixteenth to the eighteenth century), but no serious work has been done on women in this period, and we are left with tantalizing glimpses, extrapolation, and plain guesswork about the lives of the early female settlers. All that we can be sure about is that women did come from the times of the earliest settlements, both as wives and daughters, and as single women who came as servants. Inevitably all their lives were both hard and hard working, and there are indications that certain traditions and divisions of labour that are current on the island today originated then. But the argument that follows is based on the more certain evidence of demography and patterns of settlement, until we reach the better-documented nineteenth and twentieth centuries.

The island of Newfoundland is characterized by considerable variation in climate and geography, which dictated variations in fishing patterns and strategies. There are also variations relating to the relative strengths of different denominations and sects in different areas, and to the origins of the first settlers and subsequent arrivals. All this has consequences for gender relations and the sexual division of labour, but because of the paucity of the material on women we cannot, as yet, make province-wide generalizations. I have, therefore, indicated which area of the island each piece of evidence relates to and how far it can be taken to be generally applicable. Most evidence comes from the northeast coast, and can only be applied with caution to the south coast, the southern shore, or the northern peninsula.

Nevertheless, I would argue that it is only by taking a larger perspective that we may be able to understand the current negotiation of gender relations.

"Soe long as there comes noe women they are not fixed": settlement, expansion, and permanence

Although European fishermen from England, France, the Basque Country, Portugal, and Spain were exploiting the bountiful supplies of cod over the Grand Banks in the summer months by the end of the fifteenth century, if not earlier, there was no attempt at permanent settlement until 1610 when the London and Bristol Company of the Colonization of Newfoundland established a settlement of 40 men at Cupids, Conception Bay. Manifestly women were needed to establish a settlement and in August 1611, sixteen women arrived, and by March 1613 the first recorded child was born.[7] Apart from that we know little of why they were, why they came, or what their lives were like — save that in the prevailing conditions there was no room for slackers of either sex. The story is repeated for the Welsh settlements at Renews (1616), the Bristol settlement at Harbour Grace (1618), and Calvert's more successful venture at Ferryland (1620). Throughout it is arguable that tough and hard working though the women were, it was less relevant to the development of their economic independence and mutual respect than their role in settlement as such.

A signal feature of settlement in Newfoundland up to the end of the eighteenth century was the demographic sexual imbalance and the effect the absence of women had on the speed and success of settlement. There was a huge preponderance of men on the island, especially in summer when the seasonal migrants (wholly men) far outnumbered the winter residents. Small groups of men (and a very few families) wintered over for one or two

41

seasons. Even among the permanent residents the number of male apprentices and servants far outnumbered the imported women. Significant as they were, the servant girls were in no way sufficient to produce a balanced population. It produced problems of order in St. John's[8] and prevented further settlement on the frontiers. As a naval captain put it succinctly in 1684, "soe long as there comes noe women they are not fixed". This situation was a double-edged sword to the authorities. Those on the ground complained bitterly about disorder "for the permanent growth of a colonial population every single man who is sent out in excess of the number of single women is absolutely useless" (quoted in J. Mannion, 1977:19). On the other hand, the English government did not want growth of the colony and was reluctant to admit that it had grown as much as it had, in which case the answer was simple — restrict the number of women immigrants. While there seems to be no evidence that this measure was ever tried, it does seem to have been on the agenda for some time (Halton and Harvey, 1883:43).

In any event, the pattern of a large summer (male) migration and a much smaller resident population continued through the eighteenth century, and so did the friction between them. In 1675, 1,200 people wintered on the island; by 1730 it was 3,500; by 1750 it was 7,300, and by 1753 it had risen tenfold to 12,000. The proportion of women at the beginning of the century was only 10 per cent (instead of a "normal" 25 per cent) and children only accounted for 25 per cent (instead of 50 per cent). By the end of the century these proportions had risen to 13 per cent and 33 per cent respectively and they climbed to normal proportions a few years later. As G. Head puts it, "the wintering population was approaching normal characteristics and no longer contained an overwhelming mass of single male labourers. With women and children the attachment to the island was firmer" (Head, 1976:141).

The necessity of women to settlement was clear, but the growth in the number of women had another important consequence. The "planters" (established fishermen with their own boats) ceased to import large numbers of "youngsters" (servants from Europe) and relied instead on their families. It is likely, given the tradition of active female involvement, that wives had always helped out on shore at peak times, but evidence suggests that the heyday of family production began in the late eighteenth century.[9]

I will examine the Newfoundland family fishery in more detail below, but first I want to complete the record of women's more basic contribution to the colony — as sexual partners and founders of families. Bonavista Bay and Trinity Bay had had scattered settlements in the eighteenth century (of 450-900 and 1,500 respectively in 1772) and a few pioneers had already moved north to Notre Dame Bay and Fogo. On the south coast, settlement was centred on St. Jacques, Fortune, and Grand Bank at the east end, and on Port aux Basque in the west, and these gradually extended to meet at Burgeo and Ramea, although the total resident population of the south coast continued to be small (about 600 in 1763).

By the beginning of the nineteenth century, new settlements were established not by new immigration from England but by families moving to a "summer station" on a less frequented stretch of the coast — as far as the northern peninsula, and later Labrador.[10] If the family was happy, they might well settle there. Those families then had children and the ensuing marriageable girls attracted further settlement. In one example, on the extreme northwest tip of the island, a tiny group of Englishmen in a merchant's employment survived until the Watts family arrived, with two sons and two daughters. One daughter married William Buckle in the late 1890s and they founded the Buckle family that spreads across Labrador to this day. The other daughter, Mary, married a naval deserter, Alexander Duncan, who changed his name to his mother's maiden name of Gould. They had three sons (from whom are descended the numerous and powerful Goulds of the Flowers Cove/Port au Choix area) and nine daughters "who grew into beautiful girls" providing a sudden bonus supply of eligible wives for the young English settlers. These couples spread along the coast from Eddies Cove to St. Margaret's Bay, populating all the coves (Firestone, 1973:23).

The demographic contribution of women to settlement has been recognized both by contemporary authorities and spelt out in recent studies, although the feminist implications have not been.[11] But the economic contribution of "the skipper of the shore crew" has been more slowly recognized. It is to her that we now turn.

Women's work in the fishing settlements

The best documented area of Newfoundland is the northeast coast and much of the discussion that follows is taken from there. The situation, for example, on the south coast where the trap fishery never developed, was significantly different. Moreover, the evidence is too sparse for any legitimate conclusions to be drawn as to whether the consequences of women's different roles in the fishing economy were as great as might be expected. At this point, all I am attempting is a description of the sexual division of labour as it developed, especially on the northeast coast, together with certain congruences with women's position as observed today.

A further caveat needs to be entered when collapsing such a long period as that between the beginning of the nineteenth century and Confederation (1949). Clearly there were profound technical changes (such as the introduction of the cod trap, and of engines), social changes (such as the more widespread education), and political changes (such as the rise and fall of the Fishermen's Protective Union in the early twentieth century.[12] Nevertheless it seems that the essential pattern of the sexual division of labour did remain relatively constant, and in this discussion I shall stress that continuity. It is in this context that I am using material such as Greta Hussey's autobiography to illustrate patterns that existed long before. It should, however, be reiterated that the context in which they occurred was changing.

The outport communities were always (up to the influx of federal money in 1949) on the brink of survival.[13] A bad year could push whole settlements into starvation or emigration. I stress this because it was women who, as always, had the prime responsibility for feeding, cleaning, and caring for themselves, the men, and the children. It would have been hard in those wild conditions even in prosperity: in poverty it was an enormous task.

A complication that affected many families was a pattern of transhumance. Families who lived out on the exposed headlands would often "winter in" the head of the bay where there was more shelter and more wood. They lived in "tilts" — crude shacks which, nonetheless, women had to make habitable. Conversely, many families lived "at home" in the winter but moved in the summer to "summer stations" or "outside" to fish. These places were often hundreds of miles away "on the Labrador". Greta Hussey describes her mother packing everything the family might need in "the Labrador box" for four or more months. They took "pots, pans, dishes, cooking gear and most of the rough grub that we lived on, such as salt beef, dried peas, dried beans, hard bread, sugar, butter and salt pork" (Hussey, 1981:5).

The range of domestic activities Newfoundland women undertook as a matter of course accords closely with descriptions given of the lives of rural women in the nineteenth and early twentieth centuries in other parts of America and Europe.[14] Feeding the family included most of the care of the animals — a few cows, sheep, goats, horses, and later chickens, who needed hay and roots to help them survive the winter. The garden was a major responsibility. Men usually did the actual digging, but women cleared or "picked" the ground of stones, planted and weeded it, and defended it against animals. Then they gathered the vegetables and dried them or preserved them (sometimes in salt) in a root cellar, as they are recorded as doing in Edward Winne's letter from Ferryland in 1622.[15] They practised rotation of crops and despised shop-bought seed because "the flies would eat it". Besides, a woman was considered lazy "if she did not grow her own seeds" (Murray, 1979:18).

If the family kept cows or goats, then the wife made butter. A major food gathering activity was berry picking, and while men sometimes did this, it was primarily the task of the women and children. Most of them relished the opportunity to get out on the barrens and the marshes. Blueberries, partridge berries, the succulent bake apples, marsh berries, currants and cranberries, raspberries and blackberries were all gathered on different parts of the island (Murray, 1979:23). Many of them were sold, and a family might well provide itself with its winter supplies of flour, margarine, sugar, molasses, beef, and pork with its "berrynote". In passing we should note that this is, in effect, a cash contribution to the family income. The rest were bottled or "jammed down". And so we enter the kitchen. The Newfoundland housewife was honour-bound to set a meal before any member of the family (or visitor) the moment they entered the house. Like many of the practices noted here, it survives today. Everyone had at least four meals a day, and in summer it often rose to seven or eight — a man's light snack in the early morning, breakfast about 7:30-8:00, a mug-up at 10:30-11:00, dinner at 12:00-1:00 p.m., mug-up at 3:30-4:00, tea at 5:30-6:00 p.m. and a mug-up before bedtime at 10:30-11:00 p.m. "Mug-ups" consisted of tea, bread and butter, and "relish" — left over fish or home-made jam, and the last meal of the day, "the night-lunch", was often quite substantial. Main meals, not surprisingly, revolved around fish and potatoes, but salt pork, salt beef, figgy duff and pease pudding, thick soups and dumplings were common. Game-meat or birds were a coveted extra. A glance at any traditional Newfoundland cookbook will show that housewives stressed quantity and weight above all else, but they were ingenious in ringing the changes on limited ingredients.

Bread-making was both a major chore and a woman's pride: "the knowledge of bread making was one skill all marriageable girls were expected to possess" and little girls would stand on chairs to make the "barm" or dough. Most housewives baked at least once a day; large families needed two bakings (Murray, 1979:121). Before commercial yeast was introduced in the 1920, women grew their own hops. Greta Hussey made her own yeast from hops and raw potatoes because she was dissatisfied with the bread made from shop-bought yeast. In times of dire poverty they would mix potatoes with the flour to eke it out.

Men's suits always seem to have been bought when possible, but most other clothes were homemade. It was another task made more obviously complicated by poverty. Coats had to be "turned", flour sacks had to be transformed into pillow cases, aprons, and tablecloths, and in the poorer families into dresses and shirts brightened by embroidery. "The coloured thread was inexpensive and with a bit of skill and a few hours work, plain flour sacking was made very attractive" (Murray, 1979:29). Quilting was less developed than it was in the United States, but hooking mats developed into a folk art (Pocius, 1979:365). This developed because the women covered bare floors with mats of brin "hooked" with pictures or designs using any brightly coloured rags they could find, thus saving the last scraps of an old garment. The results fetch high prices today and are an enduring testimony to the skill and resourcefulness of Newfoundland housewives.

Some women made sails or "twine" for the nets but such work is usually conspicuous by its absence in women's tasks — a sign and a symbol of the separation of worlds that began exactly at the shoreline, or landwash. Some women could card and spin wool straight from the sheep; but all women could knit and the list of garments that had to be turned out is staggering. Murray cites "knitted petticoats, long stockings, vamps (ankle length socks), corsocks (balaclavas), mittens, cuffs, gloves, vests, long johns and sweaters". In addition, there was the mending, a much less attractive task and one heartily hated by the young cooks who went on the Labrador fishery (Hussey, 1981:44).

Washing started with carrying water and splitting wood — both women's tasks. Before the 1930s, they made their own soap from rotten cod livers and wood ash. They took care to "blue" and bleach their whites — and even after scrubbing boards were introduced, some women would not use them because they were "hard on the clothes". The production of a faultless line of washing was another indication of a woman's pride. Even today there is a correct order in which to hang clothes on the line that newcomers flout at their peril. Health was another female concern, and most women knew some folk remedies, but the real skill resided with the midwives. Two or three women in each community won the confidence of the women with their skill and patience, at a time when doctors were frequently unavailable. Their work needs a separate account.[16]

Houses gradually became more complex (and larger) but some features endured (and still endure today). They were made of wood by the men of the family. A man's pride rested on his ability to build his own boat and house as surely as the woman's did in her "domestic" skills. The central room was the kitchen in which virtually all family activity took place, and in which the many visitors were received. Houses were kept spotless. They were repainted or repapered inside at least once a year and the kitchen was done spring and fall, including repainting the floor linoleum. G. Hussey records repapering their Labrador house with newspaper or religious tracts each year when they arrived. Floors and steps were scrubbed daily. Mats and bedding were aired. One of the heaviest and least popular jobs was washing the heavy winter bed covers when summer eventually released them. Lamps were trimmed and polished, stoves polished. There is an endless list of such recurring tasks.

The enormous extent and weight of the work, as well as the variety of the skills and the standards of excellence the women maintained are impressive, but they are not unique. What marks out the Newfoundland women was that into this crowded schedule came the fishing. The timing and length of the fishing season varied around the coast as did the species pursued and the methods used. The south coast, for instance, could pursue a winter fishery free of ice. Its proximity to the Grand Banks also made it a natural headquarters for the banking schooners.[17] On the northeast coast, the seal hunt was an important part of the economy. Herring were important on the south and west coasts. Shellfish were increasingly caught, and lobster-canning factories were established on the northern peninsula in the nineteenth century.

But these were all supplementary to the inshore pursuit of "King Cod". In most parts of the island, cod came inshore in pursuit of caplin in early summer and remained until fall. The traditional English approach had always focused on this catch, taken from small boats first with hook and line, and later in cod traps.[18] Boats were under pressure to catch as much as possible in the short season — up to five boatloads a day. The crews did not have time to deal with the much more complex and time-consuming operation of drying the fish onshore. While the shore operation never became "women's work" the way baking was, it did become an area in which women developed skills and expertise. Above all, in the context of the full-fledged trap fishery it involved considerable authority as the "skipper", that is the fisherman's wife, had charge of the whole process, including the hiring and supervision of labour.

Essentially, the fish, each one of which could weight up to ten pounds or more, were processed along an assembly line. Each load was pitchforked up onto the stage. There the "cut throat" began the operation, the "header" removed the head and guts, and "splitter" (the most skillful operator) removed the backbone. The fish were then washed and the "salter" put them in layers into barrels of salt. After a few weeks, the fish were "made". First they were washed and then carried out to the flakes where they were dried and stacked. It was an operation calling for timing and experience to spread the fish out at the correct time and then build stacks of the right size so that the fish stayed in perfect condition throughout the process.[19] "It was first taken up with a small fish placed over a large one, both back up. Care had to be taken with the big "pickle" fish when taking them up for the first time, especially if it were a Saturday. Sunday might be hot and the big ones might sunburn if left unshielded. Next evening we put four fish together, head and tails. Then small "faggots", then larger "faggots" [that is rectangular piles nicely rounded on top]. When the fish dried hard they were put in a big round pile" (Murray, 1979:16).

47

While this process was carried out by all fishing families, the degree of division of labour and the timing varied according to whether the crew was a hand-lining crew or a trap crew. It was immensely hard work. Wilson reports one woman saying "If I had but two hours sleep in 24, I could stand the week's labor; but to do without rest for nearly a week is too much for my strength" (Wilson, 1866:212). This was in addition to their usual work, which at this time of year included the preparation and clearing of seven meals a day for the equally exhausted fishermen. Luckily this intensity only lasted for two to three months with a gradual tailing off in the fall.

Economy and authority: "The woman was more than 50 per cent"

Not surprisingly, male writers have largely failed to recognize the strategic importance of women's economic contribution to the fishery until Ellen Antler made a serious effort to estimate the cash value of the women's contribution to the fishery. She argued that the drying of the fishing added $2,400 to the value of the season's catch in Labrador, $1,500-2,000 in Conception Bay. Other writers have tried to put monetary or proportional values on the total amount that women's work contributed to the family income. Alexander reckoned it was at least half.[20] But to most outside authorities, this was an invisible reality. The economic unit was the family, and the head of that unit was the fisherman. Combined with ideological pre-eminence of the fisherman as a catcher of fish, it has helped to obscure not only the real contribution of women but also our understanding of the sexual division of labour in the outports.

Josiah Hobbs, who gave the title to Hilda Murray's book, was not alone in his estimation that "the woman was more than 50 per cent . . . I should say a woman, in a fisherman's work, was half the procedure". Whenever they are asked, Newfoundland men unhesitatingly credit women with at least half the work of the family. There is an air of something like awe in the folklore descriptions older men give of the women of their youth.

The handling of what little cash actually passed in outport families reflects this trust. Women handled the "berry money", as we have seen. They also bartered the occasional dry fish for something they needed at the store. The end of the season reckoning when the fish were "shipped", that is sold to the local fish merchant, was in the hands of the man, but when he had "settled up" he gave this money to his wife (Murray, 1979:24). Money earned "away" was passed to the wife and all household transactions were handled by her. Contemporary evidence bears this out. Dona Davis working on the south coast records women handling all the domestic finances, referring major decisions to their husbands as a formality to rubber stamp their approval. Furthermore, they consider wages that they earn "theirs to spend as they see fit" (Davis, 1983:101).

All this suggests that women have earned, and been granted a place in the economic unit of the family as nearly equal partners. Yet, much evidence in the handling of family budgets suggests that while women often "manage" money it need not necessarily imply real control.[21]   This suspicion is reinforced in Newfoundland by the fact that whatever arrangements were made within the family, external economic relations were carried out by, or in the name of, men.

There is, in addition, the tradition of male-dominated fishing communities, the "authoritarianism" of Newfoundland fathers and the extreme sexual division of labour. Both historically and in contemporary Newfoundland there are particular difficulties in establishing the dimensions of "power" and its relation to "authority". The pervasive egalitarian ethic and the consequent avoidance of authority in outport communities have often been remarked on.[22]   Coupled with a stress on individualism (which is interpreted as individual families) this means that there is virtually no possibility for leadership or the exercise of power within the community. Even minor success is penalized, but on the other hand, if an individual or a family (or a community) feels wronged then voluble public protest is in order. When we look at the distribution of power in Newfoundland it is also important to remember that prior to Confederation, outport communities, in common with rural communities elsewhere, were not only politically powerless but economically marginal, with each individual family equally exploited by merchant interests.

Some writers suggest that women (partly because of their stranger status) are less susceptible to the egalitarian ethic. In another paper (Chapter 6), I pointed to one way which women had found of defining to the ethic but escaping its consequences. Dona Davis, who worked in a community that was not characterized by exogamy, found women powerful in defence of their families and their own positions in the house, but less effective in public associations and penalized if they trespassed into the male sphere. Even today it makes little sense to talk of either men or women having power in a situation when the communities themselves have such a minimal public voice.

Patriarchal assumptions permeate nineteenth-century accounts and later anthropological work. Faris, for instance, simply states "in a fishing community one might reasonably expect a sharp division of labour along sexual lines, and Cat Harbour is certainly no exception", going on to observe that virilocal residence and exogamy reinforce such divisions. Faris has been criticized for his assumption on a number of grounds. Stiles (Stiles, 1972) and Davis, who worked on the south coast, which never operated the trap fishery in family units as they did on the northeast coast, both point to much closer and more reciprocal husband/wife relationships. Regional differences are certainly important, but here I want, rather, to stress Faris's dubious assumption that the people of Cat Harbour, especially the women, gave priority to men's work in the same way that Faris himself does.

Both Firestone and Faris produce some evidence for what they see as extreme male authority in the home. It is worth quoting the passage in which Firestone states:

> The family is patriarchal. Decisions pertaining to family activities are ultimately those of the father . . . and plans of a group of brothers working under their fathers are finalized by him. In the house the woman gets a drink for her husband from the water barrel or food on demand . . . The man tells his wife to do whatever it is that he wants in a matter of fact way — neither a command nor a request — and she complies (Firestone, 1978:77).

He concludes "there is no question as to the man's authority nor to the woman's subordination". He cites as corroborative evidence a woman saying "it is best when the wife does what the husband wants". But in the very next quotation we hear a woman saying "a good woman here is one who is obedient and doesn't try to tell the man what to do . . . at least the men would say that". Thus, even on the evidence Firestone gives us, there are some contradictions. Firstly, economic decisions relating to the fishing crew might well have been taken by the skipper without infringing on the way in which domestic decisions were taken. Secondly, the apparent servitude of women in the matter of providing food applies not just to the men of the house, but to everyone, including female visitors. I suggest that rather than reflecting subordination, it arises out of poverty and the extreme skill needed to produce sufficient food and drink. It has become part of the housewife's pride that she can, and does, supply what is necessary. When I see it today, I do not notice subjugation, but rather a sense of quiet confidence in the women's control of the kitchen and the house. Thirdly, it is hard for a feminist to escape intimations of connivance in the last quotation. She was, after all, talking to a man, Firestone, who would, she assumed, also "say that".

A more overt example of patriarchal practice is that of remuneration within the family for women's work in the shore crew. Women who were hired from outside the family were paid, but while the sons who fished received a share (or more likely a part share) of the voyage, the daughters who worked on shore got nothing. On the other hand, girls who worked outside the home did not have to contribute to the household, whereas boys did. Again it was part of the economic structure organized around a patrilocal fishing crew. As Faris's unsympathetic male informant puts it, "Maids leave, so why should they get anything". What we see here seems to reflect an awkward transition from the time that a household is dependent on a daughter's labour to the time when another household is dependent on her labour as a wife.

At this level, the Newfoundland situation seems to confirm the stress that Levi Strauss and his followers put on "the exchange of women" as fundamental to the social organisation of male dominance. Yet, as M. Mackintosh has pointed out in connection with Meillassoux's arguments, because he regarded female subordination as a fact and not a problem, he slipped into illegitimate theoretical assertions that confused the relations of human reproduction with the process of the reproduction of the whole society and this led to a deduction of social relations from production relations (Mackintosh, 1977:121). Mackintosh, rightly, insists that we "should seek rather to grasp the way in which specific forms of these oppressions operate, how they are maintained and reinforced, how they are overthrown or why they are not overthrown",[23] and this brings us back to the women of Newfoundland and the problem of an extreme sexual division of labour.

In many ways, this seems to be the crux. Partly because it is so expected in a maritime society, both male and female writers have tended to take it for granted. There are, and probably always have been, exceptions, but the sexual division of labour in the outports is now and always has been extreme. There are clearly and geographically limited spheres of activity. Lists of "men's tasks" and "women's tasks" hardly overlap at all. Social, cultural, and political life is largely carried out in single sex groups.[24] Responsibilities within the household are quite separate. The problem lies in assessing what the consequences of this are, and this is compounded by the primacy accorded to the male activity of fishing. Because of the patriarchal structure of the wider society from which the outports come and in which they continue to be embedded, this carried with it (and still carries) various overt indications of dominance over the female spheres.

As the material under discussion had indicated, however, the extreme sexual division of labour in Newfoundland communities has been combined with women's vital and acknowledged economic contributions to the household economy, with the tradition of their vital role in settlement and with an ideology of egalitarianism. One consequence of this has been that women express their autonomy, control, and authority within "separate spheres". These spheres are not coterminous with the usual delineations of "public" and "private". Indeed, the whole concept rests on the interrelationship and interdependence of men's and women's economic efforts in both the household and the fishery. Rather there are various physical boundaries, which, together with the sexual division of labour, allow women

51

both the physical and ideological space they need. One of these is the shoreline, or "landwash". Men controlled the fishery at sea; women the fishery on shore. I would suggest that the acceptance of that boundary in such matters as women not going in the boats, or even making the nets, reinforces their control of the shorework and its importance in the recognition of their economic cooperation. Even more important was women's control of the house and everything in it, including the kitchen. The distinction between "public" and "private" in Newfoundland outports did not happen between "outside" and "inside" but between the kitchen, which was public, and the rest of the house, which was private. The kitchen was not just an extension of the community, but in effective terms, the centre of it. No one knocked at a kitchen door. Anyone could come and go as they pleased — but they were forbidden to pass into the "private" areas of the house. Only "strangers" (or those in authority) knocked (and sometimes entered by another door). In the absence of community meeting places, the kitchens were the places in which the community met, that is, publicly interacted, held discussions, and came to decisions. Even where alternatives were available, the absence of any effective heating except the kitchen stove would not encourage much conversation to take place there.[25] In this context it is vital that the kitchen was readily and obviously acknowledged to be the women's domain. It was impossible to exclude them in those circumstances. Present-day observation shows male conversation being carefully monitored by the women who often disguise their interest behind ceaselessly working hands. Coupled with the egalitarian ethic it helps to explain the much-noticed practice of "waiting-on-men". In this way, the women can easily intervene in the men's conversation without apparently leaving their own sphere and thus can exert a correct authority of their own.

In assessing this somewhat contradictory material the most useful comparison is with the material gathered in Scottish fishing communities by P. Thompson. The crux of his argument is that the very different gender relations and economic attitudes (past and present) in Buckie, Lewis, Aberdeen, and Shetland are inextricably linked. In particular, the "moral order" of a community, its interpretation of religion, its child-rearing practices, and its attitudes to gender affects its ability to adapt and survive in different economic conditions. Regional differences have also played a complicating part in the study of Newfoundland, although it would be hard to find such overall contrasts as there are in Scotland. However, the parallels, especially the social practices described in Buckie and Shetland, are illuminating. Shetland represents the high point in both gender relations and economic success, perhaps exemplified by their positive handling of the oil activity.[26] The situation of women there is characterized by a degree of economic involvement and genuine equality, a lack of male authority in the home, sexual freedom, and political and intellectual energy, which it would be hard to equal in Newfoundland. Nevertheless some similarities with Shetland support the argument that women's economic participation in the fishery and the non-authoritarian domestic relations in Newfoundland are integrally connected.

In Buckie, which Thompson characterizes as "the moral order of free enterprise", individualism, a greater separation of gender spheres, greater male authority, and a more deferential religious observance, create a more immediately recognizable comparison with Newfoundland. The most notable contrast is that, in the absence of an egalitarian imperative, highly capitalized Buckie boats were then among the most successful fishing enterprises in Britain. As in Newfoundland, however, Buckie women have asserted control over their own sphere, and the house operates similarly as the centre of a warm and egalitarian community — "Strangers knock, friends come in". It was an open-door community; and as today, food was always offered to a visitor — "the table was always laid for anyone who came in" (Thompson, 1983:250).

Too much can be made of these comparisons, but they help to set the material presented here in context. While Newfoundland outports are not unique and their experience is parallelled elsewhere, they operate in a specific historical, economic, and ideological situation and aspects of these may vary from community to community, making generalization even within Newfoundland difficult. The eventual gender relations and sexual division of labour will be the result of complex interaction of economic and ideological forces, not least of which will be women's active participation in their own lives.

What I want to suggest here is that women in Newfoundland — at least the wives of fishermen, that is the owners of boats (and that is a considerable caveat), have used their vital roles in initial settlement and in the fish-producing economy not to destroy the sexual division of labour but to establish its boundaries in such a way as to confirm their control over at least their own spheres. Inheritance did not matter if a woman gained a "woman's sphere" by marriage; nor did the ownership of a share if she controlled the household budget. Nor, and this is also important, did either matter in conditions of bare survival, when there was no surplus to be appropriated.

Conclusion

We can speak of "traditional outport life" at least in the sense that the outlines of the sexual divisions of labour and the basis for the negotiation of gender and power come into sharpest focus at the end of the eighteenth century with the establishment of the Planter's household unit with its inshore fishing crew and shore crew as the key unit in the fishing economy. And these outlines remain until the demise of sun-dried fish as a product in the 1950s and the access of modern goods, services, cash, and opportunities in the heady post-Confederation days after 1949. Much of what is evident today is rooted in that long experience, but the precise connections still need to be specified. Here I have restricted myself to an examination of the context of the male domination of the fishery in which the signal fact of women's contribution as both settlers and shore crew serve to alert us that women were in a position to negotiate actively in the formation and development of the relations of production. In its turn, this forces a reconsideration of the consequences of the sexual division of labour and its relationship with other areas of women's interest.

We are still a long way from a wholly adequate theory of the subordination of women. But the route lies through careful examination of the evidence of different women's lives. The fishing communities of Newfoundland offer a perspective that sharpens our view of certain aspects of the sexual division of labour, and, I hope, contributes to the gradual filling out of the complex picture of negotiation, and adaptation that constitutes the reality of gender divisions. In the next chapter, I will take up that task in the particular context of women in Grand Bank, a small town on the south coast of Newfoundland.

Notes

1. A version of this chapter first appeared in *Labour/Le Travail*, Number 15, Spring, 1985. Since then a number of young feminist historians have been at work, but with rather different focii, e.g. N. Forestall, (1989); L. Cullum, (1993).

2. Examples might include B. Taylor, *Eve and the New Jerusalem* (London, 1983); S. Oldfield, *Spinsters of this Parish* (London, 1984); P. Summerfield, *Women Workers in the Second World War* (London, 1982); J. Parr, *The Gender of Bread Winners* (1990).

3. For example, see R. Firth, *Malay Fishermen: Their Peasant Economy* (London, 1946); M.E. Smith, *Those Who Live From the Sea* (New York, 1977); R. Andersen, *North Atlantic Maritime Cultures* (The Hague, 1979); J.A. Acheson, "The Anthropology of Fishing", *Annual Review of Anthropology* (1981).

4. M. Gray, *The Fishing Industries of Scotland* (London, 1973); M. Orbach *Hunters, Seamen and Entrepreneurs* (Berkeley, 1977).

5. For male anthropological accounts of Newfoundland outports, see J. Faris, (1972); M.M. Firestone, (1978); C. Wadel, (1973); L. Chiarmonte, (1970);

6. Among the studies that supported my observations were Dona Davies' extensive studies of "Grey Rock Harbour"; C. Benoit's studies of mothering and midwifery, (1990, 1991); A. Matthews, "The Newfoundland Migrant Wife", in A. Himelfarb and J. Richardson, *People, Power and Process* (Toronto, 1980); There is also considerable descriptive evidence in autobiographies and folklore accounts, for example, Greta Hussey, *Our Life on Lear's Room* (St. John's, 1981); H. Murray, *More than 50%* (St. John's, 1979); H. Porter, *Below the Bridge* (St. John's, 1979); E. Goudie, *Woman of Labrador* (St. John's, 1973).

7. A son, to Nicholas Guy, a relation of John Guy. The mother's name is not recorded.

8. In 1766 St. John's, the rate of single Irish men to available women was as high as 17:1, quoted in C. Grant Head, *Eighteenth Century Newfoundland* (Toronto, 1976), p. 87.

9.   Similar arrangements in family economics have been documented in pre-industrial France and England by, for example, L.T. Tilly and J.W. Scott, *Women, Work and Family* (New York, 1978). For citations see C. Grant Head, *Eighteenth Century Newfoundland*, pp. 141, 232, 82, 218.

10.   There are several excellent first-hand accounts of the Labrador summer fishery, one especially by G. Hussey, *Our Life*, who did not settle there, but makes clear the process by which it happened. See also F. Barbour, *Memories of Life on the Labrador and Newfoundland* (New York, 1979).

11.   See J. Mannion, (1977); G. Head, (1970); G. Handcock, (1990).

12.   The cod trap is recorded as early as 1868 in Bonne Esperence and seems to have been widespread by later 1870s. Inboard engines did not become common until 1920s. Social changes arose mainly as a consequence of missionary activity. See W. Wilson, *Newfoundland and its Missionaries* (Cambridge, 1866); D.W. Prowse, *A History of Newfoundland from English Colonial and Foreign Records* (London, 1895). For various interpretations of the Fisherman's Protective Union see W.F. Coaker, *The History of the FPU in Newfoundland 1909-29* (St. John's, 1930); B. Neis, "Competitive Merchants and Class Struggle in Newfoundland", *Studies in Political Economy*, 5 (1981); J. Feltman, "The Development of the Fishermen's Union in Newfoundland", (MA thesis, Memorial University, 1959); I. McDonald, "W.F. Coaker and the Fishermen's Protective Union in Newfoundland Politics, 1908-25", (PhD thesis, London University, 1971).

13.   Even later their economic vulnerability made them liable to various "rationalizations", for example, J. Smallwood's Resettlement Programme in the 1960s which resulted in the extinction of several hundred of the smaller or more remote outports and the relocation of the inhabitants to more "convenient" locations. See C. Wadel, (1969); N. Iverson and R. Matthews, (1968). Indeed, there are grounds for seeing the response to the 1992 fish stocks crisis by both levels of government as a continuation of the same process (see P. Sinclair, 'The Fisheries crisis of 1990', Report to Economic Recovery Commission, 1990; P. Sinclair, 'Coping with scarcity: A critical analysis of Fisheries management in the North Atlantic', 1991).

14. For example see M. Chamberlain, *Fenwomen* (London, 1975); F. Thompson, *Lark Rise to Candleford* (London, 1945); S. van Kirk, *"Many Tender Ties": Women in the Fur Trade, 1670-1870* (Winnipeg, 1980); B. Light and A. Prentice, *Pioneer and Gentle Women of British North America, 1713-1867* (Toronto, 1980).

15. Quoted in G.T. Cell, *Newfoundland Discovered: English Attempts at Colonization, 1610-1630* (London, 1972).

16. In comparing M. Chamberlain's material (*Fenwomen*) with my own, I tentatively put toward two generalizations. Firstly, Newfoundland midwives never developed as many erudite skills, either herbal or surgical. They managed on commonsense and humility. Their hallmark was their accessibility. They would willingly buckle down and sort out the rest of the family or climb into bed with the mother for a warmup and a giggle. See C. Benoit, "Mothering in a Newfoundland Community" (London, 1990) and *Midwives in Passage* (St. John's, 1991) for a more thorough discussion.

17. While this was the original method of exploiting the cod resource, it seems to have been neglected by the English settlers until its revival in the eighteenth century (Head, *Eighteenth Century Newfoundland*, 203-6). Andersen has studied it in its heyday at the end of the nineteenth century. R. Andersen, "The 'Count' and 'Share': Offshore Fishermen and Changing Incentives", in R.J. Preston, *Canadian Ethnology*, 40 (Ottawa, 1978); R. Andersen, "The Social Organisation of the Newfoundland Banking Schooner Cod Fishery", (unpublished paper, 1980).

18. There are numerous accounts of both the technology and the economies of the traditional inshore cod fishery. See, for example, M. Firestone, *Savage Cove*; NORDCO, *It Were Well to Live Mainly Off Fish* (St. John's, 1981).

19. There are excellent descriptions of the first stage in G. Hussey, *Our Life*, 38, and W. Wilson, *Newfoundland and its Missionaries*, 211, which shows the continuity of the methods used.

20. Estimates of both the quantity and the value of the family catch appear in E. Antler, "Women's work in Newfoundland fishery families" (unpub., 1976), G. Head, *Eighteenth Century Newfoundland*; Alexander, *The Decay of Trade: an Economic History of the Newfoundland Salt Fish Trade, 1935-1965* (St. John's, 1977) and O.

Brox, *The Maintenance of Economic Dualism in Newfoundland* (St. John's, 1969). The whole exercise is more ideologically useful than analytically pertinent in that under conditions of simple commodity production, the "value" is embodied in the product, rather than in the direct remuneration (via the wage). Nevertheless the effort to demonstrate that women's (and children's) labour contributes specifically to the value realized by the family unit was an important contribution.

21. See J. Humphries, "Class Struggle and the Persistence of the Working Class Family", *Cambridge Journal of Economics*, I, 3 (1977); R. Pahl, *Divisions of Labour* (London, 1984).

22. In, for example, J. Faris, (1972); D. Davis, (1983); Chiaramonte, (1970).

23. See M. Molyneux, "Beyond the Housework Debate", *New Left Review* 116 (1979) for a similar prescription. This brief reference makes a connection with a substantial theoretical debate, contributions to which have been made by V. Beechey, "On Patriarchy", *Feminist Review* 3 (1979); F. Edholm, et al., "Conceptualizing Women", *Critique of Anthropology* 3, 9/10 (1977); L. Bland, et al., "Relations of Production: Approaches Through Anthropology", in Women's Studies Group, *Women Take Issue* (London, 1978).

24. It should be noted that Thompson's evidence from Scotland, and all the material gathered on fishing communities elsewhere, stresses the sexual division of labour and separation of sexual spheres. What varies are the consequences. See P. Thompson, paper presented to ASA Symposium on *Women in Fishing Economies*, November, 1983.

25. For a discussion of the role of the kitchen as the boundary between public and private, see L. Dillon, "Black Diamond Bay: A Rural Community in Newfoundland", (MA thesis, Memorial University, 1983). Other confirmation can be found in J. Faris, (1972); H. Murray, (1979); D. Davis, (1983)25.2; P. Thompson (paper to Women in Fishing Economies), records the same open community access to the kitchen in Buckie and Shetland Faris, *Cat Harbour*, stresses that men also met in the shop in the evenings, an arena most other observers, for example, K.K. Szala, "Clean Women and Quiet Men: Courtship and Marriage in a Newfoundland Fishing Village", (MA thesis, Memorial University, 1978), allocate to the young unmarried of both sexes. Traditionally, the "stores" — sheds on the stages — were men's

meeting places, but these were (and are) untenable for most of the colder months of the year.

26. See J. Willis, *A Place in the Sun*, (St. John's, 1991).

4 Mothers and daughters: Past and present in Grand Bank women's lives

Introduction

In this chapter[1] I approach the problem of the origins of Newfoundland women's social and economic lives rather differently from the examination of secondary sources I used in the last chapter. Simple curiosity took me to Grand Bank, on the South Coast of Newfoundland. I already knew about the organisation of the traditional inshore fishery in many parts of Newfoundland, where the catch would be brought to the shore by male family crews, and the women of the family would process it into "sun dried" or "lightly cured" salt fish. I was surprised, then, when I came across a few tantalising references that indicated that in Grand Bank the women were organized in groups working in a direct commercial relationship with the large merchant firms who owned the "banking schooners" that fished the Grand Banks.

Given the intensity with which the fishing industry in Newfoundland has been studied it seemed somewhat surprising that no one knew about this unique arrangement, for not only were women elsewhere not organized in this large scale commercial way, but they were not part of market relations at all.[2] Surely, the development of what sounded like the full scale industrialisation of traditional petty commodity production warranted more than a few elusive references in obscure texts? The unstudied existence of large scale women's involvement "on the beaches" in Grand Bank and Fortune is a good example of both how women's contribution vanishes from history and how the recovery of women's experience sheds doubt on the previously accepted historical picture.

While the "beach racket" is interesting in itself, in the course of the interviews I conducted with the older women in the community who had worked "on the beaches", I came across a line of enquiry that seemed even more interesting. Grand Bank is, by Newfoundland standards, quite large.

With a population of 4000 it is a town rather than a small fishing community. Its population, like many Newfoundland communities, is very stable: there were many families in which members of three, four and even five generations all lived in Grand Bank. In the course of the original interviews I carried out, daughters, nieces, and granddaughters would often interpret or help me understand what their mothers/aunts/grandmothers said about their work on the beaches. I became interested in talking to these women of the younger generations as well as to their mothers.

Thus I developed the strategy of talking to women of different generations in order to explore the change and continuity of "women's work". In particular, I was interested in how the women of different generations understood their work and how it fitted into the overall household strategy. In some ways women cooking meals now, with electric cookers, microwaves, and deep-freezers to aid them, are living in a different world from that of their grandmothers who had chopped their own wood and carried the water to cook salt beef and home grown cabbage on a heavy cast iron stove — but both the task and the responsibility for that task remained the same: food had to arrive on tables to feed hungry families. Thus, I wanted to do something quite complex: to describe in some detail the changes in women's work, but also to see how women who had experienced those changes understood them. Further, I also wanted to see how those changes were mediated within the family, and with what consequences for the sexual division of labour and for the nature of the relationship between mothers and daughters.

For some time I had been interested in a feminist transformation and use of oral history and the collection of life stories, both as a method for capturing the kind of material I was interested in, and also because it allowed the subjects to remain much more in control of the material. As a method and a practice it seemed to allow a more democratic and open sharing of information between researcher and subject.

As I searched the literature I was interested to notice was that the idea of focusing on different generations in the same family was not commonly explored. Much oral history takes a long enough sweep that it compares different generations, but it does not seem concerned with the way change is mediated in different families, or with the consequences for relations between parents and children and grandchildren. In some cases, it is clear that researchers have used different generations in the same family, but more as a convenience, that as a focus. A recent example is Pat Straw and Brian Elliot's (1986) interesting discussion of the way in which women experience time differently from men because of their different responsibilities, and how this enables women to control "family time", in ways such as timetabling meals. The research on which the article is based uses a sample of "deliberately selected multi-generational families". But, while the article uses material in which mothers speak of their daughters and vice versa, the relationship between the two is not discussed, nor is the material situated in particular family situations. This is not to make a criticism, but simply to register my surprise that relationships within families have not been a more common focus for oral historians, and to suggest that it might be a fruitful approach.

Of course, what I ended up doing was less ambitious than this discussion would suggest. I carried out a small pilot study in 1985, using some of the same families I had met in 1983. In all I talked to some 36 women, of whom 27 were in 9 families with 3 or 4 generations of women living in Grand Bank. I talked to some of the women several times: others only once. Often women were present when I was talking to another member of the family. Before presenting some of what they said, I must emphasize that this brief pilot study in no way pretends to be a full scale oral history of the women of Grand Bank.

Grand Bank families

Grand Bank is situated on the Burin peninsula, jutting out from the south coast of the island. It was first settled in 1657 and remained a small inshore fishing village until just after the mid nineteenth century. Then a number of merchants began to build larger schooners in which to exploit the rich fishery offshore on the Grand Banks. Each schooner would carry up to a dozen two-man dories and having reached the grounds these would fan out from the "mother" ship, and fish by the traditional hook-and-line methods. The method of payment changed over the years (see Andersen, 1978), but it was clearly a different situation from other parts of the province in that the merchants directly controlled the harvesting and paid wages (in cash or "credit") to the fisherman. When the schooners were full they returned to Grand Bank to drop their catch, and straightforward capitalist rationality dictated that the schooners must return directly to the fishing grounds.[3] Thus it came about that the merchants hired "crowds" of women to process (i.e., dry) the catches as they were delivered ashore. Each "crowd" consisted of about 20 women, and each was organized by a "boss woman". They were paid at the end of the season, half in cash and half in a credit note that had to be spent at the merchant's store. Thus employment of men in the banking fishery and women ashore went together. Employing women to process the fish was part of the merchant's profit-making strategy, but equally, the women's acceptance of the work was part of household strategies for getting by. It is this commonsensical, quotidian interpretation that I want to stress later in the paper, but I should also say here that both the technical process and the social organisation of the beach racket is interesting, and as far as I know, unique not only in Newfoundland, but in the world.

The heavily salted fish was first delivered to the shore, washed, then carted up the beach on heavy wooden trays to the drying area. Here the fish would be spread, turned, spread again, made into smaller piles, spread again, and finally made into the full-sized piles of completely dried and cured fish. Each crowd would be responsible for the fish of one schooner,and the "boss-woman" would be totally responsible for the tricky business of timing the various stages, and calculating the weather so that the fish was neither burnt by the sun, nor soaked by the rain. The women would be on the beaches by 5-6 a.m., and would not finish until nightfall, but like so much of women's work, it was not continuous. There were frequent breaks while the fish dried, in which the women could dash home and fulfil their other domestic obligations, helped, of course, by any daughters who were old enough.

> But then, I mean, we used to come off the beach and go up in the garden and spread hay and take it up. Just up in the garden there, up above the cemetery, and we used to go up and spread the hay and take it up and then we'd go down to the beach, then we used to have to go on the beach around 3 o'clock, they used to say "well 2 o'clock or half past two or 3 o'clock. Take up the fish" and then we'd have to come back then and go at the hay again. You know it was really — I don't know — really hard work. And then like when you had a lot of children it was washing everyday . . . (Harriet Welsh, p. 12, describing working on the beaches with her aunt when she was 13 years old.)

> We used to have to bake a nice little bit 'cos there was no bread to buy, see, you couldn't go in the store and buy bread and cakes and stuff like they do now, you know, you had to make your own or you had to do without it. So I used to work on the beach and I — now in them days you'd what we used to call barm. You'd put your barm about half past nine in the evening, put your yeast in soak, and then you'd put your flour in and made your barm, you'd have to put it somewhere to rise. Now when I come in the night, night time from the beach, I'd put up the bread. When I'd be going away in the morning, I'd say to her (Lilian, her eldest daughter), "tie up your hair and wash your hands and knead down the bread while I'm gone" and when I comes in off the beach dinner hour, I'll put it on in the little pans, aye. So she'd do it, she'd have the bread all kneaded down, I

don't know how she used to manage it. (Ruby Francis, p. 23. Lilian would be about six or seven years old).

Working on the beaches was as usual for women as working on the schooners was for men. In 1901, the census records 262 men and 252 women employed in "catching or curing fish", out of a total population of 1170. In 1911, the figures were 435 men and 331 women out of a population of 1427. In 1921, the last time the figures were recorded in this form, there were 359 men and 304 women, out of a population of 1605. These figures represent the vast majority of the working population at the height of the banking fishery. Obviously fewer men or women were involved as the traditional banking fishery diminished towards the 1940s. But the figures also bear out the experience of the women I talked to. Of those born before 1930, the only ones who did not work on the beaches were those who had been born elsewhere and moved to Grand Bank after the beach work declined.

Past constant losses by drowning caused Grand Bank to become known as "the widow's town". Every town family that was involved in the fishery could report the loss of a near relative by drowning. Certainly all the families I talked to could list several close relations whom they had lost to the sea. However, since 1966 there have been no major losses and the younger women have not lost contemporaries. Indeed, for the very youngest women the spectre of drowning is now very faint,[4] even if their husbands or boyfriends are fishermen on the draggers.

The other inevitable concomitant of offshore fishing and a central feature of Grand Bank lives is that men are absent for considerable periods of time. While father and husband absence was experienced by virtually all the older women I talked to, the greater variety of on shore jobs today means that not all the younger women have this experience, nor expect to have it. Again, the periods of absence have changed drastically since the beginning of the century. Many of the older women didn't see their husbands for up to a year (if they worked aboard the trading schooners) or at least six months (aboard the banking schooners).

> We were married a month and a half when he went away, and I didn't see him no more for 11 months. Then he was home for a little while, and he went away one day and he was gone a year and one day, come the next. (Louise Belbin, p. 72)

Such women would regard a month's absence as quite brief, and schedules aboard the draggers nowadays only involve 10-14 days away. Furthermore, absences are regular and predictable, and radio contact is possible. But if the pattern of absences has changed, the consequences have not. Women with largely absent husbands must take almost total responsibility for running the home and rearing the children, and carry out those tasks with very little assistance. This means, of course, that they must take care of tasks normally allocated to men in the traditional sexual division of labour, as well as having to handle decisions and financial arrangements.

> Well, in our day the women did almost the same work as the men, because they had to do it. The men had to be away and the women had to do the best they could without them. (Louise Belbin, p. 76)

Of course, there are other occupations that demand male absence. While the numbers are too few to assert that there is a general trend, two of the four young unmarried women I talk to were dating young men in the armed forces, who were away for periods of months at a time.

I selected the families I studied in order to be as representative as possible of the Grand Bank population, using such indicators as socio-economic position and religious denomination. In fact, while some families (those of skippers) had, in the past, been more comfortable and some (especially in the Salvation Army) had had particularly strict upbringings, the well-known egalitarian ethic in Newfoundland did seem to have produced a remarkable homogeneous community, sharing a common history and experiencing very comparable economic and social situations. This shared framework helped to highlight individual differences and family strategies.

While there is a steady decrease in family size, there were considerable variations in family size among the older generations. As the women tended not to mention still births and perinatal deaths, family size could also be affected by different mortality rates. Some of the older women had all their children living, often still in Grand Bank. Some had lost children either through childhood disease, or later in illness, drownings or other accidents. Such misfortune seemed to run in families. One such was Rosie Baker (born 1908) who had borne 8 children, of whom only 3 were still living. Three had died in infancy, one died of cancer and one was lost at sea. In addition, both she and her daughter Laura, lost their husbands in the Blue Wave disaster in 1956. Laura (born 1935) was left with two small children, whom she reared with the help of Rosie, with whom she still lives, and her elder brother, Wallace, who lives next door. Discussing this tragic history with her daughter Mary (now 29 and with 3 daughters of her own) shows how families act to even out individual fortunes. Laura's pension was pitiful.

> The money they collected for we, like my son only used to get $17.50 a month, right, and my daughter $15, and I only used to get $10, so that weren't very much money. (Laura Barnes, p. 25)

Yet, Mary has little memory of being materially, socially or emotionally disadvantaged.

No, I didn't find . . . I mean there were lots of kids that had a lot more than I had but I found with Uncle Wallace living in the yard, and there was Nan and Uncle Robert there. I mean he was working and everything and they was living out with us or out there a lot of the time and, I mean, they never had nobody else, right. I found that little things that I didn't have if Nan was helping mom with grocery bills and what have you, that I found that mom had little bit extras that we had. (Mary Keeping, p. 15).

Most other children had absent fathers in any case and the total family resources enabled Laura to bring up her children at the same material level as their peers. Mary is now married to an electrician in the Marystown Shipyard, who earns relatively high wages, and they live in a spacious house in a prosperous area nicknamed "mortgage row".

Another family, the Thornhills, have provided some of the best known schooner skippers in the town. Lizzie Thornhill (born 1899) was married to Jake before his death in 1980. She was born in Harbour Breton and moved to English Harbour East when she was 16 to work in a store there. She met Jake and they moved to Grand Bank so that Jake could work aboard the schooners. She had 3 children. Her only daughter, Lucy (born 1924) still lives in the same yard. She married George Snook when she was already pregnant with her eldest daughter, Betty (born 1948). George was a seaman aboard a coasting schooner, which he later exchanged for work on the draggers, before coming ashore about 10 years ago to take up a succession of shore based jobs. But Lucy brought up all three of her daughters when he was largely absent. Her oldest daughter, Betty, was also pregnant when she married Charles. Unlike her mother, Betty had enjoyed school and badly wanted to go into nursing — a possibility that was cut short by her marriage and the birth of Tina (1965).

I just started through all that, I guess, without fully realising what I was doing, I suppose, I don't know . . . it's alright things turned out as they did, but with some people it would have probably been a disaster, because some girls that's all they have on their minds is. "Gee I'm going to get married", but up to that time that was the last thing in my mind. I really didn't plan it that way . . . it just happened and, at the time, if you got pregnant you got married. That just seemed the thing to do, right. (Betty Dominaux, p. 17).

However, whereas Lucy had been content to settle down and keep house and rear children with an absent husband, Betty was not. Her husband was also a seaman, aboard the Canadian National coastal ferry boat, but Betty continued to work at a series of jobs, and currently works in the meat room of a local supermarket. Meanwhile, it was effectively Lucy who brought Tina up, and to whom Tina relates most closely.

> It just seemed the natural thing to do. I was down with Mom and those and I really wasn't used to doing anything in the house anyway, and Mom sort of took over Tina, when I was married and Tina was born that I didn't know anything about her and I didn't want to do anything anyhow, and I wasn't used to it and Mom was still home and the other two girls were older . . . (Betty Dominaux, p. 48)

George, back from the sea, was given a second chance to participate in child rearing.

> I don't think ever I thought so much about my own children as I did Tina, and I'm sure George didn't. He said the other day, "Oh, my dear", he said, "I dreads for Tina to go". Yeah, and I suppose if she wanted the car, he'd give him to her, you know. (Lucy Snook, p. 31)

Tina, meanwhile, undaunted by absent men, has been faithful to a soldier in the army for several years. She plans to take a laboratory technician's course, marry and settle wherever Craig is stationed.

Even with this skeletal account of a complex situation, it is possible to see the interaction of community and personal history; the long sweep of change, the way families intervene to even out personal fortunes and the essential stability of the family project which, at least in the minds of the participants, overshadows changing circumstances.

Change and continuity

In this section I take up three themes already touched on: change in women's work, the role of male absence, and the interaction of individual psychology and family variations within the common history.

Change in women's work

One of the methodological difficulties I encountered was that oral history methods are set up to gather material about the way things were done in the past, not in the present. It was relatively easy to build up quite a detailed picture of the work women did "in the old days" — on the beaches, rearing large families, cutting wood, drawing water, ironing, washing, baking, cooking, sewing, growing vegetables, curing and pickling and making jam, picking berries, raising animals, delivering babies and so on. It is much harder to get an equally detailed account of women's work today. Use conventional oral history questions and most women think you've gone mad, "What do you mean, how do I wash clothes? I throw them in the machine of course".

Another difficulty in charting the exact changes in women's work is that the dates are not seen as significant. It was with some trouble that I got each woman to tell me when running water, sewage, a telephone, electricity, a car, a washing machine, and so on had entered her life. In most cases, all I could reach was a hazy approximation, sometimes refined by a little by cross cutting anecdotes. For instance Majorie Mathews (born 1907) remembers water and sewage coming because her husband had had a dispute with the council over it and finally,

> So they all went and got the labour and got the pipe and put the water for us and Tom (her son, born 1926) went halves with we. Yeah, we was the first one to have water up this way. "Can you remember when that was?" I can't remember now when that was". "Well, how old was your son, Tom? Nineteen, I'd say he was, I'd say it was 20, cos he was married. He was working over St. Lawrence at the same work putting in the sewers down there. (Majorie Mathews, p. 20)

> I can remember the day we changed from wood to oil . . . it's because we lived right by the train station and the day that the oil stove arrived at the platform my two brothers, they were young, and they went out with their make-up guns guarding the stove till dad got home from work because they were so glad to have it, that they didn't have to bring in any more wood and what not, so they went back and forth with make-up guns, guarding it so nobody wouldn't harm it. (Lorraine Buffet, born 1949, p. 11)

The introduction of running water, electricity, etc. does drastically alter women's work, usually making certain tasks much easier.[5] Such innovations in the home patently affect women more than men. When such changes occur in the industrial workplace they are documented most carefully and their consequences examined by social historians. It is noticeable that these changes in women's working conditions are not recorded, but also that they are not recorded by the women themselves. This process of both forgetting and collapsing of all experience into the unspecified past and the immediate present is too complex to explicate here, but clearly women's assessment of their work has some bearing on how it is remembered.

I assumed I would find a traditional and fairly extreme sexual division of labour, tempered by both a tradition of respect and gentleness between men and women and a widespread recognition of women's economic contribution. By and large, these assumptions were confirmed, although exactly who did what varied from family to family. Two points recurred in a number of interviews. One was that women coping on their own were expected to be self sufficient. They did not regularly call on male relatives to substitute. Nor did they depend on female relatives. In times of crisis they were certainly there: more importantly, most families saw (and see) each other frequently and there is a constant exchange of services and companionship. However real the services, this interaction is seen more as an expression of social than economic relations. Thus, "Who do you turn to for help"? produces a denial that they need any help, but "What do you do when you go over and see your mother"? reveals a whole range of reciprocally helpful activities. Today this is often expressed as, for example, the mother baby sitting while her daughter does her shopping, or of them baking cakes together, and while it was difficult to collect so much detail for past mother/daughter relations, it is clearly a continuation of a pattern.

> And Grandmother used to help a lot because they lived in the same yard. We lived right next door to me grandmother and grandfather and they always seemed to, they only had three children too and their two sons were away, so it was only mom, and she was their daughter, and they sort of helped out, like when we were kids and we wanted something and mom couldn't afford to give it to us, usually grandmother came up with the little bit extra. (Betty Dominaux, p. 7)

Some indication of how important this constant interaction was can the gleaned from women who, for some reason were cut off from their families, and complained bitterly about the lack. It is also clear in those cases where female relatives have stepped in to fill a structural lack in a household, for example where a woman has relied on her mother for extensive child minding while she continues to earn wages.

The extensive but informal support from other family members does not diminish the extraordinary self-reliance women rearing families with absent husbands developed. Both the families and the community expected that by and large such women would simply do the work of two, and that the conventional sexual division of labour would vanish. Often this resulted in women acquiring male skills from their fathers.

> And he (her father) has taught me. Me through necessity and if Les (her husband) was gone and something went wrong I mean I couldn't hire somebody on every time. I fixed it myself, and to make something with your own hands, to mould something out of your own hands, to me is satisfaction that somebody can come in and laugh at it, but they can't take away that bit of pride I got in myself. (Lorraine Buffet, born 1949, p. 19)

> Dad used to make the lobster pots and he was a carpenter and whatever Dad was at, well, mostly that we was too and I mean, like, now I done mot of this house inside carpenter work. Jave (her husband) can't do nothing. No, he went away one day and he was saying about putting a wall panel on the end of the living room and so he went away in the morning and when he come in the evening I had the wall panel done. And I've done the chimney and the two bedrooms . . . (Harriet Welsh, born 1927, p. 56)

Another understandable response, given the weight of work, was simply to postpone tasks until the husband returned. Indeed, certain tasks such as digging the potato beds, re-roofing the house and cutting and hauling wood were traditionally done by men in the winter period when they were home. In Grand Bank it was also possible to use cash to buy certain items or services. The use of bought coal, for example, rather than wood that had to be chopped and hauled, seems to have been a common way to cope with the absence of men.

> We didn't have much wood in those days, apart from splits. I burnt all coal. My husband was never home to go in the woods, not for years after we were married. (Louise Belbin, p. 76)

The allocation of tasks to girls and boys and their training as children is a fruitful area in which to examine the causes and development of the sexual division of labour. I also knew, from other sources, of the extraordinary degree to which some Newfoundland mothers waited on their sons — cutting their fingernails, washing their hair, etc. — and expected their daughters to wait on their brothers. When we discussed it I did, indeed, hear accounts of quite rigid allocations of tasks and also of systematic rebellions by girls against doing things for their brothers.

> They'd come home tired and that, and of course, the girls had lots of work to do anyway, but this was a tradition in a lot of houses there to wash the men's faces, one after the other, so they asked us a time or two and right "no", and then they didn't expect it of us. (Greta Hussey, born 1921, p. 31)

But what appeared as more important was the role of child labour as a vital part of household survival, especially when the father was absent. In this case it was the boys who had to take over the absent father's work.

> The oldest, he just stepped into his father's shoes. We didn't have the water in. He brought the water and helped me whenever he could. (Greta Hussey)

What this meant was that while the girls did work hard at all of their mother's tasks, they saw their brothers as also working hard and consequently did not resent it. It has to be said that my impression remains that girls did both a greater variety of tasks and much more work than their brothers did.

When one compares the weight of work the middle aged and older women did as children, (confirmed by the older women's descriptions of their children's work), with the much easier circumstances of women born since about 1950, there has obviously been a significant change. Mothers of teenage daughters today will require them to keep their own bedrooms tidy and occasionally to help with the cooking, but that is about all.

> If I'm gone. She's fairly independent. Like we went out on Saturday, she got, like her grandmother was here but then she had the opportunity to do it because I wasn't here. If I was here I would have done it myself, right, but she got supper for everybody and cleaned up afterwards, and all, you know, she got Lacey ready for bed and gave her a bath and if I'd been here she wouldn't have done that because, well, they'd be doing other things. You know what it's like. (Mary Keeping, born 1956, about her daughter, Natasha, aged 12, p. 12)

Exploring this change with women of different ages, it appears more as a part of a process of household survival. Children's physical labour could be, had been, and might again be necessary. Mothers (and fathers) did what they could and then allocated what they could not manage to children. If they could cope with all or most of the work (as women with present husbands, very small families, slightly higher incomes or just more stamina could) then they dispensed with children's labour.

> I didn't really, I didn't do much work at all because like I say, it seemed like mom was always the one that — she wanted to do it. We couldn't go it good enough for her. I suppose that's the way she took it, you know. (Lucy Snook, born 1924, p. 10)

> We didn't do anything. We used to take off down to our grandmother's so we wouldn't have to do anything. (Betty Dominaux, daughter of Lucy Snook) We didn't, cos mum, it was the sort of thing, like, she was always home and she did all the housework and we just took it for granted. (Georgie, another of Lucy Snook's daughters, p. 11)

The idea of housework as a kind of discipline does not appear. So while it was obvious that children in today's households do a negligible amount of housework, this was not seen as a sudden break. There was no need for

71

them to, but, if there was, they would. Meanwhile, it was more important for them to work hard in school, so that they would be able to get good jobs, and thus contribute to the overall household strategy in that way.

I have spoken of the sexual division of labour among children as if all families were composed of equal numbers of boys and girls. But a point made by many of the women was that such ideal-type families were unusual. Often a family would contain all boys or all girls, or, which comes to the same thing as far as work went, an unequal age distribution so that, for example, four girls would be followed by four much younger boys. In such cases the boys would be too small for many years to perform male tasks, so the girls would take them over (if necessary) in the same way as they did in families composed of all girls. So when I asked about the sexual division of labour, many of the women would remind me that the arrangements in their family were simply inevitable because of the composition of the family. On the other hand, while girls would quite frequently take on tasks that boys would normally do, when there were only boys in the family, it was the mother who took up the slack.

> Did anybody help you with the washing? No, no, but he'd fill up the water. I didn't have to bring it. Oh no, I did that (the washing). (Greta Hussey, p. 97)

So there are fewer examples of boys baking bread or washing clothes than there are of girls cutting wood.

Family position was often more important than gender in terms of how much work children did, and what opportunities they had. Elder children were often doubly imposed on. One common household strategy, especially in large families, was to send youngsters of both sexes off to earn their living at very young ages. Several of the women I spoke to had been sent into service or onto the beaches when they were only 11 or 12 years old. On the other hand, this meant that they didn't have to step into their mother's shoes at home.

> Well, you see, I was only very young (12 years) when I left Grand Beach, aye I didn't do too much. I used to have to go in the garden and make hay and things like that. But you weren't expected to make your brothers' beds and help with the baking? Oh no, I was too young then. (Ruby Francis, born 1918, p. 6)

> That's my brother Tom, he was only 15 or 16 or something like that when we went with Gus across the gulf on a schooner. I've heard mom say that they made a suit of oil clothes for dad out of the leg of somebody's oil clothes when he went to sea. (Harriet Welsh, born 1927, p. 20)

Older children who did stay at home, especially in large families, often did have to work extremely hard. Education was seen as a low priority for both girls and boys in such cases.

Well, that's how long we could go. We couldn't afford to go after that . . . I dare say, perhaps I might have been a teacher if I had more education. "Did the boys get more education?" Oh yes, Bill did, and George. The two of them, they went to the University, and they were teachers. "Was that because they were boys and you were a girl?" Well, they were younger than me, and they tried to stay in school a little longer. Bill was the youngest, see, and Tom was the eldest. He went fishing. "So really it was actually as you got down in the family you got more of a chance?" Yes, right. That's when things started to get better then. (Tryphena Evans, born 1915, pp. 15-16)

The younger children in the same families not only got more chances, but also had a better time. When they were small they were cared for by older sisters as well as by their mother and as they grew older there were no younger siblings for them to care for. Thus they were released from work and able to attend school. Several women took me to task for not taking account of family position — pointing out that their experience was critically different from that of their older of younger sisters, especially in large families. Indeed, where siblings are spread over 25 years family position could amount to being in a different generation.

But you see, you'll find as you are older, the things I wasn't allowed to do Georgie was allowed to do. Well, she was five years behind me, see. Which left her that lots of things I couldn't do, she could do it. But by the time I came along, things were different. I used to bring Rose up to our house and we'd dye our hair and we did everything up our house. I don't know. Maybe because I was the youngest. (Betty Dominaux, born 1948 and her sister Georgie, born 1953, p. 12)

Women of all generations would testify to the sheer hard work of older generations of women. It is difficult to comprehend either the scale or the intensity of their efforts. Repeatedly, women emphasized that "times was hard then". Everyone worked hard — men and women, adult and child. Women's work was simply part of an inevitable family strategy for survival. It was not any less recognized than that of men, nor was their paid work on the beaches seen as different from the rest of their work. The perspective that divides wage work from all other kinds of work would see "beach work" as both separate and significant. Certainly, in the Newfoundland context, it was unusual. Yet to the women who did it, and to their descendants, it

73

was simply another form of work, to which you turned your hand as and when it was necessary.

So when women had testified about the hardness of the work their grandmothers and mothers did there was always a reservation. It was not different, just a little more of it and a bit harder. Time and again, when I asked about changes in women's work, I would be given details that had changed, but the overall context and the responsibilities remained unaltered. When it came down to it, women felt they did the same work as their mothers but under easier circumstances.

> Well, there is less work now than it was when we were growing up, 'cos there's everything to do your work with. But when we was growing up there was no vacuum cleaners and there weren't no washers and there weren't deep fridge and dishwashers and everything around now, you know. That's why I say but when we was growing up there wasn't enough money for to buy that, you know. We used to use just the old fashioned brooms then and mops and stuff like that. (Harriet Welsh, born 1927, p. 54)

> Basically yes, but doing it in a different way. In fact I think the woman today has more responsibilities, a lot more. Okay, mom had the responsibility of the home and the children. In my instance, dad sort of took care of mom, you know what I mean, but in my instance, I took care of myself. Les made a living which enabled me to, he gave me the tool, but he never gave me the hand. Now I don't know how Joanne (her daughter) is going to reflect on that. . . "Do you think it's a harder role, a more complicated role?" I think basically yes, but it's hard to say. It's easier in some instances as compared with me to mom because I think mom was, she still is, she thinks she had to worry over this and this and this. I don't. What is to be, I can. If I can change it, I change it, if I can't, I accept it. But mom has a lot of difficulty with that. I think the problem with the two children dying, you know, had a great effect on her. (Lorraine Buffett, born 1949, pp. 39-40)

Furthermore, despite the increasing division into paid and unpaid work, it is clear that in Grand Bank today women still see what they do as a family project, to which they contribute on an equal basis with men.

The role of male absence

I have already commented on aspects of how male absence affected, and continues to affect, women's lives and responsibilities. Here I want to dwell on two views of what it meant. Louise Belbin had already lost a previous financé at sea when she met Thomas Belbin, who, at 32, was skipper of a trading schooner.

> We had a nurse up from St. John's where I was staying to, and after I was working and she said to me one day, "Have you got a boyfriend?" I said, "Yes, I got a boyfriend down". I was here in Grand Bank a long time before I had a boyfriend. But, I said, I been called everything, by right, because there was always someone wanting to walk me home, and I didn't want nothing at all to do with them. She said, "What's his work?" I said, "Foreign going captain on a three master". She said, "You're not going to marry him are you?" "My dear", I said, "I don't know nothing at all about getting married". I said, "I might never get married in me lifetime". "I wouldn't marry", she says, "because he's a foreign going captain, he'll always be gone. I wouldn't have him". She said, "to marry a man like that, always on the sea, you got no life". Twas true for her. There's not much life to it. (Louise Belbin, p. 25)

undeterred, Louise married Thomas Belbin in 1923, when she was 26.

Now, here are Betty and Tina Dominaux discussing Betty's marriage to a Canadian National ferry seaman and Tina's engagement to a soldier in the Canadian Army.

> (Tina): We're not very close, we don't know very much about each other, because I'm not used to him being here. When he comes, you got to get used to him being here and by the time you get used to him being here he's gone again. And for me, I don't think it's really good family life. Let's say, we're not as close as I'd like us to be. We're not as close as me and Mom. But like, he wasn't there all the time. "Did you find, Betty, that it was difficult to switch on and switch off when he came and went away?" (Betty): No, because it was more of thing for me to get used to him being home all the time. You know what I mean, because I've been, I've just got used to that way of life and I'm not used to having to cope with him and he's not used to having to cope with me. "Has he come off the boats now?" No, he's still there, but they had a layoff, but he got called back just as we were starting to get on each other's nerves. Because we're just not used to it. He's not used to it and I'm not used to it. (Betty Dominaux, pp. 44-45).

> (Betty): Women are more independent that they were, a lot more independent. (Tina): I'm not. I can't say I am, I can't stand it, like you likes doing things on your own. You loves doing things on your own, but I can't stand it. If I had him to go to the bathroom, I'd take

75

him and go, that's the way I am. I can't stand being by myself. Betty: Well probably it just comes from I've had to do it on my own. If you're alone, you got to do it on your own, haven't you. (p. 55)

"If Tina came to you and said she'd got two wonderful boys and one worked on the rigs, let's say, and one worked in a shop, which one would you choose?" (Betty): I'd choose the one on the rigs. "More money?" Yes, more money. I suppose 'twould depend on the persons. Some people just can't cope, can't get by on their own. Probably that haven't changed that part of it. It depends on the individual. (p. 57)

These three women, all marrying men whose work involves absence, in 1926, 1965, and 1985 all express the same ambivalence. Is it a problem or isn't it? Do you get used to it or don't you? Does it matter — is there any real choice or do women simply learn to stand on their own two feet and fall back on their female relatives when necessary? These questions need exploring systematically, but here, I simply want to point out the way in which male absence in Grand Bank is simply part of a sexual division of labour. It structures women's work in the same way as other inevitable determinants do, but it does not alter the central project of their lives.

"Individual psychology" and family variations

I want to conclude this chapter by touching on an important theme in the women's own analysis of their lives and work. It is not done to disagree with one's subjects in interviews, but there were two matters on which they were insistent and on which I continue to reserve judgement. One of these was the claimed lack of class differences in Grand Bank. They admitted that in the heyday of the merchants those families had thought of themselves as different, and, indeed, probably were different, although not in any crucial respects. They were much more ready to acknowledge a respect due to clergy and teachers, and sometimes, to deplore the more relaxed contemporary relationship between professionals and ordinary people.

As far as the business people are concerned, well, I mean, they're only the same as yourself, I mean, when it comes to clergy, I think you should have a little more respect. (Harriet Welsh, p. 53)

There's a much more relaxed atmosphere now. Before, I tell you what it was, when I went to school — I suppose it wasn't so much then as when my mother went to school — but the teachers was sort of, they was more respected than they are now. Well, I don't know about respect. Probably I'm using the wrong word, but they was sort of put on a pedestal, teachers were more than they are now. (Betty Dominaux, p. 35)

But these were only minor deviations from a strong adherence to the idea of a homogenous society in which material differences mattered less than an underlying reality of social equality. Even those who were better off were not expected to show it in their behaviour and those people on welfare were regarded as the temporary victims of misfortune and not as members of a permanent underclass. Grand Bank is a smallish town and economic differences are not as pronounced as they would be in a city. In any case, existing differences are lessened by the way in which families act to even out individual fortunes. But the most important contribution to the egalitarian vision was the underlying adherence to an ideology of equality. Even if people are not equal in fact, they should be and that imposes its own reality. This is a well documented trait in Newfoundland culture, and I know of no evidence to suggest that it might emanate more from women than from men. But the small amount of evidence I collected in Grand Bank did indicate that it sat particularly well with the women's view of the family enterprise remaining constant in a changing world, to which each member contributed as they could, taking from it what was available. Certainly Majorie Matthew's view of her eldest grandson's promotion to Minister in the Peckford cabinet could have been expressed by any of the other grandmothers. "Well, I yeah, I thought it was good, you know, he was smarted enough to get it. Someone's got to do it". Her deliberate refusal to dwell on his success testified to the overriding imperative that his promotion should not threaten the balance of the family or of the community.

While I resisted the lack of class analysis in Grand Bank and was reluctant to see the cross-cutting reality behind what the women were saying, as a sociologist, I was even more resistant to their assertions that individual psychology accounted for more differences than class, gender or family position. "It all depends on the person" they so often said. Differences between mothers and daughters could be attributed to different circumstances, but it was much more likely that each was simply an individual solving problems and arranging priorities in her own way: "She never was a woman that liked to cook a lot". (Lucy Snook, p. 9). It was with some reluctance that women would produce the first account, and often they would half contradict what they had just said with some appeal to the personalities of the individuals. When I challenged them on these points, they would defend their views by citing other sisters and aunts who had been in similar situations, but who had responded differently.

The idea women were expressing, was that people, women certainly, operate in a world in which much is unalterable and with which you fatalistically comply; but equally, much is variable, and over that you have very considerable personal freedom. Such an ideology allows a sense of individual liberty while retaining the constant framework in which these women have found dignity and satisfaction. It also allows some escape from what could otherwise be an oppressive family structure. As a concept, it enables individual members to deviate, and to claim freedom without imperilling the common strength of the family.

Naturally, my feminist and sociological concerns are to analyse the structure of these women's lives to see how what seems unalterable could be changed and also to see social patterns in what looks like individual variation. Such a perspective may be theoretically more acceptable, but what the women I talked to were suggesting was less an analysis that a strategy for survival. Before anyone claims that this demonstrates that Durkheim was right and that women are the natural guardians of expressive values and particularistic concerns, may I warn against confusing explanations that are intended to explain the world with explanations intended to explicate the speaker's position? I would argue that what these women are saying is both complex and subtle and is, primarily, about the internal mechanisms that they have built and sustained over generations.

The women of Grand Bank have shared a common project over many generations. In terms of the family project, they have won places of considerable freedom and pride, and, indeed, flexibility. Their confidence in their own strength is clean, and so is the support and understanding they continue to give to each other within the family. The notion of individual psychological differences can be seen as part of this.

Conclusion

I would like to end this account of the study of Grand Bank women with some methodological *mea culpas*. I was using, for the most part, crude and handwrought tools. It was the only infinite patience of the women I talked to that enabled me to learn as much as I did. Indeed, it was often they who pointed out some of my errors to me. They explained how, by choosing one daughter only, I was missing both the significance of age and family position and individual differences. Luckily the presence of some sisters broadened my scope, although the omission remains a serious one.

Again, it was my informants' blank indifference to some of the information I was trying to collect that alerted me to its irrelevance in their lives. In my efforts to be a good feminist oral historian, I was forcing a concern with precise dates and chronology (and hence a predetermined view of change and continuity) on them. I was, in fact, often attending to the *wrong* detail. I learned that it is as important to notice what people do not remember as what they do.

The main object of this small study was to see how talking to women of different generations in the same family could help me "triangulate" their accounts of the past, and thus produce a multidimensional and more accurate picture of that past. Two factors in particular made this difficult. One was the women's insistence on the essential continuity of the project they felt they, mothers and daughters alike, were engaged in, and which gave their lives and their work its meaning. They thus actively frustrated my efforts to isolate and make significant differences. For this reason, I found that the most useful interviews were those slightly chaotic ones (and impossible to transcribe), where several women were all present and taking part in the discussion. In fact, these were the times when I handed over my intellectual problem to them, and they seriously addressed it out of their common experience.

The other factor was that the techniques I was using were better able to get at the details of breadmaking than they were at the detail of ideology. I suspect this may be true of much oral history.[6] In my fumbling efforts to uncover the ideas that informed these women's lives, I found myself without sufficiently sophisticated tools. It remains for later studies to piece together, with much more precision, how ideas have changed over time. What was explained to me, with considerable patience, was how these women gained access to a shared perspective that enabled them to continue to live lives of worth and integrity in a changing world.

The next two chapters move these concerns into the present day. Using a particular small community in another part of the island, I want to explore ways in which sexual divisions and ideas about them are actually constructed in the context of a small fishing community.

Notes

1. This chapter first appeared in *Women's Studies International Forum*, Vol. 11, No. 6, 1988. Page numbers after the quotations refer to the transcribed interviews from which they are taken.

2. The "truck system", and indeed all other formal relationships between the family and the state or other organisations, were carried out with the male "head of household". Women were thus rendered invisible. Note also that while the truck system ensured that families remained in debt, and any money payable to the fishermen was in the form of "credit notes", the women often supplemented the family income by selling berries to the merchants. In exchange for the "berry note" they could purchase goods. This direct arrangement was the closest many families got to cash relations.

3. The Banking Schooner fishery conducted from the Burin peninsula began in 1860s and reached its peak in c. 1911, when 26 banking schooners crewed by over 500 men caught over 50,000 quintals of fish. The schooners made trips of 2-3 weeks duration, but little time was spent ashore during the season, which usually lasted from March until November. The banking fishery gradually diminished until the 1940s, when it was effectively over. It was replaced by the frozen fish industry, caught by offshore "draggers" and processed in frozen fish plants. The first of these was opened in Grand Bank in 1955, by Bonavista Cold Storage.

4. A sharp reminder of the perils of the sea was posed by the loss of the Ocean Ranger, an oil drilling rig, with the loss of all 44 men aboard on the Grand Banks in February, 1982.

5. Though we should not assume that this makes the total load any lighter. For evidence that the amount of time spent on housework remains the same despite labour saving devices, see Vanek (1973).

6. Impressive recent attempts to get to grips with this central inadequacy in oral history have centred on the use of a combination of psychoanalytical theory and autobiography (see especially, Fraser, 1984; Steedman, 1986). The problem with this approach is that it sets too high a standard. Such magnificent insights are necessarily limited to the *writer's life*. Fascinating though this is, it does not altogether address the problem of how to use oral history to gain a similar understanding of other people's lives.

5 'Women and old boats': The sexual division of labour in Newfoundland outports

Introduction

This chapter is based on the first piece of ethnographic research I carried out in Newfoundland — in Aquaforte in 1981.[1] It is also the first chapter in this book that attempts to describe contemporary women's lives and their interpretations of them. Since I carried out the study some aspects of life in Aquaforte have changed — notably the worsening economic situation and the collapse of the inshore fishery. However, most of what I saw then still pertains today. The question I addressed then, and which I explore in this chapter is one around which I organized much of my work — the nature of the sexual division of labour and its relation to subordination of women. By the sexual division of labour I mean something altogether broader than 'men's jobs' and 'women's jobs', or how a married couple split the household chores. I mean all those things we say and do, how we say and do them and what social consequences they have that are conditioned by our gender. The impetus for the original paper came from my conviction that we needed to return to our initial astonishment that so much human activity is gender specific.

Feminist attention is often focused on societies, or groups within a society, which have demonstrated a more flexible sexual division of labour, or where women have constructed areas of autonomy or even power: where the mould of inevitability has been broken.[2] Behind this search lies the hope that such exceptions, like the swallow, will herald the summer. We have long since exposed the myth of the 'tokenism' at the individual level, but at the societal level we still cling to it — a habit which prevents our understanding how the struggles of the few can become the common sense of the many. In this chapter, however, I want to take the opposite approach, and turn my attention to a situation in which the sexual division of labour appeared to be especially rigid and intense. In this way I hope to get some purchase on the interlocking and overriding structures of male domination and capitalist exploitation. My focus is labour, rather than sexual divisions rooted in religion, forms of marriage or their ideological structures. It therefore seemed appropriate to examine a society or community that was characterized by an entirely male occupation.

Maritime communities

There are many occupations that are pursued principally by men, but fishing was isolated by Murdock and Provost (1973), along with hunting and herding large animals, as a task most often reserved entirely for men in most known human societies. Stereotypically, fishing is dangerous, requires great strength and stamina and long absences from home. Even so, there is, as Andersen (1973) says, 'no clearly natural sexually based division of labour in fishing'. Despite a number of women actively engaged in fishing around the world, e.g., in Japanese oyster fishing or in Russian freezer-trawlers,[3] it continues to be identified as something that only men can or should engage in. Occasionally, intrepid women fished in Newfoundland and the number is increasing but, by and large, the stereotype holds there too.[4]

James Faris (1972:12), like many of the anthropologists who have described outport culture, economy and social structure, took it for granted that 'in a fishing community one could reasonably expect a sharp division of labour along sexual lines'. The title of this chapter comes from one of his informants in Cat Harbour who, accounting for why they called new boats 'he' but old boats 'she', said 'You can't count on women and old boats; they'll both leak after a few years'. Indeed, Faris describes a sexual division bordering on hostility.[5] Women, if not witches, are certainly strangers and 'jinkers' who pollute the fishing so that they might not set foot in the boat or go near the nets. Here we are not talking simply about 'men's work', but about entire communities that are identified in terms of an activity that is, by definition, gender specific. In such communities women do not simply have unequal access to the means of production, as in pastoral communities; they are specifically excluded from fishing. But, as Andersen and Wadel (1972) point out, in Newfoundland women are (or were) indisputably part of the fishery. In the production of the traditional sun-dried cod, they made up most of the 'shore-crowd', who split, salted, washed and dried the fish on the 'flakes', a process that was both skilled and added considerably to the value of the catch (Brox, 1969, Antler, 1976).[6]

Thus, in the traditional inshore fishery in Newfoundland, the sexual division of labour was drawn between the harvesting and processing sectors. With the changes in the inshore fishery to produce deep frozen cod products, this division has had to be renegotiated with crucial consequences for the sexual division of labour.

There were many technological changes in the Newfoundland fisheries from the 1960s to the early 1970s. However, the vast majority of the smaller outports are still characterized by the traditional inshore fishery, heavily concentrated on cod, using small (under 30 foot) open skiffs, operated by family-based crews, and employing a variety of strategies, e.g., jigging, gillnets, trolling and lines — but with the cod-trap predominating. In contrast, the women's lives have been directly affected and fundamentally changed by the virtual elimination of the dried-salt cod industry and its replacement by frozen products. From the 1950s, the sun-dried lightly salted cod trade declined as frozen fish processing plants began to be established round the island until now the frozen fish products are dominant.[7] There are fish-plants, or at least holding depots, in virtually all communities. Instead of going to the family stages and flakes for processing, fish now go directly from the boats to the fish-plants. These plants employ a substantially female workforce, and any involvement the women have in the fishery is now as individual wage labourers in these local fish-plants. Thus, while the catching sector remains virtually untouched, both the technical means and the social relations of production have been transformed in the processing sector. Under the old system, the men who 'owned' the fish could appropriate women's surplus in accordance with the amount of fish caught. As this no longer happens women are free to redistribute their own labour and to control the wage they earn, by 'choosing' to work in the plants.

The men are fishermen, but are the women fishermen's wives?

Women in Newfoundland

I have described in previous chapters, both the shortage of research on women in Newfoundland (at least until the mid 1980s) and the consequences of the gendered, bordering on sexist, views of most of the male studies. Of these, the ones that bore most directly on the Aquaforte study were the anthropological monographs published by the Institute of Social and Economic Research in St. James in the 1970s.[8] These are, coincidentally, all written by men who tend to be preoccupied with fishing, the composition of crews, land inheritance and other androcentric concerns. Women only appear momentarily as they scuttle round doing odd chores and not being very interesting, or as the 'O's in kinship diagrams. They are, as Loftland (1974:144-5) has said 'essential to the set, but largely irrelevant to the action. They are, simply, there'. More importantly for the purposes of the present paper, male anthropologists usually talk to men, and their information is, therefore, often skewed.

Aquaforte

In 1981 Aquaforte was a small maritime community dominated by the traditional inshore fishery described above.[9] The sun-dried fish gradually gave way to frozen fish after the Fermeuse plant was opened in 1952 and the smaller owner-managed plant at Aquaforte opened in 1972.[10] The flakes and stages, which used to stand at the water's edge below each house, fell into disrepair and boats gravitated to the community wharf by the fish plant. Forty men in 14 crews were involved in fishing on a regular basis at the end of the study in 1981.

Aquaforte lies some 60 miles south of St. John's on the southern shore, with a total population of 203 in 56 households (1981). All the houses have electricity, and all but one have a telephone. Many of the younger couples have built large modern bungalows with help from the Newfoundland and Labrador Housing Corporation. Most families had at least one car or truck. There were three general stores, two garages, and the old school is used as a community hall. The (Catholic) parish church, three schools, doctor, clinic, post office and government agents were situated in Ferryland, a larger community lying on the adjacent bay to the north. Ferryland and Fermeuse also provided a few jobs, some slightly larger general stores and the bars and other social meeting points. Branch meetings of most of the voluntary associations, the bingo evenings and other social events take place in Ferryland, often in the Legion Hall. There was no bank anywhere on the shore, and for larger shops, hospitals and most government offices, they had to go to 'town', St. John's, 60 miles away.

One of the important changes in recent years was the ease and frequency with which they could do this. The road was 'made' in 1965, and paved in 1972. It was no longer an all day trek in a 4-wheel drive vehicle, but an easy 1½ hour trip. Five women and one man commuted daily, during the summer, and some through the winter as well.

In this respect, too, Aquaforte is typical of many small communities that were linked up by road in the last 15 years, thus vastly increasing both mobility and a tendency to depend more heavily for jobs, goods and services on the larger towns. This opportunity for employment outside the narrow confines of Aquaforte was especially important for the younger women, as we shall see later.

Aquaforte provided the context I needed — a small maritime community, with a traditional inshore fishery. Here I should be able to observe a clear and visible sexual division of labour.

The method I used was ethnographically based. I went to live in Aquaforte, and though the stay was too brief for a real ethnography, I was able to collect most of the usual demographic, economic and kinship data as well as conducting 39 formal interviews. But most of the time I spent where the women were — visiting, shopping, in church, at the Darts Club, Bingo and the Women's Institute — watching to see what the sexual division of labour was, how it operated and how it was interpreted. Most of the material that follows derives from this 'watching'. Let us first take, for example, two women — a widow, whose three sons fished together in their father's boat, and one of her young daughters-in-law.

Two women: Lizzie and Cheryl

Cheryl was 22 years old. A few months before I met her she had married Russell (aged 23 years) whom she had dated since she was 15. When she left school she took a secretarial course at the Trades College in St. John's and then worked as a secretary in the College of Fisheries. All her six sisters are — or were — in clerical work and all six brothers fish in her home community of Renews.

Russell fished with his two brothers, and Russell and Cheryl lived in a modern bungalow he built with their help, a few hundred yards from his widowed mother's house. Lizzie (aged 59 years) was widowed six years previously. Her three daughters were all in St. John's — one married with two children and the other two in clerical jobs. One of her sons, Steve, still lived with her and the other two were close by.

Cheryl 'called by' as many as six times a day to see to her mother-in-law because 'I get bored up there by myself'. It didn't take long to clean their newly built bungalow (with a vacuum cleaner) or to cook for the two of them (in a modern oven). In the afternoon, like all the younger women and most of the older ones, she watched 'The story' on TV.[11] When the truck was free, she drove across to visit her mother and about once a month she took her to St. John's.

When I first met her, Cheryl said she didn't want a job at the plant, 'I wasn't trained for that', and she didn't fancy standing ankle deep in water all day for less money than she got as a secretary. But when a job did come up, she snatched it. At least it was something to do, and someone to talk to. She didn't belong to any association or club, but she was pressing Russell to join the Kinsmen so she would be eligible to join Kinettes and, as Lizzie said, 'if she leans long enough, she'll get there'.

Lizzie was always aware of Steve's departure at 4:30 a.m. though she didn't get up until it was time to cook his breakfast at 9:00 a.m. After that, her days were a whirl of activity. Both her other sons and daughters-in-law visited several times a day, and Steve wandered in and out constantly, all of which kept Lizzie supplied with information, which was traded to the stream of visitors, or on the 'phone' 'up and down the road'. Lizzie knew all the ways with cod, salmon, herring and caplin. There was frozen moose in the freezer and fresh eggs from her hens. But her real pride was her knitting and her bedspreads, some of which she had sold through craft outlets. A devout Catholic, she went to mass some weekday evenings, as well as on Sundays, and she took her part in the church cleaning, flower arranging and other Women's Auxiliary activities. The church ran a bingo evening once a week which she rarely missed, sitting with her friends at the same table. A recent past president of the local WI, she not only attended the meetings but was active in the works projects, craft displays and fund raising, to say nothing of the outings they arranged. She had just triumphantly passed her post to a much younger woman, 'it's so difficult to get the young ones in . . .' With showers, weddings and funerals and going along to 'support' the guides dinner, the 4H Achievement Day and other gatherings, she was rarely at home in the evenings.

At weekends the two younger daughters came down from St. John's and Lizzie prepared even more enormous meals to sustain them through their hectic evenings at the bars and dances in Ferryland and Fermeuse.

Although Lizzie had never been in a boat and knew little of the technology, she could store the figures of the catches in her head and watched her sons' progress intently and with pride. For her, it was part of a long and valuable tradition epitomized by her life with her husband. She liked talking about the 'the old days' and much of her effort in the WI was spent preserving the old 'women's culture', and trying to pass it on to the relatively few young women members.

Lizzie was well aware of Cheryl's predicament, and worried about what would happen to her own younger daughters. One was courting a draggerman from Portugal Cove South, an even more remote outport beyond 'the barrens'. She could see clearly that for Selene to live there, away from her job, her friends, her svelte jeans and her holidays, was a recipe for disaster, but Selene was impervious to her warnings. All Lizzie could hope for was that when they married, Paul could get a job on the St. John's draggers and they would live there.

Lizzie's position of helpless concern typified the older women's desire to preserve what was left of their identify of 'fishermen's wives' in an active present, coupled with the realisation that the structural basis for that life no longer existed for her daughters.

The past was a powerful influence in Aquaforte — less the historical past, than a collective, constructed memory, hypostatized to protect them from an unpredictable and wicked present day world.

For the men, this past was bound up less with the occupation of fishing than with the identity of 'being fishermen'. Even the 23 out of the 73 adult males who had other occupations (including 4 in fish-plants) still acknowledged the primacy of fishing. Many of them fished in their spare time or intended to return to fishing when they could afford to. For the Aquaforte fishermen (in common with most of the other inshore fleets) could not live from what they caught. They, in the disparaging words of the local rural coordinator — 'fish for stamps'. In other words, their catches during the summer were chiefly valuable because they qualified them to claim Unemployment Insurance Compensation for the rest of the year.[12] Far from detracting from their status as fishermen, they, and everyone else, saw it as an advantage to have time to 'go to the woods', 'to be free', 'to be your own man'. In fact, on the basis of a relatively short season, the men won time to build and maintain their houses, their boats and their gear, cut timber and hunt moose, caribou, turrs and rabbits and pursue any number of more individual activities. The combination of cash and subsistence ensured, for most of them, a reasonable standard of living, with comfortable houses, TVs and cars. Their winter identity was just as much that of a fisherman as the actual fishing they did in the summer. 'Fisherman' means that set of plural adaptations which enabled them to continue the traditional lifestyle.

Life in the outports has always demanded this kind of flexible response in order to survive in a harsh physical environment at the end of a harshly exploitative capitalist chain. What distinguished the current set of adaptations is the way in which they have negotiated a space between capital, state and subsistence that ensures both a much improved material standard of living and a degree of autonomy.

There was very little distinction in either ideas or practice between the older and younger men. The younger ones were slightly more inclined to try new methods, and they certainly drink more alcohol, but their sense of identity was the same.

Not so among the women, for whom there was a definite generation gap between the women of about 50 years and over who can remember life before Confederation in 1949, and the women of 45 years and younger. The older women were guided by the past in much the same way as the men, and they too defer to the identity of 'fishermen'. The younger women have no such allegiance and most of them frankly dislike their husbands' role. Everyone agrees that 'fishing is a gamble', but younger women were not prepared to tolerate such insecurity, and, believing that there were alternatives, they maintained only a reluctant loyalty to the status quo.

None of the women could actually live the traditional lifestyle the way the men did. Their role as fishermen's wives had vanished. Not only were there no fish to be dried on the flakes, but virtually all other aspects of their past lives had gone as well. In particular, women had stopped having large families. None of the younger women had more than three children, while the women in their sixties had brought up eight or nine or ten children — one had seventeen. Furthermore, they had done this before labour saving devices, convenience foods or easy access to St. John's. Many of them had reared children before Confederation in 1949 had eased the crushing poverty in the outports. All the women over 50 could remember life as Hilda Murray described it: they could tell you where the fish flakes were, the variety of animals and poultry they kept, about the constant baking, cooking and washing, the wood chopping and water drawing, the gardens and the berry picking, the bottling, pickling and preserving — and the 'times', the festivals and ceremonies. Now they were left with faint echoes. The older women still baked bread two or three times a week, used traditional recipes and ingredients, knitted, kept hens, grew potatoes and cabbage and went berry picking and trouting. But it was not like it was. The women under 40 who couldn't remember pre-Confederation days showed little inclination to keep it alive. So whereas the past is still an active part of the young men's lives, for the younger women it had become mere idle tales.

This tension between older and younger women was intensified by exogamy. Men (aged about 25) married women (aged about 23) from the other villages up and down the shore. Initially, they brought their wives into their parents' house and then, when means allowed (fairly soon) they built a house close by.[13] Thus, women are separated from their own mothers and thrust into a very close proximity with their mothers-in-law. This they resisted by keeping in close contact with their own mothers, greatly aided by the telephone. Mothers and daughters in neighbouring outports rang each other at least once a day, and as local calls are free, the conversations can be lengthy. As most of the younger women also have access to a car, they can expect to visit their mothers at least once a week.

The older women's criticisms of their daughters' 'modern' lifestyle were muted by their acute sense that they themselves have lost their own place as 'fishermen's wives', and this was expressed in a grudging admission that, materially speaking, life was a lot better for the younger women. The women in their sixties admitted that 'there was a lot of fate in those days'. It was hard work, they were poor and there were no luxuries. This remembered reality meant that they didn't really expect their daughters to wash nappies by hand when they could get Pampers, or to use the local

88

midwife when hospitals were available and so good, or have too large families when it would threaten their new (relative) affluence. How can they deny a 'better' life for their daughters, when they can't assert, positively, as their husbands can, the benefits of the traditional lifestyle?

Ironically, the older women's eroded identity as fishermen's wives was reflected in their interest in the fishery and their fervent avowal of the fishermen's cause. Many provided details of the fish, the traps, the problems and the politics. Many of the details were wrong because the older women had rarely been out in the boats and had no direct connection with the fishing. Nor did they go to the many meetings called to decide the trap-berths, to vote on the price of fish or to protest at the depredations of the inshore draggers. But they were keenly interested and listened carefully when the men discussed such things in the kitchen. Some of them handled all the paperwork, most worried about getting the men up in the morning at 4:30 to go off fishing. When the fishing season starts, the 'phones buzz with an efficient information network, so that within minutes of the boats returning, every house will have the details of sizes of catch and who caught how much and where.

Whenever I returned after a few days away, my landlady's opening remarks all had to do with the fishing, how many pounds her son had that morning, what it was like in Renews, or, if it was bad, 'it's so quiet it's like a place in mourning'. The younger women took part in the information network — especially in terms of relaying details of catches from other outports via their mothers — but they usually disclaimed all knowledge of the fishery and even resisted being drawn into the white hot debates of the day, for example, whether someone should lose his trap-berth when he went to work on the oil rigs or how to stop the inshore draggers from trespassing inshore. On the other hand, they were less inhibited about actually going in boats and quite a few enjoyed a Sunday's jigging, though this was never equated with fishing proper.

Let us now look more closely at these younger women.

And this little piggy went to market . . .

More girls than boys continued in post high school education. A few boys and girls went straight to work in the fish plants. A few boys went fishing, and a few girls baby-sat for the women working in the plants. A majority of girls who went to university became teachers and nurses, and they, like the male graduates from this town, will not return to Aquaforte, but will marry and settle elsewhere on the island, Labrador or the Mainland. However, the boys who went to Trades School returned as soon as they finished their courses, and went directly into fishing if they could. If not, they worked on the roads, the forestry or in garages, until they found a berth. For the girls, it was different. Usually, after a Trades School secretarial or clerical course, they got jobs in St. John's, for there were no jobs in Aquaforte and precious few (e.g., as doctor's receptionist) in Fermeuse or Ferryland. Some of these girls might well commute up to St. John's daily, at least during the summer. Their rest 'come down on week-ends' specifically to go to the bars and the dances — to have a good time and look for husbands. In this they were usually successful. Very few of the young Aquaforte secretaries married 'off the shore'.[14]

So within a few years of leaving school, men and women had opted for two contrasting worlds. The young men had returned to the ways of their fathers, but the young women were wholly absorbed in the modern, urban, sophisticated and materialist life of the big city. In dress, manners, assumptions and ambitions they were indistinguishable from millions of North American women. They enjoyed their financial and social independence. They dressed smartly and travelled afar — to Florida for the holidays or to Alberta to visit emigrant relatives. Yet unlike their sisters who were teachers and nurses, they remained firmly attached to the shore, and, above all, they married on the shore. When I talked to them at weekends, they accepted that they would, one day, have to give up their jobs, independence and lively social life because 'there's no work down here'.

And this little piggy cried 'wee wee' all the way home

When it actually happened, it came as an acute shock. Even if, at first, the young couple lived in St. John's, they were unable to afford a house there. And, inexorably, when the babies came, they returned to their husband's outport. This is the point of maximum disillusionment. The young married women in Aquaforte were, of course, from neighbouring outports. They confessed openly that they were bored, lonely and frustrated.

Why, then, did they do it? Marriage and return to the shore were not inevitable, as the experience of their more qualified sisters shows. Yet, it had not occurred to any of the young women I spoke to that they would do otherwise. A combination of very expensive housing, acute unemployment and low wages forced the issue once the young couple married, but it did not answer the question as to why the girls did not move to the mainland, or marry boys with good St. John's jobs or even marry boys from one of the other towns with more clerical jobs.

It was not, of course, seen as choice. Such 'choices' rarely appear as obvious as they do to watching sociologists. In the social determinations of the young St. John's typists the option not to marry was not appealing; nor, indeed, were the wages and prospects good enough to offer a long-term career. And through the rosy spectacles of romance there were clear prospects that offered some trade-off beyond the immediate disillusionment. They would secure a modern house, a car and a decent standard of living. They would all insist on acquiring all the material accessories they knew to be vital — the electrical gadgets, the luxurious furnishings, the large picture window. Nor were they blind to all the real advantages of outport life. They enjoyed the lack of traffic and the healthy environment for their children.

As the babies came the young mothers saw more of each other, and dedicated themselves to building a reproduction Canadian suburban lifestyle. Soon, too, they were drawn into the energetic activities of the voluntary associations[15] — Women's Institute, Kinettes, Darts Club and the Legion, to name but a few. Most of the Voluntary Association activity was dominated by older women who saw in it not only some outlet for their own energies but also a way to involve younger women in the activities of the community.

Indeed, after the initial singles 'hunting' sessions in the bars, the two sexes drew apart for the bulk of their social life, only coming together for the big banquets and garden parties and certain Church and Legion events. Apart from the meetings about the fishing, men were out very little, especially during the fishing season. Thus, in the evenings, you would find the men in each other's kitchens, visiting and babysitting, while the women were more frequently out than not. In this, the older women's frustration at being deprived of their traditional role combined with the younger women's frustration at being deprived of their suburban Canadian role to create a defensive but effective 'women's culture'.

Men, women and power

The ideology of male dominance is strong in Newfoundland culture. A combination of the male culture of fishing, a strong Church presence,[16] and a kinship system which separates women from their own community, seems to ensure an ideological domination which reflects the male control of the technical means of production. But we have already noted that while men controlled the harvesting sector of the fishery, it was women who commanded the processing sector. They also showed other signs of economic self-reliance and female solidarity, e.g., selling berries, taking jobs as telegraphists, selling bait to schooners, etc. Ideological domination, indeed, did not seem to reflect the much more complex economic reality. As we have seen in the previous chapters the material on traditional outport life makes it clear that both sexes accepted the sexual division of labour; both men and women worked unremittingly hard and everybody was poor. Nobody had any real power, being helpless in the hands of the merchants and the 'truck system'. Family cooperation was a matter of necessity, and beyond that emerged an equality of respect. 'Outport men can turn their hands to anything'. 'The woman was more than 50%'. While a certain ideological authority was invested in the man by the outside world (Church and merchant), it had less reality in the practice of the family. For without the women, the men could not operate. They were manifestly dependent on the women not only for the usual 'servicing' of cooking and caring, but to realize the value of their catch.

Returning to contemporary Aquaforte, we find evidence of some ideological skewing (though not as much as Faris reports). The Church was still powerful and both men and women accepted the place of fishing and fishermen at the apex of community esteem. But what does this mean in practice? Is ideological dominance reflected in real power? What, in other words, do the women lose by not fishing?

It is women who, by tradition, ran the post office. They also ran all three shops. Few women were active on the public political stage, but two who were, have gained places at the provincial level. Marriages are long-lasting and, in conditions where the couple are in close physical proximity, there is little apparent tension. Nor is there much deference. On the contrary, women speak their minds, come to decisions jointly with their husbands and lead independent social lives.

The sexual division of labour is strong, but while to an outsider (and to the men) fishing is valuable, exciting and skilful and men's activity is, therefore, evaluated as more significant than women's, it is hard to see that this assumption is justified by the correlation of economic with ideological dominance.

Conclusion

The mutuality of the relationship between men and women based on the traditional division of labour between fishermen and fishermen's wives has been broken. Men no longer depend on women to 'make the fish'. Yet the economic independence shown by women has been transferred to their new position as wage labourers in the fish plants. In many households, their wage is not just crucial to the family's economic survival, it may even be more than the men's contribution from fishing. What has altered, then, is that the women now have a direct relation with capital as individual workers.

Even since Joseph Smallwood took Newfoundland into Confederation with Canada in 1949, there have been disputes about how to support the scattered outports of the island, and the outcome has been a conflict within the capitalist structure that the inshore fishermen have been able to exploit. Fluent in the complex vagaries of UIC, licensing and quotas, they have carved a niche that is an amalgam of welfare state and subsistence. Despite the obvious disadvantages and drawbacks of outport life — high unemployment, low wages — the outport men have retained dignity and independence. Their time is their own, and few would swap it for the dehumanized existence of a Hamilton assembly line or an Alberta oil rig. But the younger women have rejected this package of plural adaption. Deprived of their substantive share in outport economic life, they not wanted the suburban lifestyle, and that means more money. They, therefore, put pressure on their husbands to 'go to the rigs' or at leat to get a job on one of the big draggers working out of St. John's or Trepassey. They also demanded more services on the shore, not only for their convenience as consumers but also to provide them with the jobs they so desperately wanted.

The sexual division of labour in Aquaforte has been transformed by the intervention of the capitalist means of production in the processing sector. The men and women occupy wholly different positions in the relations of production. The sexual division of labour cannot be understood simply or even primarily as a matter of subordination; and without clarification of the role of the sexual division of labour, we are unable to understand this complex social formation. Here, I can only raise certain questions and indicate some possible consequences.

While the existence of the generation gap among the women and the consequent fracturing of the 'women's culture' seem clear enough, it is by no means certain that the combination of a reasonable material standard of living and increased involvement in the culture of the voluntary associations would not, in time, erode the younger women's resentment. There is nothing inherently antagonistic about the new sexual division of labour.

Nor is it clear what would be the consequences of the pressure from the younger women for clerical jobs resulting in, for example, the establishment of a bank on the shore. On the one hand, clerical work pays better wages than the fish plants and could result in both a greater discrepancy between the women's economic contribution and the men's from fishing, and also between families with a wife so employed. On the other hand, a bank would certainly make life easier for the fishermen. Would it, at the same time, intensify the encroachments of capitalistic 'rationality' on one of the last outposts of petty commodity production? There is no doubt that most of the women, if they had the choice, would take any clerical or service job in preference to work in the plants. Would they be replaced by male labour for which the companies have an undisguised preference, and would that drive the women even further from any involvement in the fishery?

Such questions involve us taking seriously both the concept and the complex reality of the sexual division of labour. Much has changed on the Shore since this study was carried out but there is no inevitability about capitalist development or capitalist change. The Aquaforte men cannot either resist or redirect the forces of capitalism without the active help of the women. They are still dependent on them: women are still 'more than 50%'. Nor can the women retain their economic independence and social autonomy without that space that the men have guarded so carefully. The fractured sexual division of labour has to be renegotiated to enable men and women to construct their own lives in conditions of their own choosing and to resist the current encroachments of economic collapse.

Before I take this question further, I want to examine one way in which the women of the Southern Shore did assert both their difference and their control over their lives. This, in turn, involves a re-negotiation of the concepts of politics and culture, itself a useful antidote to taking such terms too much for granted.

Notes

1. This chapter was originally presented to the Conference on *Gender and Society*, in Manchester in 1982. It was later published in one of the volumes arising from the Conference, E. Garmanikow et al. (eds.). *The Public and the Private* (London, 1983). At the time that I carried out the field work on which this chapter is based, the inshore fishery in Aquaforte had already had a number of poor years. But it was still an active fishery and the focus of the community. Noone imagined that only a few years later the fishery would be closed down.

2. See, for example S. Rowbotham, (1972); P. Caplan and J. Bujra, (1978); or E. Croll, (1978).

3. For other examples, see Hornell (1980).

4. Before the war, the youngest daughter frequently went as a cook aboard her father's boat for the Labrador 'floater' fishery. In addition, women have always jigged for squid for bait for their husbands and, as Szala points out, in offshore ports where the men are away for long periods, the women must catch enough for their own subsistence. There are occasional references to women fishing with hook and line either with their husbands or on their own but these were rare until 1981 when a change in Unemployment Insurance regulations made it worth women's while to fish. Since then, a considerably larger number of women have entered the fishery, but nearly always fishing with their husbands in the vulnerable, small boat, inshore fishery.

5. There have been similar accounts which stress rigid and hostile sexual divisions; for example Wadel on Norway; Tunstall on Hull; Cohen (n.d.) on Whalsey Island and Clarke (n.d.) on Peerie Island.

6. On the Labrador 'voyages' where the catch of several months was brought back 'saltbulk', the women's task was even more important. There are also indications of women organising to negotiate conditions (G. Storey, personal communication).

7. Although the frozen fish division of the industry is clearly dominant, it should be noted that between 14% and 35% of fish caught is still salted, mainly by or through the Canadian Salt Fish Corporation. Work on both the health and safety and technological change aspects of the fish processing sector has been pioneered by B. Neis (1986, 1992).

8. e.g., Faris, (1972); Firestone, (1967); Wadel, (1973).

9. There is no such thing as a truly 'typical' outport. The variety among the 1000 or so outports resists oversimplified categories. For my purposes, Aquaforte's 'typicality' serves. However, I should note some obvious peculiarities. Firstly, it was the only largely Protestant community on the Catholic dominated southern shore. This may have rendered the church less powerful in the community. Secondly, it was relatively close to St. John's. Some communities were nearly 500 miles away, some still only have communication by sea. Thirdly, the Aquaforte fishery was a poor one, and incomes from the fishery were below those of neighbouring outports, e.g., Fermeuse. One consequence of this was that it was one of the few outports to have no longliners. This discrepancy mattered less in 1981 when all the incomes from the inshore fishery were low because of the poor season.

10. The plant at Fermeuse was opened in 1952 under NE Fisheries. It was then bought by Bird's Eye and then by Bonavista Cold Storage which became a part of the vast US based Lake Group. It is a year round plant with two offshore draggers based on it. Aquafisheries was opened in 1965 by a local man, Don Graham and a partner. It is now a substantial operation employing 65 people.

11. This horrendous institution, 'The Story', runs from about 2:30 p.m. to about 5:30, usually consisting of three Dallas type epic soaps and is an occupational hazard of all research work among women in Newfoundland (cf. Davis, 1979). A nodding acquaintance with the main characters is essential, and a quick check on the plot means that other conversations can go on simultaneously.

12. The fishing seasons vary around the island. In Aquaforte, it begins with the herring in March/April and proceeds through salmon to cod. these are caught in cod traps in the early part of the season (the summer voyage) till August and then by jigging and hand lining until October/November. This delicate balance of commercial activity, skilful use of transfer payments and subsistence activities has been shattered by the recent collapse of the cod fishery.

13. The men learn in Trades College how to read blueprints. With the aid of prefab parts, they still build their own houses with a little help from friends.

96

14. While this general pattern still holds today, 10 years after the study was conducted, the drastic down turn in the economy, culminating in the cod moratorium has meant that very few young people of either sex can look forward to any employment at all.

15. See Davis (1979) and Chapter 6 of this book for further discussion of the importance of female voluntary associations in the creation of a specific 'women's culture'.

16. Religion is strong all over the island but different denominations predominate in different areas. Especially noticeable are the Catholic and Salvationist areas. Aquaforte is situated on a Catholic shore.

Women saving firewood

Drying fish on the family stage

Cutting fish on the stage

The 'Beach Crowd' drying fish in Grand Bank

Early telegraph operators in an outport post office

The local store as the community meeting place

6 'The tangly bunch': The political culture of Southern Shore women

Introduction

A conservative tradition attests that women are 'not interested in politics'.[1] This, of course, flows naturally from the parallel assumption that women's concerns are inevitably the privatized ones of home, family and personal relations. Even if it were true that women were not 'interested in politics', we would need to ask not only why, but what kind of politics they are not interested in. In any case, does exclusion from the world of politics, voluntary or forced, matter? Feminists are committed to challenging and changing women's subordination, and we cannot, therefore, dispense with the ideas and structures of power. For women either to vacate this political arena or to participate on male terms has equally negative effects on the creation of a female politics.

There have been two defensive responses to this situation. One has been to point to the considerable advances that have been made — to the women who have established themselves publicly and to the greater space created for women.[2]

The second response has been to argue much more positively for a 'women's culture'; to argue that politics as we understand it is so thoroughly contaminated by male concerns that it has become gender specific, and that, therefore, what women create on their own, whatever that is, is more important. This response draws strength from the flowering of self-help women's health groups, women's music, feminist publishing houses publishing feminist novelists and poets and all the other evidence of a vibrant women's culture. But with the exception of instances such as the Women's Peace Camp at Greenham Common, where feminist political action is seen as the expression of feminist culture, this approach all too often seems to accept that women will be marginalized in the key processes and decisions.[3]

98

I want to draw these various strands together, and, in particular, to examine what we mean by 'culture' and 'politics' in women's experience. For it seems to me that we have colluded in a circular definition that asserts that what is male is political and what is female is not. Faced with women's undeniable activity, we have tended to call it culture and thereby relegated it to the peripheral and the secondary.

Raymond Williams (1976:76) confesses that 'culture' is 'one of the two or three most complicated words in the English language', and 'politics' is hardly less so. Heuristically, I shall assume that to make a distinction between the two will revolve around, on the one hand, the public operation of power and organization, and, on the other, the creation and expression of community identity. Such a recognition need not presuppose that culture and politics are polar opposites; nor yet that they are mutually exclusive. It is my contention here that gender is a crucial factor in the creation and operation of both concepts; that there is a sense in which we can say that women have built their politics within their culture while men have separated the two and elevated politics over culture.

In this chapter, I want to examine what we mean by "culture" and "politics"[4] in the experience of a group of rural Newfoundland women, and to see how women express their values, dreams and priorities both in their own communities and in the wider world beyond.

An evening of political culture

The variety, profusion and energy of rural women's voluntary associations has been documented by Dona Davis in her study of social structure in Grey Rock Harbour. In Chapter 5, I touched on their role in creating an active women's social life and their significance in the sexual division of labour. Here I want to look at them as expressions of "women's culture".

The 1981 Annual South Avalon District Meeting of the Women's Institute was held in Trepassey at 8 p.m. on May 20th. Trepassey lies on the peninsula closest to the oil- and fish-rich, but fog-swathed, Grand Banks. In this wild and treeless spot, the little wooden two-storey houses look scarcely strong enough to survive the winter gales, despite their bright-coloured paint.

But on a summery, sunlit evening it was a lovely ride up there. With fourteen other women, I joined the bus in Calvert, which then picked up some fifty more women from Ferryland, Aquaforte, Fermeuse, Renews and Capahayden before trekking over the barrens to Portugal Cove South and Trepassey. At each stop delighted confusion reigned. Plump, carefully decked ladies clinked aboard, and always there was someone late, someone missing or someone in the wrong place. Were we to pick up Janet here, or would she be over with her mother in Renews? Was Sophie working at the fish plant? It was a cheerful process that not only enabled the organizer to actually locate and collect all her members who could come, but kept all the occupants of the bus up with the latest information, either by conjecture — "she's at the plant, the caplin must be in to Calvert then", or "if she's with her mother, her husband must be still in hospital; that will be a hard-off crew", or by direct openings — "She had to go up there to cook tea because her chimney went on fire this morning". As Meg, my sponsor, said, in a voice of happy satisfaction, "Women together, they're a tangly bunch".

Settled in their seats, the women kept at least one eye on the sea to our left. As we passed notable fishing marks, like the Renews Rock, the conversation turned to the fishing topics of the day — such as the depredations of the new inshore draggers operating from Trepassey. Each trapskiff, moored by the buoys of the cod trap while it hauled up the heavy house of net with its catch of cod from below, was identified and its potential catch estimated by experienced eyes.

In between, the chat returned to those perennials of female communication — child-care and development, potential marriages, recent social events and knitting patterns. However, this was not a group of isolated suburban women, but the female half of a closely knit, active and productive community. I also learnt about kinship details, the power relations between different interest groups and which fishing boat had fitted new gear. There were certain "women's subjects" but they were not separated off from other matters. The surface chat was thus embedded in, and carried forward, the entire socially constructed knowledge of the community.

At the high school in Trepassey, twenty-five local members had prepared the polythene-covered "dinner" of such events (turkey salad, cookies, tri-colour jelly and stewed tea with tinned milk), as well as a daunting display of handicrafts, including a large traditional hooked mat of Trepassey.[5] Mutual cooing was interrupted by the President, Dot Mackay, who in her spare time had a part-time job as a mail-carrier, ran the Weight Watchers, helped with the Brownies, was active in the Progressive Conservative Party and brought up three sons. The paper-covered tables laid out in an H-shape had an obvious "high table", and someone had to sit at it. Dot herself had no choice, nor had the Vice-President, but the rest of the committee ducked and feinted and, by and large, retired triumphant to their coveys of friends. Pressed women, pink of face, took their places. It prefigured the central event of the occasion.

The dinner, the speeches, the group reports, the chanting of the Women's Institute ode followed a familiar pattern. They testified to a hard-working, comprehensively active and efficiently run organization. Then came "the

100

Voting", the highlight of the evening. A number of women had mentioned "the Voting" in tones that led me to expect some tense politics, but what actually happened was quite unexpected and it repays analysis.

Dot Mackay was clearly nervous. She checked the procedure in her book. We were to elect a president, a first vice-president, a second vice-president, and a secretary-treasurer, and each branch was to elect two members at large. No nominations had been received and none were vouchsafed now. Dot said she hoped it wouldn't be like last year, but to make it easier they could "cluster in groups" (i.e., each outport contingent, together). The noise level rose in anticipation, and I heard Anna Maitland's urgent whisper that "the trouble with this is you can't nominate anyone in case they nominate you back".

Operating now from clearly defined community groups, the nominations for President began. Ferryland opened up with Joan Curran: "I nominate Meg Bond [of Calvert]". Meg Bond rose promptly to her feet and said "I decline". Now Dot Anson (also from Calvert) nominated Joyce Walsh of Aquaforte. Joyce declined, and then Vera Sullivan (of Calvert) "nominated back" Helen Waite (Ferryland), who declined, and so on for seventeen nominations, of whom fifteen declined. A ballot could now be held between the two women who had allowed their nominations to stand: last year's Vice-President, Anna Maitland of Ferryland, and Mary Kenny of Calvert. When the slips had been counted and checked, Anna won by a handsome margin.

The same procedure was then repeated for the position of first Vice-President. Mary Kenny was re-nominated and some fifteen nominations and declinations later, Dot Anson also allowed her nomination to stand. Predictably, Mary Kenny won the subsequent ballot. By the time all the four main positions were filled, each woman had been nominated at least once. The pattern was that a nominator got "nominated back" by someone from the same outport as the woman she had nominated. Only four women did not decline, and they filled the posts. It took nearly an hour to extract what were, in effect, four volunteers.

It was an outcome that satisfied everyone, and the evening would up rapidly with some formal speeches of thanks, and we tumbled, tired, into the coach for the return trip down the now dark coast.

Women's culture and voluntary associations

Before I explore some of the implications of that evening, I need to return to the context in which it took place. Voluntary associations are a major part of outport women's lives. Apart from the very young, newly married women, virtually all women participate in some activity. A few limit it to

101

a weekly game of bingo or cards, and attend the numerous social events. But most are actively engaged in at least one association and the majority have a number of such involvements. Along the Southern Shore, the main ones are the Catholic Women's League, Royal Canadian Legion Ladies' Auxiliary, Women's Institute, Kinnettes and the Darts League. There are also support activities for Girl Guides, Brownies, Pathfinders and 4-H, more transitory groups like Weight Watchers, softball and badminton and a continual succession of weddings, showers, banquets, prize-givings, graduation celebrations, "garden parties" (summer community socials on church grounds), dances and fundraising events, all of which are organized and provided with food by groups of women.

Some activities are directed towards traditional good works like Christmas baskets for the elderly, and some, especially in the Women's Institute, focus on preserving traditional handicrafts, such as the hooked mats and country crafts. Associations or ad hoc groups also channel money into communal projects by applying for grants or supervising Government schemes. For instance, the Calvert Women's Institute repaired their centre and built a park and playground on two Canada Works summer programmes. All the work was organized and carried out by women, including all the building work. Women were also responsible for the project that extended the Legion hall, although in this case they overreached their technical skills and the new roof leaked, giving rise to much male banter.[6]

The resulting hectic round of activity involves all women in at least some aspects of the associations. Many are engaged in community activity of some sort every day. It is easy to see the significance of this activity in involving women socially and in terms of the impressively efficient communications network. But to what extent could any of it be described as cultural, or, even more problematically, political? Certainly much of the craft-works and the perpetuation of traditional entertainments and gatherings (e.g., mumming, garden parties) could be seen as "cultural" in the sense of "folk culture". More importantly, the level of involvement and the enthusiastic sociability create a social space to which all women are attracted. Furthermore, to associate as women was seen as the positive attraction, and women-only social events were, if anything, more popular than mixed ones.

Guided by a preconception of the Women's Institute and similar associations as inherently conservative and dedicated to upholding traditional sex roles and the importance of the family, it is easy to dismiss much of what they did as simply "servicing" the community in a way that was analogous to individual women servicing their families in the home. Were they not simply valiantly underpinning the deficiencies of state provision and supporting male initiatives?

Dona Davis, from a vantage point on the south coast of Newfoundland, has argued that women's voluntary associations are essentially to do with play, rather than with work — which happens at home. Moreover she sees the family as the only "politicized centrally organized multi-purpose group" in a society characterized by its egalitarian nature (Davis, 1979:199). Before I comment on these ideas in terms of the content and style of women's culture expressed in the voluntary associations on the Southern Shore I need to consider an important factor that affected the women of the Southern Shore more than women in some other areas, such as the south coast.

Local but not isolated: the road to integration

Settlements along the Southern Shore are scattered at about five- to ten-mile intervals. They vary in size and importance from hamlets of less than two hundred people, mostly related, to administrative centres like Ferryland with a population of 795 (1982).

While the Southern Shore is a clear cultural and geographic entity, subdivisions are more complicated. All the formal agencies have different ways of segmenting the Shore. In Ferryland, the RCMP, the doctor, the Department of Social Services, the Roman Catholic and Anglican parishes, the Rural Development Officer and the Unemployment Insurance Commission office all have different boundaries along the Shore. Electoral and census boundaries confuse matters still further. The voluntary associations follow suit. Some have branches in each community; some only have branches in the larger communities; thus people from Aquaforte have to go to Ferryland for most of their activities, while Calvert has its own Women's Institute branch, but goes to Ferryland for Legion events. The Women's Institute local area runs from Calvert (north of Ferryland) south to Trepassey. The Southern Shore Development Association, contrariwise, runs *north* along the coast from just south of Ferryland.

The result of these arrangements is an extraordinarily profuse and complex set of connections between all the communities of the Shore. Thus, although most communities are small enough to allow face-to-face contact between all the members, the totality of the Shore is sufficiently geographically extended (some hundred miles long) and densely populous to produce a more formal *Gesellschaft* context. The whole area also integrates vertically with Provincial and Federal structures, thus linking Aquaforte, for example, ultimately with Ottawa. But it is the women far more than the men who operate on this wider level, and they are more involved than the women discussed by Dona Davis. One reason is exogamy. A man would marry a girl from a neighbouring outport. He then built a house close to his parents' and, by extension, to his brothers'. Fishing crews were still composed

103

predominantly of close male relations. Men, therefore, lived among their kin, kept their boats at the community anchorage, fished with their brothers and other close male relatives, and sold the fish to the local fish plant. The women, separated from their own families of birth, kept in close contact with their mothers and sisters by means of both the phone and frequent visits. With roots in two communities and with sisters in others, women start with an inherently "wider world" than the men.

A second reason is the importance of voluntary associations in women's lives. The sheer number of women involved and the social mesh produced by their cross-cutting memberships together with the fact that nearly all the local voluntary associations are linked with levels of activity beyond that of the individual outport or small cluster of outports mean that women frequently meet women from neighbouring settlements on a regular and structured basis, and, less frequently, women from further afield. It is no accident that in Aquaforte alone the two people active politically at the Provincial level at that time were both women.[7]

Accounts of life in the traditional outport of the past emphasized their isolation. Transport was not easy, and was in the hands of men. Most communities had contact with others along a coast or bay by boat during the summer and by sledge during the winter. This is still the case in Labrador and along the South Coast, areas which have few connecting roads. But elsewhere, the coming of all-weather roads and widespread car ownership have transformed women's mobility. The men still dominate the all-terrain vehicle and skidoo trips to the woods; but the women have taken to the roads. No place on the Shore is now more than one or two hours' travel from anywhere else, and while winter conditions are not easy, the cars and trucks are robust enough to keep moving. Combined with the telephone, easy access to road transport has given women freedom of association, and they have taken it up with gusto. Quite apart from shopping, many women travel for meetings, banquets, tournaments, weddings and showers, conventions, concerts and prize-givings and on any other pretext.

Women's public activity, then, is not only greater but less restricted to the immediate locality of the settlement. It also gives them a virtual monopoly of the informal communication network, a point I shall return to later.

Men's "politics"

The men, on the other hand, tend to stay at home. They do not involve themselves in voluntary associations as frequently as their wives. However, Lions, Kinsmen and the Canadian Legion flourish and most men attend the events that have been organized by their wives and the big social events of the year. Male associations have a structural dominance. Province-wide, the male "service" associations decide on the annual "cause", which both the male and female associations' fund-raising supports. Membership of some female associations, e.g., the Kinettes, depends on having a husband who is a member of the male equivalent association.

A small group of men, drawn from the actual or aspiring local bourgeoisie and the local professionals, "do a lot". They hold the key positions in the local associations, run the Fire Brigade, drum up support for good causes, chair meetings of the Development Association and similar local groups that deal with snow and refuse clearance and generally act as "local leaders — visible and articulate. It is noticeable that there is no such visibility of the much greater number of women who "do a lot"; nor do the active women come so often from families of higher status. Otherwise, the young single men (like the young single women) roam the bars in packs, go down to St. John's and generally "party around". During the winter, when fishermen have leisure, most of the men prefer to "go to the woods" in small groups — to hunt, cut timber and drink.

Yet despite a relatively low level of public activity, it is the men and male groups that dominate those public expressions of what we, conventionally, call politics. The Fishermen's Committee in each community is a small elected group, usually about four people, always men. They wield the only overt local power, and they have considerable authority. They supervize the draw for trap berths and salmon-net berths at the beginning of the season. This involves determining who is, and who is not, eligible as a "fisherman". Each crew has one or two berths, but the berths vary enormously in their ease of access, in their danger to the trap, and, most important, in their productivity. The trap fishery is an entirely passive one, and the location of the berths is a major factor in the success or otherwise of a crew. Fishermen's fortunes, then, are largely dependent on the draw. The committee is also responsible for settling minor disputes, for representing the interests of a community in cases of "poaching" by residents from neighbouring communities, and for enforcing the myriad complex regulations imposed by the provincial and federal government fisheries departments.[8] Disputes or issues that the committee cannot handle go either to the Union or to the relevant official. Members of the committee have a great deal of knowledge as well as authority. There is much discussion of fishing issues by both men and women, but only men, i.e., fishermen, go to the meetings to discuss them formally. Attendance at such meetings is high, although few men apart from the "local leaders" actually speak.

All fishermen were also members of the NFFAW[9] and local meetings were held in which officials discuss the negotiated fish prices and other issues. In addition, some leading fishermen attend meetings in Trepassey and St. John's to discuss issues such as licensing and quotas. These are usually organized by government, local professionals such as doctors, or the Union. Ad hoc committees and meetings to respond to such issues as the Mobil Oil Impact Study tend to be convened by local professionals and dominated by the local leaders.

The Southern Shore Development Association is a wider organization covering the whole Shore. Its meetings provide some of the few occasions when men meet men from other outports in a structured way. Inevitably fishing issues come up, but the meetings focus mainly on general community problems, e.g., response to oil-related development, refuse disposal, community grant applications, demands for road surfacing, etc. Yet few women, except one or two especially "public-minded" women, attend these meetings.

What I appear to have described here, then, is both men and women being involved in formal public associations, but with a difference. While the women are engaged in cultural or "play" activities, or else in supportive functions such as catering, the men continue to control the more serious and "political" activities, what Peggy Sanday calls "the public", i.e., "political or economic activity which relates to the control of persons or things" (Sanday, 1981:190).

Rural Newfoundland, then, presents us with a public life divided according to gender in a particularly clear way, and it also exposes that circularity of definitions of *culture* and *politics* that makes them correspond so neatly with men's and women's activities.

men	=	fish, roads, oil	=	politics
		bake sales		
women	=	community projects	=	culture
		money-raising		

This is the point at which I want to look again at the voluntary associations, particularly in terms of their content and their style. It is an examination that takes us back to the Women's Institute meeting in Trepassey.

Cultural politics and political culture

We should notice, first, that the meeting was set up, organized and run by local women themselves, not by local professionals or government officials, nor even by provincial officials of the Women's Institute. Only the outgoing President, Dot Mackay, remotely resembled the pattern of the male "local leaders". Her husband had a government job, although as he worked elsewhere on the island he was invisible locally. Neither Dot nor her husband had been born in the area, and this "stranger" status might have given them links with the local professionals, but, in fact, they did not associate with them. They lived in a trailer home. Dot's job as a part-time mail carrier was hardly prestigious and, generally, she had more in common with the other women who made up both the outgoing and the incoming committees. By and large, the women came from "good" families, which were merely a reflection of the "respectable" membership of the Women's Institute as a whole. The Darts Club, for instance, had a much more socially mixed leadership. Apart from the principal of the school in which we met, who was there as a private member of the Women's Institute, there were no local professionals. Nor, as one might expect (and a number of writers, including Dona Davis, support this), were there any wives of professionals.

Secondly, the area represented at the meeting, half the total Shore, involving seven communities, was too large to be merely local. This level of association was only open to men who attended the Southern Shore Development Association and ad hoc fishery meetings, neither of which involved structured links between the men of different outports in the same way as that available to the Women's Institute members. While the meeting had its own autonomy, it was also aware of its position within the framework of the provincial Women's Institute — to meetings of which the new president and vice-president would go — and beyond that, the federal Women's Institute, and indeed, beyond that, the world.

The main business of the evening was "the voting", and to understand this it is necessary to recognize the strength of the ethic of egalitarianism among Newfoundlanders. This has been well documented by sociologists and anthropologists, who have pointed out that the refusal to either accept or grant leadership positions can both foreclose local initiative and prevent effective resistance to outside encroachment.[10] In other words, what may have been an essential mechanism for social survival in the days of harsh merchants and grinding poverty may be less appropriate in changed conditions.

The egalitarian ethic clearly throws some light on what went on. In so far as these positions were leadership positions, or were perceived as that, it would be compulsory to refuse them. In the male associations (and in the one described in Davis, 1979), the vacuum was filled by local professionals or by aspiring "local leaders". Thus, by degrees, male outport society was becoming more stratified. On the other hand, the fishermen's committees, which did have a wider spread of members, often had their authority challenged. This was usually expressed int terms of it being morally wrong to accept a leadership position. Much of the discontent stirred up by a refusal to allow one crew in Aquaforte to continue to use its berth after its skipper had gone to work on the oil rigs centred on the credentials and imputed partiality of the current committee, rather than on the merits of the decision itself. Similarly, in Calvert, one elderly man was still not speaking to his nephew because, during his nephew's term on the committee, the man had been refused the right to draw. The uncle's enduring rage centred upon what he saw as his nephew's prior obligation to him, based upon kinship.

Clearly, the Women's Institute committee did not have, and certainly did not exert, that kind of direct authority over its members. But it had some, notably the right to expel members who behaved inappropriately or who failed to attend meetings. Looking at what happened during the voting shows how the women have tacked the problem of the conflict between egalitarianism and authority. I have already pointed out that what they ended up with was actually four "volunteers". One was very young, and none were from high-status families. Yet, because they had not transgressed the egalitarian ethic, their subsequent leadership gained ready acceptance. Also, because nearly all the women had held position in some association, at some level, at some time, there was a much greater understanding and sympathy for the conflicts of office.

So I want to argue here that while the men remain trapped between an incompatible egalitarian ethic and a democratic mechanism, the women have found a way of using the mechanism without betraying the ethic. Their solution allows both authority and decision-making and also the retention of a strong sense of identity as a group. Comments at that meeting and heard from many other women show that they regard such leadership positions as jobs with some perks, not status positions. There is no question of anyone "handing on" (symbolized by the abandonment of the high table by the outgoing committee). There is constant pressure to involve younger women, newcomers, outsiders, women considered "not as well-off" or even "unfortunates". Nor does the committee impose itself more than necessary. Members meet only as often as they have to and the general membership remains involved in the bulk of activity. Indeed, the sheer scale of that activity presupposes an entirely active membership.

The women have a structure of extraordinary efficiency and power that has no parallels among the male organizations. Combined with all the other women's organizations, it ensures a formidable command of communications. We have already noted that while the formal activities of the groups fell into the categories of recreational, cultural or supportive, the communications are not so restricted. The women do talk about fishing issues and resurfacing the road. The point here is that their discussion is rarely set up formally and never as confrontation. It is interlaced with other concerns. In fact, it is clear that in the minds of the women they are not really separated. Why, then, don't they simply take over? They have both the means and the energy.

One answer could be that the men would resist them, as they undoubtedly would. Yet the few women who do take part are eminently successful and there appears to be little overt sexist exclusion in the public sphere.[11] As a hypothesis, this is difficult to test. In any case, a more immediately obvious answer is that they simply don't want to.

Another covert connotation of politics identifies it as "important", in contrast to culture, which is not. Looked at from the outside it is easy to assume that women ought to prefer to be involved in the "politics" of the inshore draggers, rather than the "culture" of bake sales. One anthropologist who has questioned this is Rogers. She argues that it is both sexist and Eurocentric to assert a *priori* that the public and formal sectors of society offer greater rewards than the private and informal sectors (Rogers, 1978).

Yet it is not simply Marxists who argue that the economic has to be prior in some sense. It is worth noting in this context that the whole edifice of the women's materially comfortable lives which enables the voluntary associations to be so active rests on the success of the fishery, and on the continuing operation of the local fish plant. A year later, after a disastrous season's fishery, the Aquaforte plant closed down. It reopened shortly after with government aid, but it alerted the people to their extreme economic vulnerability. In other parts of the Province such closures have led to local action, but so far these have been male-dominated, usually co-ordinated by the local development association or branch of the fishermen's Union.[12] Where are the women at a time when the well-being and indeed the survival of the entire community are under threat?

The sexual division of political action is all the more striking in the light of Newfoundland women's significant economic contribution. There is a long tradition of women's active economic involvement in Newfoundland. Even now that women's contribution to the family economy in the production of sun-dried fish has ended, women work in the fish plants and manage the shops and post offices, frequently bringing home more than their fishermen husbands. In this case it does not make sense to equate political power with economic activity.

This point raises the question, again, of what the term "political" includes. During some research I carried out in a United Kingdom city (see Porter, 1983) I asked, "Do you think men know more about politics and things like that than women do?" Most of the men and some of the women thought that men did know more than women. But many more women either defined politics as what women *were* interested in, or else dismissed politics as "men's business" but then said that what women were interested in was "Oh, health and education, and food prices and the old people, and things like that". Apart from being a tidy lot of exceptions to any definition of "political", these responses also reflected both a sense of priorities and a sense of powerlessness. For both men and women, "politics" boiled down to elections, industrial disputes and a few newsworthy issues, problems which were out of their control anyway. So, indeed, were prices and education at a national level; but women could, and did, confront these issues locally in their shops and schools, as individual consumers and parents. It seemed to me that the absence of a community equivalent to a trade union forced the women into frustrated individualism.

In Newfoundland, the situation is reversed in that it is the women who have the strong grass-roots organizations while the men remain trapped in inappropriate political structures and relative isolation. In contrast to women, the men seem to be operating out of their depth in structures that have been imposed on them. In many ways, men reproduce the structures of oppression. There is patently little that the weak and isolated inshore fishermen can do to control or challenge either the proliferating obscure regulations of the state bureaucracy or mainland firms that would like to eliminate them in favour of "more productive" units.

We have already noted that while women's voluntary activities fell into the categories of recreational, cultural or supportive, communication was not so restricted. In Aquaforte, everybody talked about fishing issues, but the men and women discussed them separately. Information necessary for discussions was traded in the family. The women needed details of the menfolk's catching problems, waterfront conversations and results of formal meetings of exchange with other women on the phone and face to face. The men relied on the women for all information about other crews in different parts of the community and in other settlements up and down the Shore.

Where more general issues were concerned the men and women did not rely on one another for information. Whereas the men would "talk politics" — about the Constitution, the impact of offshore oil development or its failure, and the crisis in the fishery — the women remained silent about such matters in public, and even in private they usually confined themselves to moral commentary on such events as the assassination attempt to the Pope or the *Ocean Ranger* oil-rig disaster.

When I questioned them about these wider political issues the Aquaforte women, like the English women I talked to, said that "politics" was not interesting, or was simply depressing, and, most significantly, that nothing could be done about it. In the English research I had found that women often said that men's concerns were "more important" than their concerns. This meant that men could talk about what interested them — from motor bikes to civil wars. Meanwhile, women got on with the "really" important matters of personal relationships, caring concerns and the family. Like their English counterparts, the Newfoundland women disclaim their activities as "not important", and by this they mean that they do not consider them "political".

Women do talk, though less dogmatically than the men, about locally important issues. They also talk about all the other important aspects of the shared life of the Shore, and they act in powerful co-ordination to forward those things they approve of and to discourage those that they oppose. In their voluntary associations women have established a kind of freedom, autonomy and material confidence in which they can make their own politics. They have established control over certain aspects of the shared life of the community which they see as central. But by accepting that their interests are by *definition* not political, that is, important, by refusing to involve themselves in those that are and by hiding behind the camouflage of the "tangly bunch", what they have engineered is in effect a retreat from an apparently uncontrollable outside world to one which is more manageable.

Conclusion

In this chapter I have had two objectives. One is to raise the question of the use of the concepts of "culture" and "politics". I have suggested that the use of covert assumptions leads to the misinterpretation of the evidence, which then slips into preordained categories, rather than being accurately examined on its own merits. Once a speech or an action has been defined as "cultural", it is difficult to remain open to its "political" consequences and dimensions. The second is to present some of the activities of the women of the Southern Shore in the voluntary associations, and to ask certain questions about these. It is clear than the women possess certain tools of considerable political potential. Their command over channels of communication is in itself a considerable strength. So are their organizational sophistication and the accomplished ease with which they organize and co-ordinate various activities. Yet they do not use their potential power in open conflict with the state, or with capital. They have deliberately separated their resources from the men's albeit powerless efforts to affect economic and political decisions involving the whole community. In other words, they have turned their backs on politics as they understand it, and have built instead a "political culture" which remains powerful in controlling the culturally meaningful parts of the environment of its members providing that the economic and wider political reality in which it is embedded is unthreatened. While there is a certain perspicacity in their sense of powerlessness it is, essentially, a negative position. The women have achieved a piece of subversion that should not go uncelebrated, but the latent power of the organized rural women of Newfoundland is, as yet, unrealized.

As one frustrated Bristol woman put it, "Women together: that's the greatest power in all the world". The society that gave rise to the voluntary associations and to the institutions and priorities that these women value is under economic threat, and the potential power of "the tangly bunch" to act in its defence should not be underestimated or forgotten.

In the next stage of my efforts to understand the ways in which Newfoundland women constructed their lives and ideas, I moved to a different part of the island, on the north east coast. I also began to use methods that would help me to draw together the strands that were beginning to emerge, and also to move, cautiously, towards a more general understanding of women's lives in Newfoundland.

Notes

1. The material drawn on here was collected in Aquaforte, south of St. John's, between February and July 1981. The research was supported by the Institute of Social and Economic Research of Memorial University, and I gratefully acknowledge the help of R. Hill, Director of the Community Services Council project on "Work and Unemployment in Newfoundland", and J. Cag, both of whom gave me access to their data and helped make contacts in Aquaforte. A version of this chapter was published in *Newfoundland Studies*, Vol. 1, No. 1, 1985.

2. See N. Adamson, L. Briskin, and and M. McPhail, *Feminist Organizing for Change* (Toronto, 1988); V. Randall, *Women and Politics* (London, 1982); M. Stacey and M. Price, *Women, Politics and Power* (London, 1981).

3. See D. Thompson (ed.), *Over our Dead Bodies: Women Against the Bomb* (London, 1983); P. McAllister (ed.), *Reweaving the Web of Life* (Philadelphia, 1982).

4. The dichotomy between culture and politics, especially as typified as male and female areas, relates closely to the dichotomy between 'public' and 'private', which has been much discussed in feminist writing see, e.g., P. Sanday, 1974, and also to the formal/informal dichotomy used in other contexts.

5. For a scholarly account of these vibrant works of art see G. Pocius, *Textile Traditions of Eastern Newfoundland* (Ottawa, 1979).

6. Various summer works programmes were aimed at the unemployed. They provided the much coveted stamps that entitled the holder to claim unemployment insurance. One of their deficiencies was that they operated at the height of the fishing season when many men, unemployed during the winter, were busy. In this case the slack had been taken up by the women. There has always been considerable controversy about the merit of the so-called 'make work' programs, (see House (St. John's, 1986)) but they remain — for the moment — as part of the rural communities survival strategy.

7. Jean Payne in the Liberal Party and Joyce George in the Progressive Conservative Party.

8. By and large the federal body, the Department of Fisheries and Oceans, deals with the live fish i.e., matters of quotas, licences; and the provincial Department of Fisheries deals with the dead fish, i.e., hygiene arrangements in fish plants. The NFFAW negotiates fish prices for all the province's fishermen, as well as representing the fish plant workers and the men working on the draggers.

9. The Newfoundland Fishermen, Food and Allied Workers Union (NFFAW) split in 1987 (after this study was carried out). Two unions now represent fishermen and plant workers. The FFAW (Fishery, Food and Allied Workers), in close association with the powerful autoworkers union, CAW, continued with the old leadership and the majority of members. The other union is the UFCW (United Food and Commercial Workers). There is also a vocal Newfoundland Inshore Fishermen's Association (led by Cabot Martin), and the equally vocal Petty Harbour Fisherman's Coop (led by Tom Best).

10. Davis also argues that leadership positions threaten the stability of the "trading" between individuals and families. In Grey Rock Harbour they therefore foisted such positions onto strangers (Davis, 1979). For accounts of how this situation has changed since 1979, see Davis (1990,1991). However, when I visited a fieldworker in South East Bight in 1989, something similiar happened to me, when I was manoevered into making the 'draw' for the allocation of Summer Works Programme jobs to the local youngsters, so that noone on the local RDA committee could be blamed

11. It is no coincidence that the Mayor of Trepassey, a woman, was one of the most vocal and effective leaders of the resistance to the income of the major National fish plant there in 1990, winning some community compensation.

12. A notable exception to this is discussed in B. Neis, 'Doing Time on the Protest Line' (1988) where women were actively involved in resisting the closure of the plant at Burin.

7 Time, the life course and women's work in Catalina

Introduction

We come, now, to another stage in trying to understand the central theoretical problems raised in this book. The Catalina study, which I introduce in this chapter,[1] was carried out in 1987. It served as a pilot to the much larger *Women's Economic Lives* project, which I will be discussing in subsequent chapters. However, in this chapter I want to reflect on the Catalina Study, and the Grand Bank study (discussed in Chapter 4) and what they tell us about women's experience of work. The intention is, and was then, to use this material to provide a solid foundation for a wider-ranging examination of women's economic lives as they are experienced in different parts of the island. Various connections had been forming in the back of my mind. Some continuities and discontinuities were becoming apparent and the limitations of my existing conceptual armoury were daily more obvious.

More interesting, however, was the fact that other people, working in different contexts, were having similar thoughts. At a very general level these thoughts have to do with the connections between gender, power, and material life. As a loosely conceived tendency, we seem to be increasingly dissatisfied with the answers provided by glib "facts", going far beyond a traditional scepticism about quantitative methods. At the very least we are now more concerned with how these facts are collected and what they mean to the so-called subject, as well as to the researcher (Cain and Finch, 1981; Stanley and Wise, 1983). We are also increasingly preoccupied with the historical dimension of the material we use. Again, this goes beyond writing in a conventional "historical background", amounting to a sustained attempt to de-privilege the present. The concern with the research process, increasing seriousness about the "subjective", and a recognition of history have all led to a growing interest in, and practice of, biography, autobiography, and oral history as important research methods.

115

Using some material from the Grand Bank and Catalina studies, I shall explore how we might look for possible answers. My object is to bring together some of the material from both projects that, when I came to consider it later, seemed to fit together. In particular, I want to suggest that both studies point to two significant discontinuities between men and women in their actual experience of work and how they interpret it. In both these studies the women seemed to focus less on the actual work they did and more on the context and purpose of their contribution, and its benefit to their particular household. The reverse side of this perception is that these women saw greater continuities between their lives and those of their mothers and daughters than men saw between themselves and their fathers and sons. The other discontinuity is in how men and women perceive "time", especially in relationship to the life course. In the context of the Catalina study, especially, it was this perception that led women to make different decisions about how and when to enter the labour force, as well affecting their evaluations of their economic contributions.

The problem of time

Just in these opening remarks, I have used a number of rich phrases that signal a host of concerns and ambiguities. The title of this chapter, alone, contains at least four — "time", "the life course", "work", and "women". I do not intend to get bogged down in attempting precise definitions or exploring the theoretical jungle that they open up, but some operational machete work is necessary.

Time

In a sense, some sociologists are new to "time". This is not altogether a disadvantage. Historians tend to take it for granted. Anthropologists notice it rather more, but often focus on the way it takes on a different character when it is organized according to ritual or to symbol. E.P.Thompson (1967) was perhaps the first writer, and certainly the most frequently read, to look at the political dimensions of time, of how ordinary people negotiate the boundaries of "work" time. Indeed, he discussed the origin of the very notion of the separate "working day", and how this working day then was alienated as "time" along with all the other aspects of social life that were restructured under capitalism.

Oral historians and sociologists (when they are acting in this capacity), have learned how to deal more sensitively with time and its relationship to an individual's life course (Bertaux, 1982; Thompson, 1981). While it would

116

seem much easier to collect a life story that is nearly over than one that has only just begun, if one takes seriously that the "story" will change according to the individual's subjective perception, this bias toward older people's life stories is a serious limitation.

There have, nevertheless, been some imaginative attempts to recreate the past experience of whole communities as well as individuals (Harevan, 1982; Thompson, 1975). Harevan's comments on using this method in Manchester, New England point to awareness both of the problem and of the inherent limitations of the method.

> More than being a source of factual evidence, a reconstruction of reality, oral history is a recreation of people's memories and perceptions — it teaches us what people remember, why they remember it and how they remember (Harevan, 1982, p. 373).

More recently, feminists working with gender, especially in terms of collecting life stories and material gathered through life stories, began to point out that the experience of time was different for men and women. Replacing the term "life cycle" with "life course" reflects "the notion of individual progression through a series of fairly fixed and predictable life stages, in favour of a more complex notion of individual progression through a life span which admits more variation in patterns of experience" (Finch, 1988:11). There are ways in which the greater number of potential biological events in a woman's life (menstruation, childbirth, and menopause) would seem to lock her more firmly into a life cycle. Yet, women either do not follow the expected progression or their individual course aligns less than neatly with a family one. More important, the existence of an actual and potential biological "course" forces women's pattern of life away from men's. The of British Sociological Association (BSA) volume on *Women and the Life Cycle* (Allat et al., 1987) explores a number of the consequences of this.

Straw and Elliott (1986) take another approach. They contrast the ways biological rhythms are mediated into significance.

> . . . so that males and females somehow acquire or are taught to have a different sense of and feel for time. This comes in part from the distinctive sequences described above but also from the fact that a female's sense of time is continuous throughout life in a way which a male's is not (Straw and Elliot, 1986:36).

It means that women are more involved with what Leach (1971) has called "non-recurrent time" and what Straw and Elliott (1986) call "generational time". Women "manage the great events of the life sequence of birth, marriage and death" (Straw and Elliot, 1986:38) and thus become "gatekeepers of family and community history" — remembering certain events, forgetting others, creating a moral order. It also means the women oversee both the internal and external timetables of their families.

> Within the house it is mainly women who decide who is to do what and when; but they also determine, to a large extent, how outside time demands, in terms of leisure, are accommodated to fit in with the rhythms of family life (Straw and Elliott, 1986:41).

While Straw and Elliott are concerned to demonstrate the power that this control over time gives to women, I have quoted from their article principally because I want to direct attention to the complexity of the decisions that women make. Time, as a number of writers have pointed out, is a scarce resource in the lives of working class people, which are characterized by scarcity. Some control over time, some flexibility in its disposal is, therefore, extremely important. If we accept that women are traditionally more aware of the family project and their own contributions to it that are other family members, their decisions about the allocation of time both in the short term and the long term will be closely related to the project of family survival. This is not to say that only women are involved in the family project, but it is to suggest that if we examine women's decisions about "time" we will also learn about women's perspectives on the larger project.

Different studies: common themes

There were, of course, certain common strands in the two studies I am bringing together here. Essentially, they were both pilot studies,[2] carried out in small Newfoundland towns, rather than larger urban centres or small fishing communities, and both were focused on women's experiences of work and the economy in the broadest sense.

I described Grand Bank, and what drew me there in Chapter 4. We need, now, to turn to the quite different town of Catalina. Like Grand Bank, Catalina is a small town dominated by its involvement in the fishery. Historically, this has included both the inshore fishing conducted in small boats and processed by family members, and the Labrador fishery, involving larger boats, but not including women as part of the wage-earning labour force. Like Grand Bank, Catalina's economy is now dominated by a large fresh fish processing plant employing 1,000 workers, both men and women.[3] My intention in Catalina was to explore women's labour-force participation and the nature of the labour market they had available to them. I also wanted to make use of Pahl's (1984) work on household strategies to explore women's invisible economic contribution to their families.

Change and continuity in Grand Bank

I learned a great deal about women's work inside and outside the home in Grand Bank from the mothers, grandmothers, and great grandmothers who talked to me. As I described in Chapter 4, I had more difficulty documenting exactly the work women do today. Nevertheless, I did learn enough about the way women's work had changed, and what they thought about it to arrive at some conclusions.

One was that despite the obvious differences in both the techniques and scale of the work women did in the different generations there was a continuity in the central project and women's responsibility for it. Women, as I said there, felt they did the *same* work as their mothers, but under easier circumstances.

Women of all generations saw their work as a *family* project and they had a very clear sense of both the dignity and worth of that project and of their own essential contribution to it — at least equal to that of men. It was the women's insistence on the essential continuity of the project they felt they were all — mothers and daughters alike — engaged in, that gave their lives meaning. In my fumbling efforts to uncover the ideas that informed these women's lives, I found myself without sufficiently sophisticated tools. It remains for later studies to piece together, with much more precision, how ideas have changed over time. What was explained to me, with considerable patience, was how *these* women gained access to a shared perspective that enabled them to continue to live lives of worth and integrity in a changing world.

Women's economic decisions in Catalina

In Catalina, I was primarily interested in how women's work in the paid labour force and in the home was connected to an overall household strategy. In particular, I wanted to understand how decisions are made, and by whom, as to what jobs women take, how their paid work is viewed in the household, and how it relates to other work carried out by both the women and the men in the household. I suspected that the kind of jobs women got, and the sequence of jobs in each woman's work history, were integrally connected with household strategies. The question was whether it was household decisions that led women to take certain jobs, or whether it was the

119

availability of (usually rather poor) jobs that led to women taking certain roles in the household, or whether the two were connected in more complex ways. Having learned to take seriously the concept of the "household" as the pivotal economic entity, I was also concerned to break it apart and understand something of the relations and negotiations inside the household.

Older women gave me an account of their work prior to the Second World War that, apart from the "beach work", was very similar to the testimony of women in Grand Bank. Mrs. House, for example, whose father was a foreman on the railway and who lived in East Point, kept a garden, cows, hens, and, usually, rabbits. She made butter and hay and cleared the land of stumps. She even helped her father slaughter animals. At the age of 11 years, she cooked for a "crowd of 19" — nine siblings, two cousins, six boarders, and her parents. Later, when she was married, first to a fisherman who later went to the woods, and after his death to a seaman who came ashore to work at Mifflins, she herself painted her house, fixed the fence, dug ditches and hauled up the water from the well to the house. She spun wool and made yarn. She picked and sold berries. She also carried milk to the south side of Catalina to sell. After her first husband died, she took up midwifery. She estimates that she delivered 100 babies. She never lost a mother, although three or four babies were stillborn. Her mother-in-law lived with her for 24 years, bedridden for 4 of them.

One feature this account illustrates is the way in which women were infinitely flexible in their economic contributions. It is clear even from this brief summary of Mrs. House's activities, that she could and did turn her hand to whatever was necessary. The point was not exactly what women did, but the expectation that they would contribute economically in whatever way was available. We come across the same features when we examine contemporary women's work histories.

The current situation for women is distinguished by, on the one hand, the availability of jobs at the Fishery Products International (FPI) plant, and, on the other, by a labour market characterized by a rigid occupational segregation by sex. Practically all women work in jobs *only* held by women, in working groups comprising *only* women — usually with direct male supervision. Women's jobs are concentrated heavily in the two areas of production work at the plant (and within that in the trimming and packing grades) and clerical work. Men's occupations, on the other hand, are not only much more varied, but also include a greater number of managerial and professional occupations.

Some workers are employed on make-work projects. For women, the most important are the SAR (Social Assistant Recipient) projects, which employ Social Assistance recipients in order to give them sufficient stamps to transfer them to the (federal) unemployment insurance (UI) roll. At the

120

time of the project, two women were employed as domestics under this program and ten were employed in a knitting project.

Catalina women take the major responsibility for all domestic labour. In fact, evidence from the women themselves and from local professionals (e.g., doctors, teachers, nurses, and social workers) suggests that Catalina men do even less around the house than is usual for the province.[4] This means that in most households women are doing all, or virtually all, the shopping, cleaning, washing and ironing, cooking and washing up. Our best estimate is that in somewhat fewer than half the households, men cut and haul the supply of firewood. Men also, usually, shovel snow. They also undertake a variety of household repairs, although this can vary from knowing where the fuses are kept to undertaking major rebuilding work. Very few households keep vegetable gardens. When they do, it was our impression that it was slightly more likely to be men who looked after them. Some men hunt and/or fish. Most women pick and preserve berries.

In addition, Catalina women take almost total responsibility for the care of their children. The only significant exception is where both partners work opposite shifts at FPI. In that case the husband usually looks after the children when his wife is on the night shift and he is at home. A significant and growing aspect of the caring work undertaken by Catalina women is the care of elderly and/or sick relatives. These include her husband's relatives as well as her own. The problem seems to be more acute in Catalina than elsewhere and is obviously exacerbated both by the lack of dense kin networks and by the cutbacks in social and medical services.

It is impossible to generalize about the routes women take between and through all this paid and unpaid work. Most women I talked to, certainly those under about 50 years of age, saw paid work as a normal and natural further economic contribution they were expected to make in addition to their domestic and caring work. What I was interested in, however, was how they established priorities between the two kinds of work, how they reached their decisions, and, indeed, how much "choice" they had.

Two women's stories

Here, then, are accounts of two women's paid working lives. Edith was born in Clarenville. She left school at the age of 16 and went to work in the office at Eaton's in Toronto. "I went to St. John's, but they had to have someone with experience. My brother and his friend were driving back and they took me with them". She stayed at Eaton's for 3 years, although she hated Toronto. When she came back to St. John's she got a job as a sales clerk in the sports department of Ayre's Department Store. After a year she moved to Eastern Canada Savings and Loan and worked as an office clerk.

121

A year later she seized the opportunity to work nearer home and took a job as a telephone operator with CNT (Central Newfoundland Transport) in Clarenville. By this time she was married to a driver with Clarenville Transportation, so when CNT closed down a year later, she took a job as a cashier with Clarenville Pharmacy rather than relocate to Gander. Two years later she left to have her first child. At the same time her husband moved from his job as a driver to Easy Save,where he stayed for the next 22 years, working his way up the hierarchy.

Edith was out of the labour force for two years, and then went back full-time, working as head cashier in the Chain Stores. Despite the responsibility that reflected her, by now, extensive experience, her pay was still very low — barely enough to show a profit after she paid her live-in babysitter.

When she got pregnant again she left her job and remained at home with her newborn twins. When she returned, it was as a buyer in Price Choppers, a clothing store, but after 18 months (and a brief stretch working at Woolworths), she gave up the unequal struggle to find, and pay for, adequate child minders.

At this point, 5 years ago, her husband was transferred to Catalina as Manager of Mifflins Grocery (which is owned by the same company as the outlet in Clarenville). Since then, she has been unable to find any work at all. This is not only because there are fewer clerical jobs in Catalina, but also, as she clearly perceives, because she has no local kin to speak for her. Because her husband has a "good job", Edith feels that she is discriminated against for those jobs that are available. "They know your husband has a good job so they put your right on the bottom of the list". She is currently taking a bookkeeping course at the Vocational School in Bonavista, but without any real hope of it leading to a job.

She is president of the Parent Teacher Association (PTA) at the children's school, is president of the very active Navy League, helps to teach the junior and senior choirs in her church, and has helped with the local 4-H group. While the fact that her husband earns a reasonable salary means that a paid job is not essential to the household economy, it is essential to Edith's own feeling of self-worth. She expresses anger, boredom, and frustration because she cannot find one.

Edith is clearly an able, competent, and experienced worker. Why did she enter such a sequence of low-grade jobs and how did she reach her present position? At 16, Edith left school without any intention of continuing her education or acquiring qualifications. For her, what was important was to begin earning as soon as possible. Any work would do, but clearly she saw clerical work as both more attainable and more "suitable". The only qualification any of her jobs required was experience of previous similar work. Once she had "thrown her six to start", at Eaton's in Toronto, she was launched on a series of more or less similar jobs. While astute employers clearly gave her considerable responsibility, they did not reward her commensurately and she rarely earned much more than the current minimum wage. At no point did she take further courses, or return to further education. Given her present predicament, her course of action may seem ill advised and short sighted, but looked at in the context of her domestic responsibilities and the overall household economic strategy, it makes perfect sense. As a member of her family of origin, her first contribution was to remove herself as a cost as soon as possible. Having done this, she manoeuvred her way back to employment in her home town of Clarenville. Here she met and married a man who had a "good" job. Her continuing employment enabled them to save and establish themselves as a young couple. Her domestic support helped him to hold down the stressful work of long-distance bus driving. After his move to Easy Save, and his entry onto a "career ladder", her wage became less important, especially because both of them saw the responsibility and costs of child care as resting solely with Edith. When her husband was offered a promotion with the move to Catalina, they had no choice but to accept. His increased salary would compensate for the lack of opportunities for her.

In some way, this work history can be seen as illustrating the classic "supplementary wage" notion of women's work. Edith has never been able to earn more than a fraction of her husband's wage. Clerical work (i.e., women's work) simply does not pay as much as bus driving and grocery management (i.e., men's work), and this fact alone would dictate that her wage could be sacrificed more easily than his. But it is not as simple as this. Edith has never seen her paid work as more than one element in her total contribution to the household, and, to be fair, neither has her husband. Her "choice" of clerical work both reflects this pattern, and perpetuates it. Viewed from the perspective of an individual, Edith's work history seems bitty and inconsequential — a series of short-term solutions to the underlying problem of her weak position in the labour market. But it was clear from the interview that each job was the result of a fine calculation of household needs and the balance between her financial and nonfinancial contribution. The net result is an effective household economic strategy. Edith's household is considerably better off than many in Catalina. And yet it is vulnerable, precisely because the sexual division of labour is so rigid. It would only require Jim's disability or unemployment for the whole complex strategy to founder. It should also be evident that the major costs of the strategy are borne by Edith. Her contribution has always been at least as great as her husband's. Yet it is her personal fulfilment that is sacrificed.

This pattern is repeated in other examples, but Edith's history should serve to illustrate the point that women's position and decisions in the labour force make more sense viewed in the context of a total household strategy. At the same time women's own positions and ranges of opportunity are only visible when we deconstruct that household strategy.

Madeline's history illustrates both the varied strategies adopted by families less fortunate than Edith's and the way in which government benefits are integrated into an overall economic strategy.

At 50 years of age, Madeline currently works as a domestic on a home-aid project funded by the Department of Social Services. She provides house cleaning services to senior citizens, working one day a week in each home. To qualify for employment on these projects the applicant must be a Social Assistance recipient. Madeline and her husband have been receiving Social Assistance since 1985 when Madeline's husband was disabled due to illness. His disability pension could not support them and they had to turn to social assistance. Madeline then tried to find work, and was eventually placed on the home-aid project, which will give her 10 weeks of work, thus qualifying her for unemployment insurance. People on such projects are paid $200 per week for 10 or 20 weeks (whichever is necessary to qualify them for UI), after which they are entitled to draw UI at the rate of 60% of $200, that is $120 per week for one year. If no work is available after a year then the recipients have to return to Social Assistance. Madeline is also providing a service for a diabetic man whom she visits twice a day to give him his insulin injections. As she is paid for this service she will not be eligible for UI when she finishes the home-aid project. Madeline's work situation is thus far from satisfactory. It is also in no way reflects her ability and experience. Let us examine how she came to reach this point.

Madeline graduated from high school in 1953. She attended Teachers' College in St. John's for two summer school sessions and taught for 6 years successively in Upper Island Cove, Bareneed, Bay L'Argent, Goulds, Blaketown, and Catalina. Each time she was forced to move on because of the need for her to have more formal qualifications.

In 1959 she married and had her first and only child, remaining at home for 3 years as a homemaker. Then she took a job as a part-time clerk in a local store, holding it for 2 years before the store was taken over by new management. Her next job was as "Girl Friday" in an office. It lasted a year and a half until the company went broke. After that, Madeline was unemployed for 2 years before finding a part-time job as a receptionist in a doctor's office. This lasted another two years until the doctor left the community. After a brief period of unemployment, Madeline found work teaching food preparation at the vocational school. She was forced to leave 3 years later because she did not meet the new qualification requirements.

Her next employment was as a cook, a job that lasted about 1½ years, before she left it because of domestic pressures at home. She stayed at home for the next 2 to 3 years, until her husband had to leave his job because of ill health. The only work Madeline could find then was as a babysitter at $65 per week. She left the job when she was offered the Social Services project.

About 7 years ago Madeline's daughter, her husband, and their three children moved in with Madeline and her husband. Her son-in-law is currently unemployed. He works as an inshore fisherman, and his work is seasonal. Madeline's daughter now performs much of the domestic labour in the house — cooking, baking, packing lunches, shopping, washing, ironing, and caring for her children, her husband, and her invalid father. When Madeline is not working, she also participates in these activities, although neither of the men is reported to help with domestic work. Madeline's daughter has never had a paid job.

Neither Madeline's work history nor her current situation are atypical. Madeline is clearly an able, intelligent, and energetic woman, capable of much more challenging work than she has at the moment or has had in the past. She is now the sole wage earner in the family, although not the provider of all the economic support. Other members of the family variously qualify for such benefits as invalid pension, child benefit, and UI. Nevertheless, Madeline's financial contribution is vital, and her very low pay imperils the economic standing of the whole household.

Like many women, including Edith, Madeline did not take her education and training seriously. She got enough to qualify her for an immediate job, and left it at that, a lack that has haunted her throughout her working life. She now bitterly regrets not getting more qualifications when she was younger. As she rightly realizes, she could be holding down a job in the local elementary school, and looking forward to a good pension. But, like many women, by the time she realized the vital need for qualifications, or by the time they were required, she was not in a position to obtain them. For one thing she did not have the financial resources to pay for training courses, and for another she could not leave her domestic responsibilities for the time required to go to St. John's for the courses. There are many women in Catalina ready, able, and in need of training courses who cannot take them because there are none available within commuting distance of their home town.

Like many of the work histories we collected, Madeline's was characterized by short-term, dead-end, low-skilled, and low-paid jobs. It is also characterized by her capacity to take any job — however unpleasant or badly paid — and do it. I was constantly impressed by women who have willingly taken any job that came their way, according to what was available and how it could be fitted into their domestic responsibilities and the economic needs of their households. The resulting work histories look patchy and inconsistent, and the reality is that the women are trapped in jobs at the bottom of the pile. Yet this is not an adequate reflection on the women's abilities or why they took the jobs. They fit, rather, into a complex but coherent pattern of household survival. Women take jobs in accordance with the needs of their families, not to forward their personal careers. Thus their willingness to take unskilled, badly paid work reflects not only the reality that there is nothing else available for them, but their own perception that this was only part of their contribution to the household. The labour market is not structured around this logic, and consequently such women are severely disadvantaged within it — a fact that becomes crucial for the whole family, and for the community — when the overall economic strategy breaks down. This can come about because of family breakup, invalidity, unemployment, or changes within the labour market. The result is the situation in which Madeline and her family find themselves. Their economic strategy was sound and satisfied deeper and personal and family values. Through no fault of their own, but because of ill health and unemployment, the strategy has failed, and the result is a family dependent on a variety of inadequate state subsidies and the tiny wages that Madeline can command.

Households are a crucial concept in understanding how people structure their economic lives. It has enabled us to recognize the unpaid economic contribution that women make, but it has also drawn our attention to the ways in which women's own lives become subservient to ensuring that the economic unit of the household survives. Looking at these women's work histories it is clear that the choices women make with regard to the jobs they take are highly contingent on the overall demands of the household. This puts them at a further disadvantage in the labour market, which in turn reduces their power in the household.

Women's positions are in many ways worse now that the cash nexus prevails. When all members contributed economically to the household, but none of them were paid, it was easier to see women's contribution for what it was — equally important to men's. Now it is different. On the one hand, unpaid economic contributions are less recognized, and on the other, when women do take paid work, it looks less valuable than men's because women are paid so much less than men.

Conclusions

What, then, do the experiences of these women from Grand Bank and Catalina have to tell us about the discontinuities between men and women that I pointed to at the beginning of this chapter.

It is clear that women have always worked very hard and continue to do so. It is also clear than this work does not always benefit them as individuals, but is crucial to the survival of their families. Men also work, and have worked, very hard. The difference is that men's work has been much more completely subsumed into the individually waged work of the capitalist economy. The relative amount of work that men do in the paid sector is both much higher than women's and much higher than it was in the traditional economy. This work is individually rewarded and this fact has greater consequence in an economy almost entirely dependent on cash. Men are thus encouraged, both by the individualist ethic and by the economic needs of their families to pursue "careers". Women do in fact spend more of their time in paid work than they used to. But they do not regard this contribution in terms of an individual career. Nor, given the dead-end nature of the jobs they get, could they. Paid work for women, therefore, has a very different significance both to the women and to their families. It is simply another form of economic contribution; necessary, but no more valued than doing the laundry or making jam. Women, therefore, do not see their lives as divided between "organizational time" and "family time". It is all, in a sense, family time. They certainly do not see themselves as occupying two different worlds the way their husbands do.

The continuity of women's lives was perhaps more explicit in Grand Bank. But by making clear the logic of their decisions, the Catalina women reinforce the continuity of the family project. Neither group of women was in any doubt about either the value of the enterprise or of their own contribution to it. Yet, while the power and dignity so clearly expressed by the Grand Bank women also infuses the Catalina accounts, it is left to the Catalina women to point out both the sacrifices they make and the contradictions they contend with. The project of creating valuable and dignified lives for all the members of the working class families is central to all these women's experience. What concerns me is that they seem to end up holding up a good deal more than half the sky and *still* their contribution remains largely invisible and unrewarded.

We are now ready to move on to consider the results of the study that grew out of the Catalina study. It is wider canvas, encompassing three very different communities, but many of the intellectual concerns remain the same: so does the determination that Newfoundland women show to make the best of what they have.

Notes

1. An earlier version of this chapter appeared in *Women's Studies International Forum*, Vol. 14, Nos. 1/2, 1991.

2. The Pilot Project was written up in M. Porter and S. Pottle *Women and the Economy in Newfoundland: A Case Study of Catalina* (St. John's, Women's Policy Office, 1987).

3. Fishery Products Ltd. began construction on a fresh fish plant on the border between Port Union and Catalina in 1954, and the plant opened in 1957. The opening of the plant created a large number of jobs. Fishery Products International is still by far the most important employer of both men and women in the area. It also introduced a new technology as well as modern styles of labour organization and management. That these were not entirely problem free has been well documented by B. Neis and her team in their report on *The Social Impact of technological Change in Newfoundland's Deepsea Fishery*. By 1991, Catalina was the only FPI deepsea plant on the island to remain in operation, although at the time of writing (1992), the collapse of the cod fishery and the moratorium had reduced the plant to a pitiful remnant.

4. Felt and Sinclair, using impeccable statistical methods discovered that 62.8% of the men in their study of the Northern Peninsula scored zero on their Housework Index (Felt and Sinclair, 1992).

8 Towards an analysis of women's work in Newfoundland

Introduction

In this and the next chapter I will be presenting some conclusions drawn from the comparative community study *Women's Economic Lives in Newfoundland*, which I carried out with a small team, 1988-1990.[1] While the study had a number of components, including a labour force survey in Grand Falls, the main focus was on the comparative observations of three ethnographers who lived in three communities for periods of up to a year. I discuss some problems that arise from using this method in the next chapter, but here my focus is a distillation of what we learnt about the character of women's work, and how they constructed their 'economic lives'. First, let me introduce you to the three communities.

Three communities

Catalina, which appeared in the previous chapter, was the basis for a pilot project and then became a constituent community in the main study. The other two communities were chosen to contrast with Catalina in ways that I thought would best illuminate the character and conduct of women's working lives.

Catalina

The oldest community, Catalina was historically dependent on the Labrador fishery. It is still dependent on the fishery, but since 1956 in the form on a Fisheries Products International deep sea processing fish plant, which employs 1000 men and women.[2] It is close to Bonavista, from which it derives most of its services, although it also acts as a centre for its own surrounding communities.

There have always been higher levels of waged work for men in Catalina than in the surrounding communities and since World War II women's labour force participation has also increased. First, they were employed mainly as servants, and then as shop assistants. Today the plant is the most important employer, though the shop and office jobs are regarded as highly desirable. The plant work is wet, hard and stressful.[3] It is operated on a two shift system (week of days/week of nights), which causes multiple difficulties for women working there. There is no formal day care available in Catalina and women rely on a variety of arrangements, especially the use of poorly paid young baby sitters. Some couples work opposite shifts and *he* takes care of them when *she* is on nights and *she* hires a babysitter when *she* is on days.

Because of the pattern of settlement extended families tend to be less common in Catalina, so women have relatively little help from female relatives. On the other hand parents move into Catalina when they are too old to care for themselves so Catalina women *do* have considerable amounts of caring work to do.[4] This is compounded by the fact that Catalina men have the lowest rates of participation in domestic work of any community we studied.

It was during a Pilot Project in Catalina that we first examined women's work histories in sufficient detail to see, firstly, how women took on substantial, exhausting work of all and every kind, paid and unpaid for the *household*. We began to recognize that paid work was only part of the load and got fitted in with the rest of a woman's commitments. Thus women didn't get training, couldn't move to get work and ended up taking low paid, unskilled work. Secondly, it became apparent how invisible much women's work was, especially caring or health-related work. Early in the project we were testing an interview schedule with a woman in her kitchen. She had already told us that she did no unpaid caring work apart from her own daughter. At this point the door opened and a young lad, came in, went to the oven, took out a dish, covered it, and left. When we asked about it, it turned out that every day this woman cooked dinner for an old man who lived close by, and his nephew collected it for him on his way home from school, 'caring work' that was as invisible to her as it was to the outside world.

In the main study, we found our picture of women's work confirmed. As well, Catalina illustrated the dependency of Newfoundland communities on *one* employer as well as the importance of the tertiary sector for women's employment. Plant workers earn at least provincial average wages, and thus Catalina women contribute substantially to the household income, although a family without both partners earning will soon fall behind. Many women

130

in Catalina would give their right arm for a chance at the clerical jobs available in Grand Falls, although they openly reject the respectability, stuffiness and conformity they associate with Grand Falls, and they do, in fact, reject the social organization. They refuse to organize at all — formally or informally. Even the Kinettes collapsed for lack of support. Catalina women send cakes but don't attend fundraisers and events that are organized (mainly by the church). The older women expressed nostalgia (mostly misinformed) about the old days, but they do point — accurately — to the greater autonomy and respect the women had then.

Despite, or may be because of the hardness of their lives, Catalina women present themselves confidently, relying on their conviction that they can and will survive. But they don't look for solutions within the community. The only answer they see is either to simply endure it or to move away — a solution many young people opt for. Women's economic position gives them considerable leverage even within the patriarchal culture of Catalina and there is also a strong women's culture, which is expressed among themselves. Catalina women care for each other. Problems such as violence and alcoholism are monitored by informal women's networks, which also provide some practical assistance.[5]

Grand Falls

Grand Falls was founded as a company town in 1910 by the English print baron Lord Northcliffe. Abitibi Pryce, as it now is, is a US based multinational paper firm with an increasing number of plants in Latin America. It seems clear that Grand Falls is not the jewel in Abitibi Pryce's crown, and recent evidence of this came in February 1991 when they announced the closure of one of the three machines. Grand Falls has been an independent, incorporated community since the 1960s, but 'the Company' is still a prevalent influence, and still contributes substantially to the town, directly in the form of financial support and indirectly through a sizeable contribution to the municipal tax base. It is one of the most prosperous communities in Newfoundland, with an average household income of twice the Provincial average. As well as the Mill, the Regional hospital, a large shopping mall and numerous government and other offices are all located in Grand Falls.

Windsor, which is virtually coterminous with Grand Falls, began as a shanty town 'across the tracks' for people who were not employed by the Company and were thus not entitled to live there. While many Windsor residents take jobs at the Mill and the hospital, Windsor is still a conspicuously poor community in every way. Grand Falls and Windsor constitute, in fact, one community divided rigidly by class.

131

The Mill employs 1000 people, nearly all men. The policy of firing women when they married continued until the 1970s. There are still no women in production jobs. There are two women engineers and about 30 female clerical staff. Grand Falls also has a high proportion of people employed in education, government and other offices and services — especially health services and the hospital. A very high proportion of men are employed in middle class professions at rates much above provincial average salaries.

Whereas one can speak of Catalina (and South East Bight) women as a homogenous whole, without great economic, social or religious differences, Grand Falls is divided. There are some poor people in Grand Falls — though mainly they are pushed into Windsor (e.g. through resistance to the locating of a Transition House or CMHC housing in Grand Falls). The big distinction in Grand Falls is between the conforming middle class couples (with one or both partners employed) with children, and the non-conforming — the poor, single, unemployed, disadvantaged, outsider or just odd. This includes foreign doctors, single professionals, single mothers, divorced women, the elderly etc. The middle class standard of living is very high — car (two cars), large, opulently furnished house, cabin, all-terrain vehicle, holidays, VCR, microwave, kids' sports equipment, etc. But this lifestyle needs a professional income, or two middle class incomes, to support it all. The establishment and sustenance of the ideal life style is a joint project and women see their role as two-fold — the social performance of 'the labour of ornamentation' and the provision of an additional income. Women are, therefore, desperate for work, which is as hard to get in Grand Falls as anywhere. Furthermore there is no notion of a hierarchy of rights for work as there is elsewhere — where the community decides who shall get a job on the basis of family need. In Grand Falls a ferocious dog-eat-dog competition to 'get to know' someone prevails.

Our survey of employers in Grand Falls found that all jobs were sex segregated and all women's jobs paid less than men. The only exceptions were some in middle band jobs (draughtspeople/hairdresser/government offices/the Salvation Army). The professional teachers, doctors and nurses are mainly imported and women from Grand Falls don't necessarily get professional jobs even if they are qualified. Most women's jobs are in the conventional clerical, shop assistant and bank clerk categories. It is not unusual for job openings to attract a hundred applicants. In the vicious competition for jobs, there is some evidence that young single (pretty) women got preference — especially in the Banks, which appear to seek applicants who look like sex objects but will endure unskilled work.

There are three daycare centres, but between them they can only take a tiny proportion of the children who need it. Nor is there a great supply of teenage baby sitters. There is also a middle class ethnic dictating that children must be 'stimulated', do numerous sporting and cultural activities, read early, play instruments, and 'achieve' — and, of course, the responsibility for this, falls to mothers.

Grand Falls life is dominated by an obsessive and oppressive round of social and community activities.[6] Respectability, conformity and social success are vital to ones 'status' in Grand Falls. There are a never ending series of tests — parties you must go to, dinner parties and barbecues you must give, fundraisers, banquets, carnivals, competitions, sports events, official events, religious events, municipal events. All these must be organized, catered for, run and appeared at, dressed for and ENJOYED. Women do the bulk of this work, though the men are also active. What is noticeable is that women do most of the work around children's equally frenetic lives (except for boy's hockey and scouts) and that women take the back room roles. Men do the 'fun' clubs, such as Rotary, political parties, sports clubs and Masons. There are very few 'recreational' women's organizations. One of the few is the Curling Club, but that carries with it the hurdle of entry and it appeared to be confined to prosperous, middle class women. Apart from the Curling Club, women-only organizations were limited to women's church support groups.

Most Grand Falls women are thus doing three jobs — domestic work, paid work and the work associated with the 'social life'. Plus the load of caring. In this regard, Grand Falls women are ostensibly better off than women elsewhere because of the presence of the hospital, Carmelite House (a Senior's House), Social Services, etc. But relatives come to Grand Falls precisely *because* of these facilities. They then need visiting, and their other needs taken care of. Nurses are supposed to be 'good at caring'. Therefore a high proportion of nurses we talked to cared for a relative at home as well as performing their official nursing duties. The middle classes tended to put their relatives in homes — but the poorer women endured the worst situations of any we met. One woman had total care of her bedridden 75 year old mother, her 90 year old grandmother, physically spry but mentally unreliable, as well as her two teenage daughters. She also held down a paid job that she did at night, while her daughter 'baby sat' the elderly women.

The discrepancy between the incomes of husbands and wives is greater in Grand Falls than elsewhere, with consequent greater dependence by wives on their husbands. This is coupled with a rigid sexual division of labour inside and outside the home. The sheer weight of work women perform was certainly greater in Grand Falls than in the other two communities in the study — especially among the poorer and more isolated women. It was also clear that social and family pathology, such as family violence was more easily hidden than in the other two communities.

South East Bight consists of just over 120 people in thirty households scattered around three small coves, linked by small foot paths. It lies far down a peninsula in Placentia Bay. It has no road so access is by boat, ferry or helicopter. It is incandescently beautiful. The original date of settlement is unknown, but South East Bight achieved some local fame as one of only two small communities in Placentia Bay to resist the Resettlement programme carried out by Smallwood in the 1960s. It, therefore, has a very strong community identity. Indeed, the only real division in the community is between the families who 'stayed' and those who 'came back' after Resettlement.

South East Bight depends on the inshore fishery together with Unemployment Insurance and 'make work' projects. It has fought for, and got, the necessary services to survive — ferry, collector boat, school (but only to grade 10); the doctor, nurse and priest who fly in 1 or 2 times a month (if the fog allows); electricity (but water and sanitation needs must be met by individual households).

While young people do have to go away for education and jobs, there is a strong feeling that they do so reluctantly and will come back when they can. Youngsters try to marry within the community. The only 'jobs' in the community belong to three teachers, two merchant families who run small stores, a couple who run the Government wharf and one man who looks after a generating station. Women, therefore, have half the available jobs. Women also take more of the make-work projects in the winter, to enable the men to hunt and cut wood. Women fish, and have done since the early 1980s (because of the change in the Unemployment Insurance regulations) — usually with their husbands. Women also go to the woods and drive skidoos and ATVs. South East Bight was threatened by the crisis in the fishery, but more directly by changes in Unemployment Insurance which made it difficult for individuals to survive and which also changes the make work projects from useful wharf repairs and building skidoo trails to 'training' projects perceived in the community as 'useless'. The community is adept at manipulating government regulations to its best advantage. Indeed it is clear to the community that such manipulations are both legitimate and, indeed, the *only* way to survive as a community. Economic survival is seen as a household and a community project — and one in which women are equally involved.

There are some obvious contrasts with the other two communities. South East Bight households have an average income of half that of Catalina and one third that of Grand Falls. They do have electricity, TVs (with dish aerials), fridges, microwaves, ATVs, motorboats and even some cars (parked at Monkstown) but their houses are much smaller, and there are no thick pile carpets, 36" TVs or voluminous settees and flashy ornaments such as are found in Grand Falls. Dress is startlingly different. Far from the suburban respectability of Grand Falls, in South East Bight both women and men dress for rough outdoors work. A very few smart clothes are kept for 'best'. They have few formal organisations. The Rural Development Association totters and exists mainly to allocate make-work grants. The church and school have support frameworks. The annual Garden Party is a big event, and there are also weddings, Christmas, etc. — all of which involve the whole community in an orgy of cooking, baking and cleaning.

Men, women and older children work at domestic, subsistence work and fishing. There is a sexual division of labour but there is much more overlap, for example, women fish: but he steers the boat. Women garden and pick berries: men hunt and chop food. Men do domestic work in the winter when women do make-work, but in the summer, women will get up at 4:00 a.m. to fish, return at 2:00 p.m. and then do 'their work'. This work consists of all the usual housework, cooking and cleaning to the high standards of traditional outport life, including baking the family's bread.

Older children, especially girls, share the labour, although on sex divided lines. Girls care for younger children. Families are still bigger than the Newfoundland average and extended families are the norm. Grandparents live next door and are cared for by women. But they also help, especially with child care and the care of the mentally handicapped — 'she does for me and I does for her' as one women put it describing her relationship with her elderly mother who lived next door. There are no very old or sick people in the community at present. Such people have to be shipped out to Marystown, which has the medical facilities to care for them.

So — South East Bight women work hard. There is a division of labour, and women do more than men but the context is physically, economically and socially undivided. Both men and women work and live largely outside the wage economy and direct their efforts towards the achievement of a clear household project. They are clearly equal in the household, especially in decision making. We could find no evidence of violence or child abuse, though we looked carefully.

Beyond this, there is a clear and articulate determination by women, even more than men, that this is the way of life they have fought for, and which they intend to keep. Their role as women is wider, is closer to men's and has a greater recognition in the community than in either Catalina or Grand Falls.

Three women in three communities

To encapsulate the material I am trying to understand, I want to represent the data on the three communities in the form of 'typical' or 'composite' cases. These are not real cases because I want to draw attention to the maximum number of features that require our analytical attention. I want to sketch a situation so as to pose the question — which theory best takes account of what we find? In particular I want to address two questions — "what is the nature of women's work and what is its connection to women's place in the household?" and "when women work, do they do so as ungendered subjects, as non-men, as wives and/or mothers (or potentially so) as women in households or as 'essentially feminine'?"

In order to make the 'ideal type women' more comparable I shall describe women who are all at the same stage in the life cycle and who all live in households of similar composition, i.e., they will all be in their mid-thirties, with three children aged 3-10 years.

Cathy Clarke: Catalina

Cathy Clarke lives in Catalina, with her husband and three children. Their house began life as a trailer home, but has been built on to and improved so much as to be unrecognizable. This was work that Chris did, except for the electrical work, which he can't handle. Some of that was done by a cousin who lives in Port Rexton. Cathy, herself, does all the painting — aiming to do the inside once a year. She also does all the housework, laundry and shopping, although Chris helps with the Sunday dinner. Inside, the house is not luxurious; it does have all the accoutrements of a TV, VCR, microwave, deep-freeze, etc. It is also immaculate, with ornaments and framed photos (of the children in various stages of graduation, and artfully posed 'family photos'). They have one truck, which Cathy can drive, but she doesn't use it every day, and often Chris takes it to work.

Chris has worked as a cutter at the FPI plant for 13 years now, and, by Catalina standards, he earns good money, approximately $26,000 per annum. This is because his long experience gives him excellent bonus, and he is top of the list for any overtime there may be. He has no formal qualifications. He finished Grade 11 and then went to Toronto where he worked mainly on building sites until he got the job at FPI. But as Cathy doesn't have a job at present, their household income is limited to Chris's pay, and child benefit for the three children.

Cathy dropped out of school after Grade 9 in order to babysit for her older sister. She was sorry about this because she'd wanted to train to be a children's nurse, but somehow that ambition seemed very distant and impractical, especially as her grades weren't very good. From there she had had a number of temporary, low paying jobs — as a babysitter, as a casual worker in the crab plant in Bonavista, as a temporary shop assistant (also in Bonavista), which she had much enjoyed. At one point she had gone to St. John's, to stay with a friend and look for work. But she hadn't been able to find anything that enabled her to more than barely survive, so she came back to Catalina. Then, when she was 23, she landed a job at the fish plant as a packer. She also met, and married, Chris, who lived in Port Rexton, but had also just got a job at the plant. All went well until the children arrived. With two salaries they were able to buy and build up their house, and acquire the consumer durables to go with it. Cathy went back to work after her first child was born and for a while they managed on a combination of help from Cathy's mother, working alternate shifts and employing a young schoolgirl to fill in the gaps.

This wasn't satisfactory, and put both of them under a lot of strain. Cathy was increasingly unhappy about leaving Carl with the young babysitter as he got older and more demanding. Then shortly after their second child was born, Cathy's mother developed thrombosis, which led to the amputation of one leg. This rapidly shifted the helping shoe from one foot to the other, and Cathy had no choice but to give up her job. Not only did she have two children to care for, but she had to spend inordinate amounts of time (and money) taking her mother into the hospital in St. John's and visiting her there. Cathy's father, who had been employed as an electrician with the telephone company before his retirement, had proved virtually useless in caring for his wife, and indeed, needs attention himself. Cathy had two brothers in Catalina, and a sister who lives in Gander, but virtually all the caring falls to her. She doesn't feel bitter about this, but she is worried that Chris's parents, who live in Port Rexton and are becoming frail, may decide to move into Catalina and add further to her cares.

Since she gave up her job at FPI five years ago, Cathy has repeatedly looked for other work, preferably part time, but with no success. She has no qualifications and not very varied work experience. She is obviously able and hard-working, yet the chances of her finding suitable work seem virtually nil. This distresses her, partly because while their economic situation at the moment is acceptable, it is likely to fall behind as the children get older and Chris's income falls behind the rate of inflation. In any case, Chris's job is far from secure, especially with the troubles in the fishing industry and Cathy worries about what would happen if FPI closed, or even went onto short-time work. But Cathy also worries about her own situation. While she is fully occupied with caring for her children and mother now, she can see a time when that won't be the case and she will find herself idle and frustrated. She bitterly regrets not getting training when she was younger, and has tinkered with the idea of doing a clerk/bookkeeping course in Bonavista, but that would involve expense and babysitters with no guarantee of a job at the end.

While the Clarkes do a considerable amount of maintenance and improvement on their own home, they do very little self provisioning. Chris occasionally goes to the woods with his brothers or cousins and gets a load of wood, and Cathy used to pick berries with her mother. Cathy does not knit or make clothes (though occasionally her sister will make up a pattern for one of the children). She does enjoy embroidery, and once took an evening class in it. They do not grow their own vegetables — and Cathy complains of how expensive and limited the choice of groceries in Catalina is.

Cathy is not a member of any voluntary association and only goes to church (Anglican) on occasion, but all her children are involved in numerous sports and other activities. Chris is a member of the voluntary fire brigade, and also plays softball in the summer. They don't do much entertaining outside the family, but they do try to go out 'once in a while'. Social life is, in any event, disrupted by Chris's shift work.

Cathy has a fairly traditional and pessimistic approach to life. She takes no interest in politics, and is dismissive of political attempts to solve Catalina's or Newfoundland's problems. She adheres to a quite rigid sexual division of labour — both in her own life and in what she sees as 'suitable' for men and women to do. She is, however, resentful of where this has landed her, and hopes all her children, including her daughter, will get qualifications and good jobs, even though that means they will leave Catalina.

Cathy does not appear to have many women friends. She only sees her sister occasionally. She is quite friendly with one of her sisters-in-law, with whom she goes shopping in Clarenville every few weeks. Otherwise, she sees one or two of her neighbours, but she doesn't go out in the evenings with them. For external stimulation and enjoyment she seems to depend solely on the radio, the VCR and her husband.

Like the other women I will describe, Cathy is a good hearted, honest and hard working woman. What comes over from talking to her is an air of fatalistic pessimism and puzzlement. Things are bad, and likely to get worse. Even though she doesn't interrogate her own situation (apart from that of her family) that closely, it is obvious that she is frustrated. She doesn't seem to have a fierce attachment to Catalina as such. She just doubts that life would be any better anywhere else, though if Chris loses his job, they will doubtless try their luck on the mainland.

Glenda Ford: Grand Falls

Glenda Ford, in Grand Falls, presents a very different first impression from Cathy Clarke. She and her husband Gary live in quite a large house (3 bedrooms) in a 'good' part of town. The furnishing are much more sumptuous — the carpets are thick, the three-piece suites obviously expensive, the TV is massive, the bathroom suite is coloured and sports exotic fittings, the kitchen is large and equipped like a restaurant kitchen; there is a massive mock granite fireplace and so on. The Fords also have two cars, an ATV, a 'cabin', which sounds pretty luxurious in itself, and quantities of sports equipment. Glenda is always dauntingly well dressed with matching accessories, makeup and a general air of urban sophistication: she works as a bank clerk at one of the chartered banks in Grand Falls and Gary has a good job at the mill as a machine tender. Gary, who was born in Grand Falls, and whose father also worked at the mill, completed school, and then did a trades certificate and had to wait less than a year before being taken on as a regular worker. He clears at least $33,00 p.a. Glenda grew up in Springdale, where her father managed a fish plant. She left school and took a one year course in St. John's and then worked for two years in Stephenville before she moved to Grand Falls. There she met and married Gary. She stopped work for a few years after her first child was born, and was lucky to get her job back when she decided to return. She did this with some misgivings, because she enjoyed being at home. She likes babies and loves 'doing little things' for the house, which includes making all the rich curtains. She also loves cooking, especially making cakes. She donates many of these to fundraisers, but she also occasionally earns money by making special cakes — for graduations or weddings. She managed to continue these activities when she went back to work. Gary works shifts, on a complicated rotating pattern, so working out when and if they see each other is a problem in itself, although the fact that Gary is often at home when Glenda is working does not seem to relieve Glenda of a task of finding childcare.

Now a senior teller, Glenda still only earns $18,000 p.a. The conditions at work are stressful and unpleasant. Glenda has to stay on her feet virtually the whole time and often has difficulty getting a few moments off to go to the toilet. While she still maintains that she enjoys her work, she is resentful both about the sequence of young (male) managers who arrive from elsewhere and establish their dominance by insisting on rigid routines and about the opportunities she feels are given to 'pretty young things', who come in 'knowing nothing but how to flash their eyes'. As a bank teller, Glenda has to be smartly dressed — itself extra work and entailing considerable extra expense.

When she gets off work she feels utterly drained and exhausted and then has to turn to and deal with the children and attend to the housework, shopping, cooking and an extensive social life. She doesn't know how long she will be able to handle it. She does it partly because she enjoys being something other than 'just a housewife' but mainly because without her income they would never be able to support the style of life they lead. This is important only partly because of the ease and comfort. What is more important is that she feels 'we have done something with our lives'. Her family is better established than her parents, and her children have better chances than she did. She mentions 'class distinctions' in Grand Falls sufficiently often to reflect her underlying worry that their position in the carefully delineated social scale depends directly on their keeping up their material standard of living.

Childcare has always been a major problem. Glenda has tried unsuccessfully to get all her children into one of the few daycare centers in Grand Falls, but the minimum waiting list is two years. Two of her children are now in school, though this doesn't lessen the problem. She still has to deal with after school, holidays and illness and additionally has to cope with their involvement in numerous out of school sports and activities. These all involve her in chauffeuring and in parental support — buying and maintaining sports gear, making costumes, fundraising and attending numerous performances and matches. Gary, it seems, takes no interest in any of this — except in his oldest son's hockey, which he attends when he can. When his shifts allow, he does look after the children, but ensuring cover is obviously Glenda's job, as well as all the housework and childcare. Glenda has managed to work only by means of a series of not terribly satisfactory child minders, whom she employs in her own home. She doesn't like to hire very young minders, preferring older women. But these experienced women also have their own ideas about discipline etc., which Glenda worries about. She pays her current helper about $150 week out of her own net pay. The whole issue of day care adds considerable strain to Glenda's life and she feels strongly that cheap, good quality day care should be available. Her own preference would be for her employer to provide a good creche and after school centre and for there to be some tax relief for what she pays for home based help.

Gary is active in a number of sports and service associations, especially Kinsmen and hockey. This involves Glenda in some support activity, especially as she is an active member of Kinettes. He also likes to go out to their cabin at weekends — sometimes with her, and sometimes with buddies. In any event, it is Glenda who has to look after the children. Glenda supports and encourages her children in all their school and other activities. She is a member of the school PTA and has helped make the costumes for numerous performances. She also helps out in her daughter's Brownie pack — going along on excursions and providing back up for special events. Last year she got involved in organizing the Kinsmen's music festival for children. In addition she is active in the Kinettes, and also in her church group — the Anglican Women's Guild. This last is mainly devoted to fundraising and she has contributed much of her craft work as well as helping to organize their bake and other sales. For relaxation Glenda belongs to, and enjoys the Curling Club, but she finds she often doesn't have time to be a member of a regular team.

Both Gary and Glenda lead an active social life, which mainly revolves around the fundraisers and charity functions they are involved in. Glenda will frequently find that what with her work and the various other commitments, she hasn't had an evening at home for several weeks.

One shadow that Glenda sees looming over her life is that her father has just died of a heart attack, leaving her mother who has always been frail and dependent. What Glenda fears is that her mother's frequent trips to the hospital in Grand Falls will become more frequent and that eventually she will decide that she wants to move in with Glenda and Gary. Glenda faces this prospect with trepidation. She knows from the experience of several people she knows or knows of, how difficult the situation can be, with resentful husband and children poised against the incoming mother. Glenda has a clear agenda for her children, and Gary is not the most flexible or cooperative of husbands. A frail and difficult older woman could easily be the straw that broke the carefully constructed edifice. It would also, of course, add to Glenda's intolerable work load. Yet, she also knows that she would be expected to cope even if her mother became bedridden.

Glenda has friends, mostly at work and in the various organisations she is involved with, but they seem more in the nature of colleagues, even competitors. She doesn't talk about intimate matters with anyone. Nor does she have relatives close by, though it is doubtful if she would confide in them even if they were closer. Nor does Gary seem that supportive or understanding about her situation. Glenda has achieved what she set out to do — but the struggle is far from over. It depends on constant, unremitting hard work and a certain amount of luck. They both have to keep their jobs, the children have to remain healthy and high achieving, the marriage has to stay together. Even quite small setbacks could send them plummeting down the Grand Falls social scale — a fear that undercuts the manifest 'success' of Glenda's life.

Sue-Ellen Black has also achieved what she wanted, and her achievement is also fragile and at risk. But beyond that the resemblance ends. Sue-Ellen's family was one of the few that never left South East Bight. She was one of nine children, only two of whom have left the community, and one other goes in the winter to work in Toronto. Most of them married within the community. Sue-Ellen and one of her sisters married two brothers. Sam's family did leave at the time of resettlement and Sam spent his school years in Arnold's Cove. However, he came back then, and went into fishing — first with his uncle, later on his own and now with Sue-Ellen. They own a trap skiff and all the attendant gear, which they keep in a stage just below the house. Sue-Ellen only has grade 8 schooling, but it has never stood in her way. She has spent just one year of her life outside South East Bight, in St. John's. She hated it, returned to the Bight, helped out around her parents work for a couple of years and then married Sam.

They began by living with her parents and then built a house just a few yards down the hill. Sam built this, with the help of brothers, brothers-in-law and friends, and Sue-Ellen also helped out. She enjoys the outdoors, and dirty, heavy work has never daunted her, although she prefers plastering and painting.

Sue-Ellen began fishing with Sam about eight years ago, when the Unemployment Insurance regulations changed to allow them both to claim stamps. She began fishing simply as a measure to bring more money into the household, but now she enjoys it so much she'd find it hard to give up. While both the fishing income and the Unemployment Insurance is reckoned for them as individuals (with Sam getting higher money as 'skipper'), both Sam and Sue-Ellen see it as a joint effort, even though Sam does more of the skilled boat, gear and engine maintenance. Sue-Ellen has also bought in money in recent years by taking make-work construction projects on the wharf. Again, she enjoys the work and the company of other women doing it. While places on all make-work projects are keenly contested, the allocation, by lot or on the basis of family, is generally deemed to be fair.

The household income fluctuates a good deal, but for the past few years the fishing has been good — providing about $15,000 in direct income, plus another $9,000 in Unemployment Insurance. Make work projects and child benefits bring their average annual income up to the mid $20,000s.

Of all the families I describe here, the Blacks are by far the most self providing. Not only do they do all their own house building (with help from their family) and improvements, but they also chop their own wood, grow vegetables, hunt meat (rabbits, moose and turrs) in the winter, pick berries and catch fish in the summer, bake bread, knit and sew and crochet. In all, they use their skills and energies and their time in the winter, together with those of their relatives, to reduce to the minimum what they have to buy with cash.

Sue-Ellen still takes primary responsibility for the house and three children. Sam does very little in the summer, which is especially hard for Sue-Ellen. In the high season she is up by 4:00 a.m., back from fishing at 2:00 p.m. and then starts on her housework, including her twice weekly baking. The time Sam does help is in the winter when Sue-Ellen is on make-work projects. Then he gets the children up, makes them their lunch, tidies up, prepares the evening meal and does some laundry. What really lightens the load for Sue-Ellen is the proximity of her family. Her parents are still hale and hearty and her mother, especially, has energy to spare. She still has Sue-Ellen's youngest sister living with her who is slightly mentally handicapped. In addition she knits sweaters for all her grandchildren, bakes for Sue-Ellen when she can't manage and 'keeps an eye' out for the children. Two of Sue-Ellen's sisters also live close by with their husbands and children, so there is no lack of eyes to look out for children — or other hands to help with the various domestic tasks that are easier with more people — spring cleaning for example. Sue-Ellen's children are still too small to be much use, although they seem to help with more chores than their peers in Grand Falls or Catalina. These are allocated along sex lines, e.g., the boys bring in the wood and the girls care for the babies, but Sue-Ellen is actively trying to break this down, citing her own ability to do 'male' tasks as a good example.

Two other factors about Sue-Ellen's life help to make the sex role distinctions less glaring. One is that Sue-Ellen's house is less luxurious and gleaming than the houses in Grand Falls or Catalina. It is perfectly clean, but less oppressively tidy. It is smaller, the furnishings are less opulent, there is a denser use of the space. There is simply less to look after and the standards are not so dauntingly and unnecessarily high. The Blacks have much the same household appliances — TV, VCR, microwave, ATV, skidoo, children's bikes, etc., but they are small and less state-of-the-art than in Grand Falls. They do not own a car. When they take the boat into Monkstown, they borrow a brother's car based there to run into Marystown or up to St. John's. Nor do they go very often — not at all during the fishing season. Neither of them like it and as Sue-Ellen says — if you don't go to the shops, you can't buy much, - although the groceries that are available in the Bight are both more limited and higher priced than on the mainland.

The other factor is the style of dress customary in the Bight. Sue-Ellen's everyday garb, like that of everyone else, is jeans or cords, shirts and sweaters and sneakers or working boots. She is manifestly not prevented by her clothes from doing any work, male or female and she certainly doesn't depend on her everyday clothes to present herself as female. Nor do clothes afford the chance to assert status distinctions within the community. Indeed, by and large, when Sue-Ellen speaks of herself or her family, she means the whole community. The sense that everyone in the Bight hangs or falls together is very strong.

At the moment, Sue-Ellen has no additional caring work. In fact her mother and sisters contribute to her work. Nor does she worry about it in the future. If care has to be given it is shared around, and she feels sure she would never have to take too much. The lack of immediate access to medical help worries her sometimes, especially when she was pregnant. There have been some near scrapes in the community, but so far they have all ended well and Sue-Ellen sees that as one of the prices she has to pay to live in the Bight. She is much more concerned about the school. At the moment it serves her children fine, but she resents the fact that they will have to go away to do Grades 11 and 12. That, indeed, is a key worry — that her children will not be able to stay in the community she loves so much. She also worries that what she values in the community — much of which depends on its isolation, could so easily be destroyed — by a road, for example.

Sue-Ellen is not formally a member of any voluntary association — although she takes her turn at cleaning the school and the church and participates in school, church and community activities. She was a member of the RDA Committee, but she disliked it because that was the body that had to hand out make-work jobs and she disliked the negative griping that inevitably ensued. Of all the three women I have described here, however, Sue-Ellen has the clearest political views, especially with regard to the fishery, Unemployment Insurance, and the politics in other local communities, such as Petite Forte. But she is also much more vocal about provincial and federal politics. She is no more active than Glenda or Cathy but she does take more interest and seems convinced that something could be done, if only people in communities like South East Bight had access to more power.

This leads back to Sue-Ellen's enduring concern about the survival of her achievement — i.e., South East Bight as it is. She knows full well how fragile are South East Bight resources, especially the fishery and the Unemployment Insurance system. She sees both levels of government as blind and uncaring, noticing how every change brings about a worsening of the situation. This, however, has not led her to Cathy's fatalism. She knows her project is worthwhile and she draws on the history of community resistance in South East Bight to sustain her.

Women's work and women's lives

Using these composite women let us see if we can focus on the questions I asked earlier. I should note that I have deliberately chosen women who live in traditional, and relatively successful, households. These women are the ones who benefit most from the household economic formation and who are most deeply embedded in it. While fewer at the moment, the women-headed and otherwise 'deviant' households are growing in number and in importance in terms of understanding how Newfoundland 'households' of *all* kinds actually work. However, let us start with the 'easy' cases. In the following discussion I will try to focus first on the features that tie these women's experiences together, and then focus on the ways their communities specifically structure their lives.

All three women, Cathy, Glenda and Sue-Ellen work extremely hard. Only Glenda has a full-time job. Cathy is currently 'unemployed' and Sue-Ellen is seasonally employed. They bring varying amounts of money into the household. Cathy brings hardly any cash (except for child benefit). Both Glenda and Sue-Ellen bring in substantial amounts. Sue-Ellen brings in nearly as much as her husband. Glenda has a comparatively well paid (for a women) white collar job, which requires a good educational level and considerable skill and experience. She still, however, earns little more than half what Gary earns — a discrepancy that affects the power in the household in explicit ways. Glenda and Gary work in very different jobs, polarized by the sexual division of labour. Neither has the experience of working alongside members of the opposite sex. Sue-Ellen brings in more or less the same amount as her husband does. More importantly, she acquires it in the *same* occupation, doing closely similar, when not shared, work. Furthermore, the wage, and related benefits are a less important part of the total economic resources of this household.

Of the three women, only Sue-Ellen's work is relatively undivided by sex. Yet even she performs a different (and subservient) role in the boat and performs different work both in the domestic and maintenance sphere and in the self-provisioning sphere. This is counteracted by the fact that the work she performs takes place in the same physical and psychological space and even the formal market activity of fishing is less tied to the individual wage economy.

Glenda's work is among the best paid work commonly available to women. Yet bank clerks are not only a nearly totally female work force, they are usually directly subservient to male managers and administrators. The combination of bank clerk or nurse/mill worker is a common one in Grand Falls and higher up the scale so is teacher/doctor. Sometimes in the case of the nurse/mill worker combination, the salaries are nearly equal, but usually there is still a discrepancy between what husbands and wives earn. While the household project is clearly at the forefront of Glenda's consciousness, she carries out her share of it in a sex-segregated world — and that includes the mass of work I have described as 'social' or 'the labour of ornamentation'.

Cathy is clearly the most disadvantaged in the labour market. With no formal qualifications and her commitments to children (and mother) she has the least access to economic activity. Nor is it coincidental that her husband is probably the worst off in real terms. While the money coming into the household is greater than the Blacks, the Blacks have many more sources of labour and perform many more forms of work — to use the concepts developed by Ray Pahl. They also have fewer outgoings to take care of. Like Glenda, Cathy has always worked in sex segregated situations. Even at the fish plant, the trimmers and packers were both physically separate and paid less than the cutters.

Glenda and Cathy also contrast with Sue-Ellen in their desperation to get jobs and their willingness to sacrifice to keep them. Both Cathy and Glenda have enormous domestic and caring loads, with very little help from either husband or family.

I have not chosen particularly extreme examples, but it is clear that all three women work enormously hard both inside and outside the formal economy. Paid work is, indeed, only one activity in a total effort to 'get by'.

If we now look at the questions — "what is the nature of women's work and what is its connection to their place in the household" and "when women work do they do so as ungendered subjects, as non-men, as wives and or mothers (or potentially so) as women-in-households or as essentially feminine?" we can begin to lay out some parameters.

Firstly, all these women's work is different to men's, (with Sue-Ellen's less categorically so). They perform different work in the labour market, but that is not so different as the work they perform outside the formal economy. Secondly, the women's non-economic obligations constitute a major constraint over their participation in the formal economy which can only be overcome by massive sacrifices of both time and energy. Thirdly, the women do not separate their paid and unpaid activity, although they do accept an equal duty to bring money into the household. Fourthly, women see all their efforts, paid and unpaid as directed towards the *household*, rather than for their own individual benefit.

These women's histories, and evidence from younger women, indicate that this exclusive focus on the household does not begin until they actually have a household to focus on. In other words, younger women, without husbands or children, organize their economic activity differently. Aside from the obvious fact that they do not have the same load of domestic and caring responsibilities they approach paid work differently. In the case of women we have studied, few take it seriously as a career. In this respect, nurses are unusual, though even they do not typically look beyond their single years to a life of nursing. Even fewer recognize the choices they will have to make later in their lives. For most young women, the first requirement of the labour market is to provide them with immediate cash both to relieve their families of part of the burden of supporting them, and to put them into a good position to meet and marry a suitable husband.

While women in the age bracket of Glenda, Cathy and Sue-Ellen have long since lost their illusions, younger women we studied still believed that with diligent seeking they would find someone only just short of Prince Charming, whose earnings would relieve them of the need to earn, or at least to earn much. Compounded with the structure of the labour market, it is not surprising that more women find themselves in Cathy's situation that in Glenda's (difficult though that is). Little of this applies directly to Sue-Ellen, precisely because of the integration of the wage and non-wage labour and of the lack of separation between young and old as well as men and women in South East Bight.

Conclusion

So, women never perform as ungendered individuals. As young women they enter the labour market as potential wives and mothers (of an idealized and long out of date type). It is only later that women's relationship to both the wage and non-wage labour is transformed by their entry into their marital households. Now everything is mediated through that institution, and it is difficult to even see them as separate individuals. This is not the case for their husbands (though I haven't discussed them in detail here). For one thing men enter male labour markets with clear expectations of commitment and permanency (and concomitant rewards) that carry the implicit message of future or present 'family responsibilities'. While their total economic support of the family is illusionary, the dangerous illusion of the family wage carries enormous *individual* benefits for men. They not only bring more money into the household for the same number of hours work, which in a cash dominated society will confirm their superior power in the household, but they also come with the ideological justification that whatever domestic or caring responsibilities they (voluntarily) take on, will always be secondary to their wage labour.

Women are thus caught in a circular trap which revolves *through* the household. Ironically, this means that women have to commit untold effort to ensuring the survival of the household, because without it, their position

147

as women outside households or women in women-headed household would be, in most cases, economically pitiful. The greater the financial disparity and the power imbalance between the married couple, the greater the woman's vulnerability and the more intense her efforts to preserve the conditions of both her oppression and her survival.

That this is experienced most intensely in Grand Falls and that Sue-Ellen's experience is, to a significant degree, different, suggests to me that part of the reason may be the role of the wage in these two communities — Grand Falls is a nearly completely urban society. Cash rules: class divisions flourish: situations of manifest oppression exist. It is dominated by the highly competitive, privatized, isolated nuclear family in which the wage (and status) of the man (usually nearly twice that of the women) establishes the family in the social order, but in which the women's wage is also crucial. While women like Glenda share in the family project whole-heartedly and with good reason, their position as individual women is both exhausting and precarious. They are also confined in their responses by rigid social codes so that if circumstances change they will find themselves excluded, and forced to exist on the underside of the visible, affluent Grand Falls.

Sue-Ellen's experience is marked by a greater integration. In particular, whereas Glenda sees her needs subsumed into the household, but in competition with the rest of the community, Sue-Ellen sees hers as continuous with her household *and* her community. But crucially, Sue-Ellen's life is not dominated by the wage. Money is important, certainly, but it doesn't come exclusively through wages, and when it does, it is not associated either with a rigid sexual division of labour, or with absolute male superiority. This leads Sue-Ellen to *feel* freer and more independent in her individual responses, even if as a community they have fewer and less variety of economic resources. It leads her to take possession of the external work as a confident individual — gendered to be sure and bound up in her household and community — but still an individual. None of this fully answers the questions I suggested. Nor does it enthrone any existing theory as king. Instead, we have a little more clarity, and more questions.

In all the communities I studied, and probably throughout Newfoundland, Pahl's concept of the household and his attendant notions of 'forms of work' and 'sources of labour' help us to understand the context in which most men and women conduct their lives. We need, now, to explore the growing number of variations on the traditional household, and lone individuals outside any households, all of whom raise different questions.

The household in our study remains, to some extent, a locked box. The generality of the survey and the style of our ethnography did not enable us to explore fully the dynamics and power struggles *within* households. What I can be certain of is that our evidence will *minimize* such imbalances, especially where those power difficulties result in consequences such as physical violence.

The exact balance of forces between the labour market and household commitments in constructing women's economic lives is still hazy. The easy answer is to suggest that there is a connection with the different roles of patriarchy and capitalism, with patriarchy largely constructing the household and capital determining the outcome in the market place. I am inclined to reject such a formulation. If either concept is to be complex and subtle enough to help our analysis then it cannot be confined to particular institutions in that way. Surely both patriarchy and capitalism construct both the household and the formal economy? While this may not seem helpful as a conclusion, it does suggest why Newfoundland communities differ so greatly in the contexts they provide for women.

Work, which I am equating with various forms of economic activity, constitutes and intersects two of the central institutions of our society — the household and the economy. Formal and informal women's economic activity takes place in this complex interaction, and because it is gendered, allows the examination of the role of patriarchy. Newfoundland communities exist within an overarching framework of western capitalist, patriarchal society. But they differ from one another, and these differences allow us to expose at least some of these complex intersections.

Notes

1. This study was funded by the Social Sciences and Humanities Research Council (SSHRC), under their 'Women and Work' focused research programme. I discuss some of the problems of carrying out research under SSHRC's auspices in the next chapter.

2. Or did until the recent collapse of the Atlantic cod fishery. At the time of writing (1992) it remains the *only* FPI deepsea plant open on the island, albeit with much reduced activity.

3. For a detailed account see the section on Catalina in Fishery Research Group (B. Neis), *The Social Impact of Technological Change in Newfoundland's Deepsea Fishery (St. John's, 1986)*.

4. For discussion of the consequences of caring work for women see Dalley, 1988; Evers, 1983-1985; Finch and Groves, 1983; Graham, 1983, 1985; Government of Canada, 1980, 1987, 1988; Meller, 1986; Lewis and Meredith, 198; McCay, 1987.

5. Health care professionals, social workers attested to the extent of 'social and domestic problems' in Catalina, and our own observations confirmed the picture of Catalina as the 'Black Sheep community' of the peninsula. But we also found extensive, but informal network of support in the community.

6. One field worker, after a visit to Grand Falls, lent me *The Stepford Wives* — a sci-fi thriller in which the men in a suburban town replace their all-too-human wives with perfect robotic look-alikes. I did, indeed, see why she had lent me the book.

9 'Secondhand ethnography': Some problems with feminist methodology and community studies

Introduction: on the perils of not looking before leaping

In this chapter[1] I want to take up a very different aspect of the *Women's Economic Lives* study — the methodology I employed. The reports of sociological projects often have a section on methodology, but frequently it turns out to be an ex post hoc rationalisation of what the researchers did. All too often it obscures the problems, traps, difficulties and mistakes that were made. This is a pity because they are often the most interesting part of the study — and not only because of other researchers' natural tendency to *schadenfreude*.

In this case, at least some of the problems I encountered are common to much sociological feminist research, and while I do not think I have solved the problems, I do think that they are ones we would all be well advised to consider.

At the time I applied for the SSHRC grant to fund the *Women's Economic Lives* project (a full year earlier) the reasons to do so — both political and theoretical — seemed compelling. My own work had reached the point where I was frustrated by the lack of data of any kind on women in the province, including province-wide generalisations and statistical data. There was also sustained pressure from the feminist community in St. John's on women in the university to do studies that would provide 'really useful knowledge'. Women, involved in various kinds of feminist activism — from the Women's Policy Office to anti-poverty groups — wanted 'facts' in order to bring pressure on government and other official agencies. What more useful 'fact' than a university accredited 'statistic' demonstrating the point? It was also, I was persuaded, my feminist duty to access academic research funding, to provide employment for qualified feminist research assistants and to produce the kind of academically respectable material that was made possible by my position in the university.

151

A year later, when I actually began the study, things looked different. The original potential Research Assistants had long since been snatched up by other employers or had left the province; my encouraging colleagues (while still encouraging) were too busy to do more. I was on my own — facing a large sum of money, an ambitious proposal, a university bureaucracy that seemed more than usually obtuse and some previously unconsidered factors. These included practical matters, such as the time and exhaustion involved in driving to the study communities, especially in normal Newfoundland winter conditions of snow/fog/ rain/ice/gales, as well as some theoretical, methodological and moral problems I had previously skirted.

The project was a large scale one with a budget of nearly $100,000 over two years, and as such, its organisation seemed to drift inevitably into hierarchical structures. It employed a variety of methods, and, as well as intellectual motivations, it had a feminist political purpose. All these aspects turned out to be problematic. In this paper I want to examine some of these that have a particular bearing on whether, and how, it is possible to extend feminist ethnographic methods to larger scale projects. The increasing feminist commitment to small scale qualitative methods pose serious problems for the steady accumulation of knowledge.[2] Qualitative feminists/sociologists tend to concentrate either on tiny 'ungeneralisable' cameos or on high level theory. Research that focuses on middle range data tends to employ quantitative methods. There has been a tendency, then, for feminists to exclude themselves from the acquisition of middle range data, including the 'useful facts', demanded by activists. In the project I report on here, I took the option of including quantitative methods, but as a result of that experience, I want to argue for other ways of expanding the range of qualitative methods.

The approach I have taken, in this chapter, is to retrace the methodological decisions I took, the (apparent) reasons for them at the time, and their consequences. In the course of doing this, I found that what my reflections were uncovering was not only shortcomings and errors, but a richer way of interrogating the relationships between the members of my research team and the data we produced and worked on — a process I have come to call 'Second-Hand Ethnography'.

It was a 'feminist project', in the sense that the declared allegiance, theoretically, methodologically and politically was feminist. Certainly, each stage of the project was enforced by a desire to develop a feminist piece of research. But if I was sure what that meant at the outset, I am much less sure now. It is a topic I will return to throughout the essay.

A choice of methods?

I shall look, first, at the original theoretical basis for the project, especially for the methodology I proposed. In particular, I want to examine some of the slippages and assumptions I uncovered as the study progressed.

The proposal to SSHRC included the use of a variety of methods, but concentrated on the qualitative ones I felt most comfortable with. The bulk of the study was to be a comparison of three very different communities, and the focus of each was to be an ethnography carried out by a research assistant. I had recognized that three ethnographies tacked together would not make a study, so I had added a number of other elements that would, I argued in the proposal, both provide a basis for province-wide comparisons and 'triangulate' the evidence from the ethnographies. They included historical work (such as the collection of oral histories), interviews with 'significant informants' of a conventional sociological type (union officials, social workers, teachers, etc.), a labour market study, an institutional ethnography of a hospital and a survey based loosely on the one used by R. Pahl in Sheppey,[3] as amended after a pilot project carried out in one of the three communities.

My defence for this mix of methodologies was drawn from varied and, to some extend, contradictory arguments. I rehearsed the criticisms of survey methodology and quantitative data that have been raised by feminists among others.[4] Most of this work is directed at attacking both traditional quantitative methods and the social relations in sociology that embody them.[5] Feminist writers, in particular, have been inclined to equate 'feminist' with 'qualitative' methods as a result — a point I want to return to later.

I defended my continuing use of quantitative methods partly by referring to the ongoing debates, and especially those that have either attempted to rehabilitate their use, or else are working on some synthesis between two types of methods previously regarded as hostile to one another.[6] I also made reference to 'triangulation', and the implicit assumption that 'more is better' — a concept I will take up again below.

None of the literature I cited addressed the problem of using *different* methods in the *same* project. In particular, I could not find any discussion about whether the use of one method would have an adverse effect on the data produced by others or how one would choose which set of data to believe if they turned up contradictory evidence. The standard texts encouraged a kind of methodological pluralism, though they offered no defence of it. Yet at least some conflict is implied by the epistemological underpinnings of quantitative and qualitative data. A number of writers have dichotomised quantitative and qualitative methods as 'objective' versus 'subjective', 'scientific and value free' versus 'empathetic', 'interpretive' and 'politically involved'. Anderson (1983), in particular, makes clear the incompatible roles of the researcher in quantitative and qualitative methods, yet at the very end of his book he suggests a possible synthesis between the two based on an honest acceptance of the criticisms of them — something that seems quite at odds with his earlier dichotomising description.

But what if the 'field' is full of potholes?

While I was quite open about my misgivings about survey methodology, I proposed it partly on the grounds that it would enable me to compare my communities with data collected by two male colleagues (who had a strong quantitative bias) and who were carrying out a study of economic and social adaptations on the Great Northern Peninsula, and partly because I wanted to examine Pahl's Sheppey findings in a different context.[7] This begs two important questions. How far would asking the same (or similar) questions to Pahl's actually tell us about the validity of his concepts of household strategies, the domestic division of labour, forms of work and sources of labour in the very different context of Newfoundland?

We had already discovered from our Pilot Study that many of the questions in Pahl's interview schedule were meaningless or inappropriate in a Newfoundland context. Virtually all the questions probing material possessions and self-provisioning activities had to be rewritten. Where home ownership is much higher and where public housing is limited to welfare ghettoes in St. John's and a few of the larger towns, questions relating to tenancy are simply confusing. Similarly, any documentation on self-provisioning in Newfoundland that fails to allow for hunting, or to check the availability of moose licences, for example, or which ignores the possession of a skidoo or all terrain vehicles for woodcutting would be useless. But even where the questions drawn from Pahl's schedule seemed to make sense, that didn't guarantee that the *answers* would be comparable. And how would data collected using such an instrument relate to, never mind 'triangulate with' material collected in quite other ways?

The concept of 'triangulation'[8] is borrowed from surveying and navigation. The navigation analogy is more accurate, referring to the process whereby a position is 'fixed' using, preferably, different *kinds* of measures, e.g., compass bearings, depth soundings and radio bearings or at least 'position lines' drawn from different positions. The underlying idea is that the wider the variety of evidence you can bring to bear, the smaller the area of doubt about your position. The concept is much more problematic when applied to epistemology. In any case, the concept of triangulation in sociological studies operates differently. It is less a case of checking a 'fact'

154

collected by one method, using another method, as using one method and then justifying the results by means of another. Usually, it is the survey that is the primary method. Data from informal interviews, or open-ended questions tacked onto the questionnaire or data from other kinds of sources are then used either as illustrations of the 'fact' or as an explanation. For example, a recent report on a study of women and labour market poverty in Canada is written essentially around quantitative data presented in tables and figures and discussed in the text. But every few pages a different kind of data, drawn from interviews with poor working women appears, boxed off and in a different typeface. These are either little cameos, potted biographies or direct quotes, and they are organized to support the dominant text. As the authors say in their introduction 'The interviews were conducted as part of the study and provided useful qualitative data, the human face, *in addition to* (my emphasis) the statistical treatment of the problem' (Gunderson and Muszynski, 1990:4).

My own approach was, in a sense, the reverse of this, though no less suspect. The study was exploratory. I was genuinely looking for information of as many kinds as possible that would help me understand how women's economic lives were constituted and sustained; what factors affected them, and how, and so on. Such a sweeping approach is probably valid in itself: the difficulty lies in assessing the relative validity of different sources of information, especially when they seemed to be in contradiction.

I encountered several examples of the difficulty of evaluating contradictions between different kinds of information in the course of the study. For example, in the largest community — Grand Falls, we held regular meetings with the local interviewers who were carrying out the household survey. Sometimes these meetings helped to clarify details that had been recorded in a confusing way, but quite often the interviewers would challenge the veracity of the answers given in the survey on the basis of their specific local knowledge. This was especially the case concerning matters of income and material possessions but it also arose over other matters. For example, an interviewer would comment 'She *said* her son contributed to his board, but I know he spends it on beer' 'She didn't say, but what about her Aunt up in Springdale, I know she visits?' Not only does this kind of exchange cast doubt on the rest of the data generated by the survey, but it also undercuts the whole notion of the 'impersonal', 'objective' interviewer, whether or not she could be persuaded not to modify her entries on the schedule — to say nothing of the problem of anonymity.

We also had interesting discussions, from which we learnt a great deal, when the interviewers explored their own feelings about the interviews and their interpretation of what they were told. They were meeting people outside their usual social circles, which was challenging their 'common sense' assumptions about their community. They were often horrified by the evidence of poverty, stress and overwork they found. But they were also highly sceptical of what they were told. This was especially the case when they suspected the respondent of giving a 'proper' or 'correct' answer instead of 'the truth'. They would become angry especially when they suspected their informants of 'covering up' for unhelpful, or even violent husbands.

We found the transcripts of these discussions provided us with some of the richest *qualitative* data on the community, and I did not hesitate to use the information in my report *even if it contradicted the survey findings*. Over and above my bias towards such data, there are two good reasons for this. The first is that where the data were in direct contradiction, it was either because the interviewee may have purposely not provided the 'correct' information, or because the design of the questionnaire allowed some ambiguity. The second reason was that because we were working in the community as ethnographers for a considerable time, we were able to check the interviewer's account against other peoples' accounts and other evidence. It thus became part of an accumulation of knowledge about the community, rather than about individuals.

There were other ways in which the use of different methods raised problems. The most important of these was the growing conviction each of the Research Assistants felt that their administration of the survey compromised their role as ethnographers. They all found that the administration of the survey devoured a disproportionate amount of their time, but more importantly, they felt that it adversely affected their relations with respondents. The survey was much more visible in the communities that the other methods, and the Research Assistants frequently had to explain and defend it. How was the sample drawn? how could we guarantee anonymity etc.? Especially in Grand Falls, the most affluent families were often reluctant to complete the survey if it involved revealing their income. As this was the hardest group for the ethnographer to penetrate she felt that the survey made this process much more difficult. She also felt that the fact that the survey concentrated on certain kinds of information (mainly about household resources and forms of work) made it harder for her to inquire about other subjects — health care, for example. It was as if asking about health was less legitimate because it wasn't in the survey. When the Research Assistants carried out the surveys themselves, they appreciated the access but disliked the false relationship they felt it created (I will discuss the most extreme case of this a bit later).

On the other hand, when I visited the communities I could often conduct some interviews and found the experience positive. It was partly that I had greater experience, but it was much more that I actually *wanted* to know the answers to the questions, even if I doubted the format of a structured interview. As a result I would find myself turning the occasion into an informal interview — pursuing loose ends and leads the way the Research Assistants did not, and certainly not the interviewers we employed in Grand Falls. That there was so much unevenness in the quality of the data different interviewers could derive from the survey did not reassure me about the method. On the other hand, as an infrequent visitor to the community conducting surveys myself gave me a form of access I would not otherwise have had.

Does stretching a method make it any bigger?

There were two main ways in which I attempted to extend ethnographic methods in the project. The first was to 'add on' other methods, especially the survey. The second was to expand the scale of ethnography, by placing three ethnographers in three communities. We chose the communities to represent various characteristics that we wanted to compare, and the intention was to build up the comparison so as to achieve a level of generality based on qualitative data. I now want to examine how this worked out, and especially how the process revealed the underlying methodological problems.

The root of some of these problems lies in the hierarchical model of research held by SSHRC and other funding agencies, a model that is in profound contradiction to the principles of feminist research as I was attempting to practise them.[9] In this model the Principal Investigator, who normally holds a full-time teaching position in a university, is responsible for the theoretical formulation of the project, for its administration and for writing the reports, but not for actually carrying out the research. The Principal Investigator is expected to devote his or her 'research time', i.e., time left over from normal teaching and administration duties to the project, but it is assumed that he or she will not undertake the data collection or fieldwork. While SSHRC does have a category of 'research stipend', which allows full-time academics to apply for time off, it is explicitly discouraged and very rarely granted. Instead, the Principal Investigator is expected to hire Research Assistants, interviewers, and even more lowly, transcribers, coders and secretaries. The assumption that the Research Assistants will be at the beginning of their careers and/or less qualified than the Principal Investigator is built into the conditions under which Research Assistants may be hired, and especially into the rates at which they can be paid, which are very low.[10]

This model appears to be derived from the 'hard sciences', where much research is carried out in labs, set up and controlled by senior academics, but in which most of the painstaking but relatively low level procedures are carried out by members of the 'teams' collected by the senior academics. Such a model is fairly easily transferable to survey research, which also depends on large quantities of fairly routine tasks, but I would argue that it is neither appropriate nor conducive to ethnographic projects, especially feminist ones, for at least three reasons — one practical and two theoretical.

The practical reason is geographic distance. Some science projects and all surveys depend on fieldwork which may be located some way away from the university. But even if the data is collected elsewhere, that part of the process is fairly rapid, and much more time is spent in preparing the data and then performing various manipulations with it. This is not the case with ethnographic studies where the bulk of the work takes place in the field and where the processes of data collection and analysis are hopelessly interwoven. In my case, all three of my communities were at least four hours away from St. John's and one required the best part of a day to reach. I could not, as a physicist might, drop into the lab between classes. Instead, I had to carve a few days here, a week there, to pay flying visits to my fieldworkers in the communities. The upshot was, inevitably, that I was divorced from the major part of the data collection. More importantly, I could not collect my *own* data as I have been used to doing. This was not merely an inconvenience, as I shall argue later.

More importantly, the structure envisaged and imposed by SSHRC is hierarchical. The grant was in my name. I was ultimately responsible for the project and the money; I had considerable power and authority over other members of the research 'team'. No matter how we disguised it, or how far we tried to achieve more equal relations and more democratic procedures, the inescapable fact was that I had more power than my 'assistants', and ultimately, it was my reputation that was at stake. As feminists we found this situation intolerable. By and large we worked within it, and dealt with the inevitable anger and frustration as best we could. But it is farcical to suggest that we achieved anything close to the feminist ideal of a cooperative of equals engaged in the research process.

And that was just among the 'researchers'. In SSHRC's collective mind there is a very clear notion of the division between 'researchers' and 'researched'; a clear responsibility on the former to 'do research', with few rights of reply or participation accorded to the 'researched'. It is notoriously difficult to get funds to return the research to the community in any sense, and even more difficult to get support to engage the community in the research.[11] Another consequence to SSHRC's hierarchical model was the pitifully low pay scales allowed for research assistants.[12] In my case, I felt I needed Research Assistants who would be mature and developed researchers (at or near Ph.D. level); who were excellent ethnographers and who shared at least some of my own background in feminism, marxism and sociology.

158

Such people would be well able to work independently and to develop their own research agenda within the main study. I hoped to build a team of as near equals as possible who would be able to work in conjunction with one another, especially in terms of the comparative aspects of the study. While I stated all this in the proposal, I had not fully recognized how vital it would be to acquire such Research Assistants. Newfoundland is a remote province within Canada, and the communities I selected were remote within it. The one university in the province has only just begun a Ph.D. programme in Sociology. There are, thus, no 'locally-grown' Ph.D.s in sociology. The people I was looking for would, almost by definition, be older than their early 20s, and would probably have various domestic and personal ties and commitments. Fine people, of exactly the character and qualifications I sought certainly existed in central Canada, but they could simply not afford to relocate to a remote community for eighteen months for a bare subsistence wage. The hierarchical model, therefore, imposed on me a working group very different from the one I had envisaged.

The research assistants: both researchers and researched

The three research assistants I finally hired all lived in Newfoundland, although two were immigrants — one from Central Canada, one from Germany. Gunda, who did most of the work in Grand Falls, was a woman in her early 40s. She had left Germany twenty years before (though she still retains a slight German accent) and had a varied career in USA and Canada before coming to Newfoundland to do a Ph.D. in Folklore. Her main interest was in tourism. She had no sociology or marxism and she came to feminism during the course of the study. She had however been trained in ethnographic methods and had a fine, organized, scholarly brain. Sandy, who worked in Grand Falls and was responsible for the South East Bight study was an extraordinary talented young Newfoundland woman in her late 20s. She had an Arts (B.A.) degree (which did not include Sociology). She had, however, worked as a Research Assistant on various projects including the Royal Commission on Employment and Unemployment. She had long been involved in political and feminist activity in St. John's although she had not read widely in the theoretical literature. She was one of Newfoundland's more promising young poets and had also edited both poetry journals and biographies.[13] She seemed to have natural ethnographic skills and was an astonishingly sensitive and intelligent observer.

Cathy, who administered the survey and worked in Catalina was the only one with a child. She had a background in social work (20 years earlier). Immensely energetic, she had since had a long and varied career as a political activist involved in a range of social concerns. Like Gunda she became more engaged with feminism during the project. Cathy had a wide range of reading and a practical commitment to social change, but she had no formal sociology and little in-depth theoretical reading. She was also the one who suffered the most frustration about the division between 'academic' work and practical activism.

All three women were talented, vigorous and intelligent. While none of them had the skills and background I was looking for, all of them brought positive and valuable characteristics to the study. Nevertheless, it meant that I could not do the study as I first intended.

I have just presented you, the reader, with thumbnail sketches of the three women who worked as Research Assistants on the project. Based on the points I want to develop subsequently and on what I conjecture are *your* backgrounds I have made a selection of features of their characters and biographies. Both the selection and the way I have presented it reflect my own interpretation. Undoubtedly, if they were to write a paragraph on what they thought they had contributed to the project something very different would emerge. But you, as reader, are dependent on me for your 'knowledge' of these three women.

This is an obvious, but crucially important point because of the way the study developed. I could not do my own ethnography. Essentially I had to depend on my research assistants to do it for me. On my field visits, I did some interviews and as much watching and listening as I could arrange. Much of this was directed at 'training' the research assistants — trying to get them to see the things I was seeing and ask the question I would ask. What I soon found I was doing was studying my own ethnographers. Only by understanding how they saw and heard the community could I 'interpret' 'their' 'data'.

Even had I been working with the ideal ethnographers I had in mind this same process would have taken place. I would still have been dependent on *their* eyes and ears; their social experience and their interpretation of it. The process may have been blurred because we would have had a larger common theoretical framework and vocabulary with which to exchange information, but it would still have been 'second-hand ethnography'. I became acutely aware of the problems and limitations of using other people to 'do' one's own ethnography because of their diverse and less than comparable academic backgrounds. But I would argue that the same methodological and epistemological problems arise in any study set up on these lines. What I am attempting in this paper is to make explicit the processes that were set in train and the consequences that had for the 'results' of the study.

When the field work was complete, the data out of which I wrote the report were of various kinds — data collected by the surveys, written material of different kinds, 'facts' and figures we had culled from informants etc. However, the richest and, to me, most valuable sources were the reports, tapes and fieldnotes of the research assistants and my own fieldnotes and tapes, which included interviews I had conducted, but also notes on conversations I had had with the research assistants. In the rest of this chapter I am going to present some of this 'second-hand ethnographic data', which is also, of course, data on the method of using such data.

'Second-hand ethnography'

I have already explained that I did not treat the quantitative and qualitative data equally. When I interpreted the data I gave a greater weight to qualitative data if any existed. When I carry out my own ethnography I rely on my own material. Where survey or other quantitative material supports it, so much the better. But if the material appears to be contradictory I will explore it on the basis that in the last resort I will trust my ethnographic eye over any other source. I am making this explicit, because it raises different problems when one is trusting *someone else's* eyes. When I write about the study, I am asking the reader to trust not *my* ethnographic understanding of the communities, but my interpretation of my research assistants' ethnographic understanding of the communities.

Let us uncover some of the processes involved in this 'second-hand ethnography'. All the research assistants contributed written sections of the Final Report as well as other papers and articles. We also presented a number of joint workshops. But they also provided me with 'fieldnotes' while they were living in the communities. These are halfway between their own personal jottings and their finished work. They were direct communications with me. In them they tried to give me the information they thought I wanted, i.e., they also contain *their* interpretation of me.

I have chosen to use these 'texts' to illustrate the process of 'second-hand ethnography' precisely because of their reflexive, self aware character. In particular, I want to make as explicit as possible the way in which one selects one 'truth' over another, and how one decides whether and how far to 'trust' an account.

Of the Research Assistants, Cathy was the most explicit about her role as an ethnographer the role of the study and my role as the Principal Investigator and as 'boss'.

> Went drinking with MP last night. The second bar was good for playing pool. A woman I'd interviewed turned out to be the best pool player around except for her buddy I met in the bathroom. Sue, the woman I'd seen before, whirled and danced, subtly, around the table.

Men would offer them advice but then they would reject it, which felt good after listening to women go on and on about a woman's place is in the home if she has small children or is 'Needed There', or that she is a natural secretary, and shouldn't be out getting dirty or lifting heavy objects. MP was being very observant and pointing at people rather too obviously, I thought.

When I stopped wincing at this criticism I thought back to that smoke-filled bar. We must both have stuck out like sore thumbs, as all strangers in small communities do. And we were plainly, both by accent and dress, not 'from here' (i.e., Newfoundlanders). But it had seemed to me as if we had been accepted round that pool table, and I was prepared to trust my judgement of what was 'happening' there. This was partly because it tallied with Cathy's, who had a very different approach. We'd talked at length that evening about the people, and what Cathy had learnt about how they fitted together. It was no accident we'd gone drinking. We both felt happy in such places. As Cathy wrote later, 'People here are divided into strict addiction categories and I think my category became obvious last night, hic'. At the time I had been concerned that neither of us should do anything that would make us 'unacceptable' to other parts of the community and also that by doing anything as positive as 'going drinking' we would 'intervene' in the society we were observing — that we would become less than the all-seeing wallpaper of participant observer fantasy — common worries in ethnography. Cathy had no such inhibitions, and as a result she uncovered significant levels of alcoholism and other 'deviant' behavior in the community. People trusted her confided 'hidden behavior' to her. She also uncovered dense and complex helping networks among the women she knew. None of this, of course, emerged from the surveys she was also collecting.

I was thrown out of one house in Catalina by the son of the older woman I was interviewing. The older woman hardly got to say Boo to the goose, because her daughter-in-law tried to answer questions for her, in spite of my non verbal cues such as leaning towards the older woman, looking only at her, and calling her by name. I had been very careful to advise the household members, three generations of whom were sitting at the kitchen table with me, that they could refuse to answer any questions and also ask me to leave any time during the survey.

As we discussed who did the household chores, the daughter-in-law claimed she did chores which later several other people in the community told me the older woman did. The daughter-in-law claimed that men never did any housework, so I told her that I knew a few men who did half the housework. She asked me "Why don't you send some

162

of those men down then? Nobody like that around here." Then we got to the income section. "Estimate all income from all sources per week in the household", I twittered.

All of a sudden I heard an incoherent blast of sound from the room off a hall leading from the kitchen. The daughter-in-law looked confused, and hurried to see what was happening. At first I thought somebody had lost leave of their senses . . . but then I realized this was a roar of rage because of me. The son of the respondent was yelling "Tell Mrs. to get her fucking ass out of this house" and "all that damn foolishness" and this went on for several minutes. "Do you mean me?" I yelled. "Yes" he screamed. "Yes, SIR" I yelled. "Don't get lippy" he screeched. I asked the respondent if she wanted me to leave. She nodded, speechless. I left, after apologising to her for making trouble.

Apart from Cathy's growing unhappiness with conducting the survey interviews (and with its eventual usefulness) part of the interest in this passage lies in the differences between this version (which appeared in Cathy's report on methodology) and the original account in her field diary, which is much more vivid, and much more revealing about the inequality and scarcely disguised violence in the household.[14]

This account, supported by other conversations with Cathy caused me to suspect that not only my survey, but others, underestimated intra-household inequality and potential or actual domestic violence that was taking place. In this case, I encouraged Cathy to focus on those issues when she was spending time in households. It also caused us to question the local doctors, nurses and social workers about their perceptions of these issues. In this case then, Cathy's report had the effect of moving the focus of the enquiry and alerting us to other kinds of evidence.

By the end of the fieldwork, Cathy was disillusioned with the research process and more than anxious to get back to her daughter and St. John's.

I am beginning to dislike intensely my position here. I go to the PO to get a stupid survey and they all snicker. Paranoia? No. Reality. Most of the respondents were people who I would never choose to spend any time with. That part is good. But it's awfully unfriendly.

When Cathy got back to St. John's, her feelings were as mixed as those of most ethnographers.

Seven hours in a snowstorm at 30-50 km per hour all the way home. I miss my landlady. She says I'm not allowed to talk about her, so I won't. I'm exhausted from nervous storm energy and no sleep and the homecoming. Catalina is a great place, and I like the people I met. (Next day) I am home, in my Privatised Space, as MP reminded me on the phone (is that the pot calling the kettle black or not?), and it *is* a luxury not to live in a boarding house where the cigarette smoke is predominant. But I miss my landlady . . . You can't really start talking about what any place is like after a few weeks there, or even a few years. You only know about it if you are going to stay there . . . Goodbye Catalina. I miss my landlady.

Cathy's field diary is a remarkable account, and it shows her creating her experience of Catalina and struggling to understand it. Yet it was clearly *Cathy's* experience and *Cathy's* interpretation of it. Had Gunda or Sandy worked in Catalina I (and other readers) might very well have got a different picture of the community.

While I encouraged all the Research Assistants to visit each other and each other's communities it was only in Grand Falls that two research assistants actually worked on the community. Grand Falls was the largest community, and with 10,000 people it is hard to tell if Gunda and Sandy were seeing different parts of the town, or the same parts differently. However, when two such different research assistants 'saw' the same thing it became powerful testimony. Only a few days after she got there Sandy wrote:

> Social class, it seems, has always been a big thing in Grand Falls. When the original company started the town, the company decided who could live there. Those who couldn't, lived in Windsor or other surrounding communities. Ida described growing up 'out on the Botwood road' and having 'no status at all'. The town was planned such that houses for different classes of mill workers were built on different streets, i.e., the labourers got one street and mill wrights got another, and on up to the top. The company did the landscaping, providing different neighbourhoods with trees for their yards, a different tree for each. So you can walk around Grand Falls and see small houses on one street with one kind of tree; the next street will have larger houses and another type of tree.

With her poet's eye, Sandy has picked out an image to explain to me a perception about the community that she can't yet 'prove' in sociological terms.

When Gunda got to Grand Falls, she soon uncovered quantities of evidence both about the split between Grand Falls and the despised Windsor — and about the severity of social class divisions within Grand Falls. Gunda wrote

> Grand Falls is a good place to live for the affluent and for old established families, who are members of the various groups and cliques. However, this 'closed', status- and class-conscious town is

164

a hard place to live for "outsiders", i.e., the less well-to-do, newcomers, single women. Even married women, whose husbands come to Grand Falls to make careers as doctors or mill engineers, often find themselves lonely and frustrated. After a year in Grand Falls, the outgoing wife of the mill engineer who had been transferred from the Abitibi Price plant in Stephenville, complained that she had not once "been invited for a cup of coffee.

In this case, the fact that Gunda and Sandy supported each others accounts allowed me to 'believe' them. This was, initially, difficult because of the widespread conviction in Newfoundland and supported by other ethnographers[15] that it is a relatively egalitarian and 'classless' society.

Gunda talked a lot about this problem, and it was clear that she was finding it easier to make contacts among single (especially professional) women and among the middle income couples. She could not penetrate the self-declared 'elite', nor could she get them to complete surveys. But, at the same time, Gunda began to uncover the social ills that lay beneath the smug exterior of Grand Falls. She found levels of domestic violence and nervous and psychological disorders, which were not surprising in themselves although the degree to which they were hidden did surprise us. Gunda followed the attempt to found a Transition House (for battered women) in some detail and recorded informal resistance as well as the open and official position, much of which was based on a flat refusal to encounter the idea that domestic violence could happen in Grand Falls. Psychologists in the next town, Gander, referred to the 'Grand Falls syndrome', meaning women who would not reveal their problems to professionals in their own town.

Gunda also became involved in the problems of working women, especially those working as clerks in the banks. In one case, she helped a victim prepare an extensive dossier to the Human Rights Commission. Gunda also documented the exhausting schedule followed by women who worked for wages, kept TV-ad perfect homes as well as keeping up a punishing social round.

But Gunda was herself a single woman, and a German. I started to wonder how far it was her social persona that was leading to her exclusion from the elite circles and colouring her view of the community. When I visited Grand Falls her view of the community seemed to be confirmed at social gatherings we attended, in conversations we had and by other evidence. I aired the problem of the 'closed', 'cliquish' and 'snobbish' structure of Grand Falls society with the informants I met. We discussed it with our interviewers and with the Community Advisory Group we had set up. Grand Falls sends a disproportionate number of its youngsters to University and to work in St. John's. I would raise it with Grand Falls natives I met, and even in my classes. The answer was consistent. Yes,

Grand Falls was like that — and more so. The stories other people told me were far more critical than Gunda's gentle, reasonable account. It became clear that Grand Falls was a-typical of Newfoundland communities in its greater prosperity, its sharp social divisions, the degree to which conventional dreams were remorsely pursued and the ferocity of its exclusion of anyone who did not or could not conform to the established patterns.

This, coupled with an increasing interest in health and caring issues led Gunda and me into long discussions as we tried to make sense of a complex, and to some extent, unexpected situation. Gunda lived in Grand Falls for over a year. Both her notes and mine reflect a growing consensus in our interpretations. Was this because I was imposing a theoretical framework on Gunda, or was it because I was increasingly experiencing Grand Falls through Gunda and learning to trust her judgement? It soon became very hard to disentangle. However, while this means that our accounts ceased to cross check each other, they did build an increasingly rich account of the community, based on two converging perspectives and a variety of information.

Gunda remained intensely self-critical of her own fieldwork, continually trying to reach new sections of the community and broaden her participation in various activities. She was also aware both of the falseness of the distinction between researcher and researched and the need to return the research to the community in a usable form. I have already mentioned that we set up an advisory group of local women in Grand Falls. The intention was that we could 'feed back' what we found to the group on a regular basis and learn from their interpretation of it. We also hoped that such a group would be able to make use of what we found in their own community projects. In the event, Gunda found herself increasingly drawn into various activist projects in the town. She worried about how her involvement in such activities would 'compromise' her role as a researcher, and solved the problem by passing the mantle of 'responsibility' on to me. As the 'professor' from the University I found myself dressing in my smartest clothes and attending functions and interviewing people that Gunda felt would be alienated by her. It was a curious process and led both of us to examine what kind of information each of us could get from different sources, and where in all that might the truth lie.

South East Bight offers a startling contrast to Grand Falls. It is a tiny community of a hundred people lying halfway up Placentia Bay and reachable only by boat. The people depend entirely on the inshore fishery, various subsistence activities and transfer payments. It is remote, wild and idyllically beautiful. Here are extracts from the opening section of Sandy's field notes.

"The boat moved through dense fog, through intervals of yellow-grey light suddenly illuminating the sea. A whale breached, and no one but

166

the "strangers" paid any attention. Close to an island a loon sang out. The boat trailed a quiet wake. I spent most of the time on deck.

An elderly man drank beer; it was eleven a.m.

"Where're you headed"? he asked, "Petitforte?"

"South East Bight."

"From there?"

"No."

"Just visiting are you, yes?"

"Yes."

"Oh," he was at a loss for anything else to say.

All through the trip he drank beer, and looked as if he didn't know what else to do. Other men were drinking too, walking for and aft, talking, then drifting off in groups again. Women, some of them young girls, carried babies about and tried to keep track of assorted youngsters. Men conferred on deck about weather and fishing. Merasheen, resettled empty home of wistful and romantic dreams, shone through the fog. First stop, Paradise . . . As we left Paradise, I was struck by the houses. Two in particular had a curious effect on me. There were traditional houses, tall and narrow with long symmetrical windows; these are the houses which let you know where on earth you are. I watched the light shine through empty windows in the ruined gardens beyond, tottery paling fences defining a wild tangle of native grasses. The skeletons of dories sat on decayed slipways. And then new houses — fishing shacks, modern bungalow, cabin-like structures, and big houses with aluminum siding like houses in Mount Pearl.

When the government resettled in Paradise no one stayed. They trickled back, and the place became a summer fishing station. Things that were abandoned were not used again, but left to rot. New houses, new boats appeared. This made me wonder about the Bight; would its past be visible, or had it been left to rot?

In the Bight, people had resisted resettlement. Six families stayed; their members began to organize, and they began to get the services the government had threatened to deny them . . ."

Instinctively, I 'trusted' Sandy's account of South East Bight. Why? Because she wrote beautifully? Because she was raised in the next Bay?

Because what she had confirmed ideas I already had? Because South East Bight was less a community than a cause? It was probably all of these things. I was aware, as I analysed Sandy's account, and incorporated it into the final report, of the dangers of seduction. Writers such as Atkinson (1990) and Clifford and Marcus (1986) have pointed out that *all* ethnographic accounts use 'poetics' (as Anderson (1987) calls it) to present themselves, and have begun to develop more sophisticated ways of understanding how it is done. If, as they aver, 'Sociology is a rhetorical activity' (Atkinson, 1990:10) then there is no reason to disbelieve an account *because* it is successful in its appeal.[16]

Sandy's sensitive use of her own background shows in this brief reference to merchants.

> I'm interested in the status Marg has in the community. Where I grew up, the merchant wielded a great deal of power because they could extend and withdraw credit. The children of the merchant next door beat and bullied us frequently; we had a bill run up there. I must find out what power these merchants — Marg and Martin — have. I know they extend credit.

> But I discovered there is a sign in Martin's store now: "As of August 1, there will be no more credit from this store. All bills should be paid in full". What is going on here?

This accords with previous ethnographic and historical discussions of the place of merchant in small communities, and raises new questions in the context of South East Bight.

My acceptance of Sandy's account did not make the interpretive problems easier. South East Bight has fought hard to continue to exist, and has found a complex way of surviving economically. It is under threat, not only from a world that has long since rejected small scale rural solutions, but from the particular difficulties confronting the Atlantic fishery and the Newfoundland economy. South East Bight might not be there is another year or two. All of us on the project found we cared about this passionately. After much discussion we were all agreed that of the three communities we had studied, the women of South East Bight lived the most complete and satisfying economic lives, and were most positively attached to the way of life they led. Furthermore, we thought that the situation of the women of South East Bight had much to teach other women in other communities. I had felt some awkwardness about criticising the way of life in Grand Falls and Catalina, arising from the feminist conviction that research should be 'for' women. South East Bight seemed to offer a more direct and 'useful' role for the research, which comforted me politically, at least.

168

So we cared politically about South East Bight's vulnerability, and we cared theoretically about what we thought we were learning from the community. The argument is too lengthy to summarize here. Suffice to say, that as soon as we expressed it we were open to charges of 'rural romanticism', 'anthropological navel-gazing' and 'wanting to deprive women of the benefits of hospitals, supermarkets and high speed cars'. All this can be rebutted — but the point I am making here is that the main basis for our argument was the material Sandy collected and some observation of my own. I trust her judgment — but should you, and how could we use it to convince the sceptics? The argument I want to make about South East Bight is an important one. What other kind of evidence could a feminist project collect to support it? Would we, inevitably, have to resort to more 'objective' quantitative data?

Was this a 'feminist' project?

I have tried, in the last few pages, to show how 'second-hand ethnography' is carried out and some of the inherent weaknesses in the practice. I have implied throughout, that this was a 'feminist' project but the only ways in which I have made that explicit are in terms of its original goal to produce 'useful knowledge' for the feminist community. I also discussed my concern that if ethnography is a distinctively feminist method and if there are feminist reasons for being suspicious of quantitative methods then we must grapple with the problem of scale if feminist knowledge is to continue to grow.

There is increasing interest in 'feminist methodology' and I looked to this literature to guide me both in the initial conception of the project and to overcome its short comings as they emerged. Some recent contributions to the problem include Smith (1987, 1990), Stanley and Wise (1983), Stanley (1990), Fonow and Cook (1991) and Eichler (1981). Between them they have gone far beyond criticising the established practices, especially of quantitative research, to developing a new epistemology. In Smith's words 'A sociology for women preserves the presence of subjects on knowers and actors. It does not transform subjects into the objects of study of make use of conceptual devices for eliminating the active presence of subjects' (Smith, 1987:105). But as Cook and Fonow point out, 'feminist epistemology and methodology arise from a critique of each field's biases and distortions in the study of women' (Cook and Fonow, 1991:2), rather than creating anew. The result, they argue, is that feminism has incorporated several underlying assumptions, among which they discuss 'reflexivity, an action orientation; attention to the affective components of the research; and the use of the situation-at-hand'.

169

I would argue that these then take on the guise of explicitly and exclusively feminist characteristics and become mandatory for all feminist projects. This, among other things, is how ethnography has acquired its prominent place as 'the' feminist method. This is encapsulated in the synopsis of a recent article on feminist ethnography — 'Many feminist scholars have identified ethnographic methods as ideally suited to feminist research because its contextual, experimental approach to knowledge eschews the false dualism of positivism and, drawing upon such traditionally female strengths as empathy and human concern, allows for an egalitarian, reciprocal relationship between knower and known' (Stacey, 1988:21). But while this sets up a political and ethical expectation that feminists *ought* to do ethnography it does not seem to me to establish a separate, distinctive 'feminist methodology'. By applying and developing the vigorous standards feminists set themselves we may arrive at *better* methods, but this only guarantees better sociology rather than a new kind of 'feminist sociology'.

While, in this sense, this seems to be accepting the denigrations of Clifford and Marcus, that would be a misreading. Feminist research is both a delicate blending of political imperatives and theoretical insights *and* a dynamic and rapidly developing discourse. To say that the end result of this is to create a better sociology rather than a distinctive *feminist* methodology does not detract from its continuing contribution.

Conclusion: towards 'linked ethnographies'

Meanwhile, we are left with the problem of scale, with the deficiencies of quantitative methods and with the need to develop methods appropriate to every level of generality and scale. While it is fraught with methodological, epistemological and ethical danger, ethnography seems to me to continue to provide one of the satisfying ways of conducting research as a feminist. I have exposed some of the dangers and difficulties of trying to conduct second-hand ethnography, but I have also shown how the examination of colleagues' field experience and field notes can be a source of knowledge itself. What is necessary is for the process to became more equal and more explicit. Let us imagine three ethnographers working together to establish a common theoretical framework and approach and then going to separate communities or other 'fields'. As they collected their material and wrote their fieldnotes, they would exchange them with the colleagues (at least every week; maybe by computer). They would meet frequently and interrogate each others accounts using all the sophisticated and sensitive tools that have been developed for such interrogation within feminist practice. They would report back to their 'subjects' and be subjected to interrogation of their

170

interpretation by them. They would visit each other in the field: they would construct joint accounts. To some extent, this is simply an extension of what we did. But it would take place in conditions of academic equality and with a clear sighted understanding of what the researchers were trying to achieve.

These 'linked ethnographies' seem to me to be both a possible and a sound way of expanding single ethnographies. The focus would inevitably be as much on the researchers and the process of the research as on the original 'subject', but that is not, in itself a weakness. In fact, it may repair some of the damage caused by our lack of self awareness in the past. It accords with feminist methodological expectations of traditional ethnography. Our experience, limited though it was, of discussing each other's material and working through to shared conclusions was one of the most positive aspects of the study.

I said in the outset that the project on 'Women's Economic Lives in Newfoundland' was exploratory. I meant that so few studies had been conducted and so little data had been collected that I could not know precisely what sort of material I wanted or how it would be collected. In methodological terms, I tried to build on existing methods to meet my own needs, and, particularly, to meet the needs of a feminist agenda. Feminism carries with it a sense of urgency and an intense desire to know, in order to change, women's experience. If the kind of failures and mistakes I have explored have sped this process, then they must be welcomed as an equal contribution to the awkward and exciting project of building feminist knowledge.

In conclusion, let me return to the thorny question of what, if anything, is specifically feminist about the project I have described. At one level, I have called it feminist because I was a feminist and a large part of its political and theoretical purpose was feminist i.e., to explore and analyse women's economic lives within a feminist theoretical perspective, with the explicit intention of enhancing those lives. When I came to select my research team, my research methods and the other choices I made in setting up and conducting the research I referred to a body of established feminist practice. For example, I chose to use certain methods in full awareness of criticism that had been made of them of misrepresenting women's experience, and tried to improve them.

The particular problem and its partial solution that I have highlighted in this chapter — that of what I have called 'second-hand ethnography' derives from feminist concerns, and I have described both the problem and its solution in terms of feminist literature. However, neither the problem, not its solution is *exclusively* feminist. It is inextricably entwined from origin to conclusion with other strands of sociological thought. As it should be. There would be very little point in my publishing this collection if my project

171

did not have a more general applicability to the project of social science. It is thus that feminism has come of age. Our commitment remains feminist and aspects of our work can be clearly identified as feminist, but the boundaries are neither so impermeable nor so limiting as they were. It was, in fact, a feminist-sociological project. So, indeed, has been all the work I have described in this book. In the final Chapter, I will try to draw all these strands together, to enable us to take stock as Newfoundland women enter the different - and even harsher - world of the 1990's.

Notes

1. This chapter is based on an article due to appear in R. Burgess and A. Bryman, *Analysing Qualitative Data* (London, forthcoming).

2. While not all feminist researchers are exclusively qualitative in their approach, there is certainly a heavy emphasis on the virtues of qualitative methods in the literature. See Fonow and Cook (1991); Eichler (1988); Hardin (1987); Stanley and Wise (1983).

3. Courtney (1982) *Isle of Sheppey Study: Technical Report*, Social and Community Planning Research.

4. e.g., Kirby and McKenna (1987); Eichler (1988); Fonow and Cook (1991); Stanley and Wise (1983); Klein (1983); Oakley (1981).

5. See especially Smith (1987).

6. The ground has been shifting recently with attempts to modify the practice and theoretical application of quantitative methods so as to make them more compatible with the principles of subjectivity. The jury is still out on the matter but interesting (of inconclusive), recent contributions include Cain and Finch (1981); Strauss and Corbin (1990); Stanley, ed. (1991), Section B.

7. P. Sinclair and L. Felt's study of *Social and Economic Adaptation on the Great Northern Peninsula* was also based on Pahl's work on household strategies, and they were also using some adaptations of his questions.

8. See N. Denzin, *The Research Act*, 1970.

9. I am examining SSHRC in some detail, because they funded this study. I have no reason to think other funding agencies — such as ESRC — are any different, especially over the conduct large-scale project.

10. SSHRC has since responded to this kind of criticism and now has a much more flexible, and generous, pay scale for Research Assistants. At the same time, it has virtually eliminated the Research Stipend, as well as the category of 'Private Scholar', both of which increase both the degree of hierarchy and the involvement of formal academic institutions in SSHRC funded research (see Ruffman, 1992).

11. These principles are now well established tenets of feminist research — see Kirby and McKenna (1980); CRIAW (1986); Kleiber and Light (1978). It is also well established in politically engaged research. In Newfoundland, for example, Don Snowden and MUN Extension developed a combination of social research, political activism and film making to help rural communities resist resettlement in 1960s — a process known as 'the Fogo Process'.

12. The maximum I could pay a RA, with a PhD was $23,000. Such a person at the time of the project would command $32,000 as an Assistant Professor at MUN and much more as a Research Assistant for the government or the private sector.

13. It is some indication for her talent that she received a grant from Canada Council to write poetry for 6 months, which entailed her leaving the project for that period.

14. When Cathy left the project she was both angry and disillusioned with the whole research process and with the structure of the project. She was also extremely concerned about the confidentiality of her material. She wrote some of the best fieldnotes I have ever seen — vivid both about her material and her own responses to the (to her) new experience of field work. Unfortunately, she has not released these for quotation.

15. This is especially true of the ethnographies published by the Institute of Social and Economic Research in St. John's in the early 1970s, e.g., J. Faris, *Cat Harbour*, 1972; M. Firestone, *Brothers and Rivals*, 1978.

16. These, and other anthropologists, have recently developed what they call the 'new ethnography'. In many cases, this seems to entail using the insights of post-modern and other contemporary discourses to develop more sophisticated validations of established ethnographic practice. The Clifford and Marcus collection is remarkable for its explicit denial of the contribution of feminist theory to recent developments in ethnography despite its 'great potential significance for rethinking ethnographic writing' (Clifford and Marcus, 1980:19).

10 Are some places more post modern than others? A brief conclusion

In this book I have described one stage in the attempt to understand women's lives in Newfoundland. I argued, at the outset, that this was a valuable exercise both because of the intrinsic interest of these particular women's experiences and because of what we could learn by applying particular kinds of theory to their situation. The decade of studies that is presented here portrays Newfoundland women at a particular point in their history. Recent dramatic economic events — especially the collapse of the fishery — seem to close a chapter in that history. As we sit here, we seem to be at a turning point: the future is more than usually uncertain. It is, therefore, a good moment to stop and take stock. It is also a good moment to recognize the continuities, not only in the harsh and uncertain circumstances that have always characterized these women's lives, but in the resources that they have developed to survive them. Newfoundland women are in for the long haul, and they will live to tell that tale to future researchers.

In the studies in this book we have been able to delineate at least some of the characteristics that have ensured Newfoundland women's survival up until now. I have described their historical role in the long and difficult period of colonization, and the way in which women secured for themselves places of security, dignity and considerable independence. I stressed that even when settlement was initially complete the circumstances in the fishing outports were always harsh, with poverty and insecurity as constants: within this context women continued to develop and practice ways of ensuring that they, their families and their communities survived.

As we move into the post-Confederation era, the story becomes more complex. Many aspects of the traditional economy and way of life disappeared, or survive precariously in small communities such as South East Bight. Newfoundland women are increasingly experiencing a way of life (and the problems inherent in it) typical of contemporary western urban existence. But we can still chart both the complex relationship of individual

175

women with their families and communities and the continuities of both their practices and priorities with those of their foremothers. I have argued that their formidable strength, organization and persistence gives Newfoundland communities a more than usually good chance of survival.

Nevertheless, I have also argued that increasingly Newfoundland women are imperilling their own integrity and fulfillment in order to ensure the survival of their families. As economic circumstances darken; as the fishery declines and more and more women find themselves in the pure wage economy I described in Grand Falls; as fewer women find themselves without even the protection of the traditional economic household, the task of survival becomes progressively harder — especially for women. When Dona Davis revisited 'Grey Rock Harbour' in 1989, she found a very different situation than the one she had encountered ten years earlier. In recent papers (Davis, 1990, 1990b, 1990c) has tried to analyse the profound differences in the position of women in this one community. The complete collapse of the economic base in the fishery has obvious and miserable consequences for the entire community. There is a collapse of morale, initiative and confidence in previously held values. Young people can no longer look forward to a predictable and appreciated lifestyle, and parents no longer encourage them to stay. But Davis is particulary concerned to show how the reconstruction of women from strong, competent 'dependable' economic and social actors to 'dangerous', media-modelled sex objects has destroyed both women's confidence and the balance between men and women in the community. Rather than a more or less equable and equitable sexual division of labour, the attention is now focussed on a 'sexual division of (unwanted) leisure' that is organised around a struggle for power between the sexes. Davis' account is not the only one; nor is 'Grey Rock Harbour' necessarily typical, and other accounts are rather more optimistic. Nevertheless this is not a happy moment to close this book; merely a logical one.

Meanwhile, the other focus of this book was to show one trajectory of the development of feminist theory and the way in which it could be used to unlock the problems around us. While both the theory and its application changed in the course of the studies described here, the main framework stayed fairly constant. The principle interest remained in the economic aspects of women's lives, and Marxism provided an over-arching theoretical perspective.

At the end of the Introduction to this book, I implied that researchers beginning to study Newfoundland women today would probably begin in a different theoretical place and with a different set of priorities. So it has proved to be. There is a rapidly growing group of innovative and energetic young feminist researchers in the province, and their focus and methods are different from those of the previous generation. Their range of interests is wider; they are using new kinds of data with new methods. They are exploring sexuality, violence, literature, arts and language, the experience of religion, the dynamics of personal relationships and the contributions of non-western ethnic groups. They are concentrating more on urban existence and on the increasing number of women living outside 'traditional families', whether by choice or not. They are working in groups and facilitating communities to research themselves; they are embodying and exploring their research in theoretical and visual ways. They are using new theory and new methods. But the underlying project is the same. They also want to give voice to and understand the unique experience of the women around them. Their efforts, like mine, are part of a collaborative effort to understand ourselves, the women around us and our society. Furthermore, the research is not disinterested about the lives it studies. Like other feminist and action oriented research, it aims to change the situations it finds: to leave people's lives better, not worse.

This sense of accountability to the so-called 'subjects' or our research, and desire for a more collaborative form to the research has been intensifying over the last decade. Yet sometimes it seems curiously at variance with the theory that it employs.

Postmodernism,[1] in all its various manifestations, is not the only new theory on the block. It is neither fair nor accurate to assume that all the new research I have alluded to falls under the general rubric of postmodernism. However, it is true to say that in the early 1990s it has a similar cachet and resonance that Marxism did in 1960s and 1970s. Very little research and writing today is entirely unaffected by the ideas and styles that have been developed as or under postmodernism or its closely associated schools of thought. It is, therefore, appropriate to hold it accountable for the direction that research is now taking; to see whether it does elucidate our experience, or merely obscure it.

My consideration here is focused on one fact of Newfoundland's recent history and present condition, and one which affects the women of Newfoundland as much, if not more, than the men. I refer to the collapse of the Northern cod fishery, embodied in the two-year moratorium declared by the Federal government in spring 1992. This focus of mine betrays two of my fundamental convictions about theory.

The first is my persistent belief that there is a real world, and that even if I cannot know it, I can know the consequences. One example is the fishery crisis. It is not yet clear what caused the collapse, or how far back those causes go, and the issues can be and are described and analyzed in various, sometimes contradictory ways, but the consequence of the crisis is real enough. There are no fish for the Newfoundland fishing communities to catch or process and this, in turn has drastic consequences of social, economic and cultural kinds, which again, are still being analyzed and debated. But the core of the matter is that there are no fish. It merits scrutiny. It has a tangible reality, and as a researcher I can, indeed, must, investigate that reality.

I also insist that any theory that I use has practical relevance; can prove itself in the 'real' world. Indeed, I am not really satisfied until I have found a radical social theory, one 'that takes up the responsibility of giving reasons why change is required, for making the demand for change accountable in terms of some standards of judgement' (Crook, 1990:59). My acceptance of postmodernism is, then, contingent upon my finding it useful and 'accountable' to problems I perceive in what I persist in referring to as 'the real world'. The crisis in Newfoundland's fishery is just one aspect of that 'real world', one whose reality is bearing more and more harshly on economically and socially disadvantaged people throughout the world. My challenge to postmodernism arises out of a disquiet that much of what I have heard and read is not simply misguided, but profoundly dangerous. We are not, it seems to me, to be living in a period when we can attend to the ludic qualities of this new philosophical or aesthetic enterprise. Our problems are too grim for that, especially in Newfoundland and especially as women. Such a situation must reject a philosophy that would reject the very concept of 'solutions'.

Perhaps I am being unfair. I should, at least, clarify what, out of the cascade of varying expressions has triggered my suspiciousness. I am, of course, sensible of the technical differences between deconstruction, poststructuralism and postmodernism, but I follow a number of commentators in allowing postmodernism to subsume at least some aspects of them all. Even Boyne and Rattansi, who are more rigorous than most in restricting the terms of a set of 'aesthetic and cultural projects' allow that 'what has made the extension of the term credible had been its purchase on a relatively widespread mood in literary theory, philosophy and the social sciences' (Boyne and Rattansi, 1990:12) — a common condition that they (and most others) label 'the crisis (or series of crises) of representation', in which 'older modes of defining, appropriating and recomposing the objects of artistic, philosophical, literary and social scientific languages (that) are no longer credible'. They go on to argue that the idea of 'crises of representation' can be extended to allow a characteristic of 'postmodern condition' as one of a coincidence between crises of representation in the fine arts, philosophy, the social sciences and 'modern political institutions', and it is this last inclusion that forces us to examine what they have to say more closely, for they are purporting to enter the domain of the economic and social conditions of Newfoundland women. Indeed, sociologists such as Bauman claim that 'the term 'postmodernity' renders accurately the defining traits of the social condition that emerged throughout the affluent countries of Europe and of European descent in the course of the 20th century, and took its present shape in the second half of that century' (Bauman, 1991:33). Postmodernism does, therefore, claim to refer to what is happening in the 'real world' and we can therefore reasonably expect it to give us an account of the problems that we — not them — define as real, even in Newfoundland. Yet, it seems to me, that in various ways, but one most important one, postmodernist writing specifically excludes places like Newfoundland from its purview.

This suspicion crystallized for me when I came across a reference in Norris's defence of Derrida to a Derridean essay on a marginal note by Nietzsche, which reads (twice translated) 'I have forgotten my umbrella'. The shock of recognition was overwhelming. Out of the miasmic gloom of disorientating, philosophical tergiversations, shone the clear light of an unmistakable sentence, with a crystal clear meaning and incontrovertible consequences. If one forgets one's umbrella and it rains, one gets wet. It happens to everyone, all the time, especially in Newfoundland. Of course, this was not how Derrida saw it. I waded through all the complex possible meaning of Neitzsche's footnote, and why he might have written it and what we as readers can possibly make of it, which included Freudian interpretations of the umbrella's shape and functions as well as the nature of the written word, but nothing about getting wet and other consequences of living in the natural world, as we still do in Newfoundland. Our irredeemable literalism is what causes us to hang onto the reality of weather, getting wet and its consequences. Hence our concern with the state of the fishery, among other things. And that caused me to notice how much of postmodern writing is posited on, contextualized by and appears to have no knowledge of a reality other than the experience of late 20th century, western, major cities and conurbations. Nowhere is there any recognition of the experience of life in rural areas, or even smaller towns.

It is easy enough to document this. Think, for example, of the acres of words — beginning with Banham's description of Los Angeles as the archetypal (if you will forgive the expression) postmodern city; of Charles Jenks and all his followers' work on postmodern architecture; of Harvey (himself a geographer) and his focus on Jonathan Raban's description of London in *Soft City* as the ultimate description of the postmodern experience. Think of the *kind* of architecture, art, film and literature so believed of postmodernist critics. It all, I think without exception, assumes or is explicitly about *big city* life. Postmodernists are fascinated and entranced by cities. They live in cities because they *like* cities. As Elizabeth Wilson puts it with such brutally revealing clarity 'it is tempting to forget that urban life has always offered advantages that cannot be matched by rural existence' (Wilson, 1991:233), or as Jameson describes our everyday experience in 'the extraordinary surface of the photorealist cityscape, where even the automobile wrecks gleam with some hallucinatory splendour . . . How urban squalor can be a delight to the eyes, when expressed in commodification, and now an unparalleled quantum leap in the alienation of daily life in the city can now be experienced in the form of a strange new hallucinatory exhilaration'. St. John's is a city of sorts, and apart from the car wrecks, which are in any event are more a feature of outport life, it's not like that at all.

I am belabouring this point, but it seems to me to be of crucial importance, especially when allied with the postmodern description of our current condition as 'post-industrial' (Daniel Bell) as 'a fully developed modernity' with all that implies, as a 'knowledge-society', 'a third great expansion of capitalism', 'a combination of new global interdependency, an emergent post-Fordism in production and consumption, a decline in dominance of manufacturing and traditional class politics' (Boyne and Rattansi, 1991:19); as the 'society of the spectacle' (Debord), as consumer society, as mass media society, or as the 'bureaucratic society o controlled consumption', (Lefevbre), to mention just a few designations of our new state of being. These epithets may or may not accurately describe some aspects of the socio-economic parameters within which we live, but the point there is that they are variously apt in different countries and different regions of the same country. What is true for London or Los Angeles is not necessarily true for Yellowknife or St. John's, and is even less certainly true for Catalina or Burkina Faso. If to be postmodern we must conform to these descriptions, then certainly some places *are* more postmodern than others.

Many of us in the Atlantic provinces have tried before to interpret our specific economic and social conditions using frameworks and typologies devised in and for central Canada and/or Europe or the USA, and we know it doesn't work.[2] W know that as feminists too. Yet, again, we find ourselves attempting to 'fit' into another framework. Are some places more postmodern than others? Is Newfoundland, in which I find it hard to locate the dominant characteristics of modernity, never mind postmodernity, simply not ready for these brave new insights? Is postmodernism simply unable to address some places, or people — such as women — because, as Lovibond has so aptly put it, "How can anyone ask me to say goodbye to 'emancipatory metanarratives' when my own emancipation is still such a patchy, hit-and-miss affair?", (Lovibond, 1990:161). In the case of Newfoundland women, what conceivable news can postmodernism bring that will bear on their present concerns?

A close reading of the attempts of such writers as Bauman (1992) to de- and re-construct the society in which he lives in postmodern terms can have contradictory effects. On the one hand such shifting sands can appear as desperate, unknowable and certainly, unmanageable chaos, and one's only reasonable response must be to hiss with panic-struck revulsion. But another response, and one which has been taken up by many feminists, is a joyful sense of a freeing of constraints and a consequent enthusiasm for continuing the destruction of metanarratives and unitary schemes of all kinds. At last, they argue, women (and other non-white/male/western/heterosexuals) can find legitimate voices; can develop their own accounts of their own experiences.[3]

Much of the work of writers such as Meaghan (1988), Weedon (1987), Nicholson (1990), Flax (1986) has opened exciting new possibilities for not only understanding women's experience but also reclaiming it. While it can certainly be argued, in theory, that Newfoundlanders like any other disadvantaged people have had inappropriate meta-narratives thrust upon them, I continue to doubt whether the postmodern ferment will actually extend much beyond the metropolises it currently inhabits. At heart, it seems to lack a seriousness about real economic and social poverty and a lack of creative political will to change anything. Even adherents like Boyne and Rattansi confirm that, postmodern politics, however construed can only 'provide a partial foundation for the re-thinking and new self-identity' that we need (Boyne and Rattansi, 1990:25). Callincos has made the same point both more clearly and more critically. He argues that postmodernism emerged less from the actual collapse of the conditions of modernity than from the disillusion of a generation of intellectuals who came of age in the euphoria of the 1960s and 1970s. These — those that are employed — are now comfortable, middle class professionals doing very well out of Rightist regimes and surrendering smugly to the temptations of affluence and consumption. Who, as Callincos points out, is better qualified to provide a rationale for lying back and enjoying late Capitalism than Lyotard, himself an ex-militant of the semi-Trotskyist *Socialisme et Barbarism* group (Callincos, 1990:114).

Of course, it is also profoundly *urban* experience, especially in its paradigmatic British and US modes. But, more importantly, it means that not only can nothing be done about Newfoundland's fish, but that they simply disappear from the discourse. They do not exist within the postmodern habitat, they are a figment of our modernist illusions. I am, here, slipping onto the side of those who argue that postmodernism is inherently, inevitably and actually a profoundly reactionary doctrine and all too well equipped to become a tool of the right. More sophisticated commentators have examined the socio-political and ideological specificity within which Lyotard and Habermas (to name two exemplars of current debates) developed their ideas — in the French and German traditions respectively. Other commentators, including some feminists e.g. Nicholson and Frazer, Wolff, and some Third World intellectuals, have argued that postmodernism is the new radicalism,

181

with profound liberatory potential. I am not going to take up this argument here, except to note that *potentially* won't do much for us in our present crisis — and nothing about the fish.

What is undoubted is postmodernism's ability to take apart and critique all kinds of authorities and traditions — a useful enough starting point, and certainly some of the fractures it has created have been fruitfully exploited. But can it go further or must it always dwindle into the self-reflexive, narcissistic and hopeless posturing if urban based intellectuals, a 'newfangled form of textual mystification, helping to keep history and politics at bay' as Norris puts it (Norris, 1991:75)?

I return to the question I posed earlier. Are we, in Newfoundland, simply behind the postmodern times? Should we aspire to do more than simply gaze through the shop window of a postindustrial, consumer, knowledge-based, postmodern condition? Or are we, as women especially, simply living a different, and maybe ultimately, more hopeful history? I say 'hopeful' because Newfoundland women have not abandoned the reality of their existence. They may, momentarily, despair, but they know *how* survival is achieved, and why it is important. These elements have been absent from the postmodern enterprise as presently constituted.

The study of the lives of Newfoundland women is not at an end. Both the lives and the ways of studying them will change. But any future study of Newfoundland women must contain at least two elements. It must find ways of recognising the reality of those lives and the achievements embodied in them, and it must share and participate in the enduring ambition of Newfoundland women — to live in this difficult place with dignity and honour. We have much to learn from Newfoundland women, about the complexity of their lives and about their strategies. The relevance of their knowledge about how to survive in a harsh world has never been greater.

Notes

1. Some ideas, presented here, appeared in a different form in a paper 'Are some countries more post-modern than others: some thoughts from the margins', presented to the CSAA Annual Meeting, Charlottetown, 1991.

2. This problem is discussed in terms of Marxist theories in Chapter 2.

3. It is impossible to do justice to the enormous proliferation of feminist postmodern writing here. Much inspiration came from the work of French scholars, such as Irigaray, Kristeva and Cixous, especially in their writings on issues in psychoanalysis and linguistics. When their ideas reached the English speaking world, they also focused on these areas, e.g. Adams and Cowie, 1990; Ferguson, 1989. From there, it has spread to the fields of literary criticism, e.g. Radway, 1987; Greene and Kahn, 1985 and cultural studies, e.g. Coward, 1985; Wilson, 1990. The heartlands of postmodern feminist work is still in these fields, but its reach is now much wider, entering virtually all intellectual discussion. What is more important, from our perspective, is the way in which the centre of attention for all scholarly work has shifted from the socio-economic-historical paradigm of the 1970s to issues of culture, psyche and life-style. It is this that I find most exciting, but also most dangerous.

Bibliography

Abella, R. (1984), *Equality in Employment: Royal Commission Report*, Minister of Supplies and Services, Ottawa.

Acheson, J.M. (1981), 'Anthropology of Fishing', in *Annual Review of Anthropology*, Vol. 10, pp. 275-316.

Adams, P. and Cowie, E. (eds.) (1990), *The Woman in Question*, Verso, London.

Adamson, N., Briskin, L. and McPhail, M. (1988), *Feminists Organizing for Change: The Contemporary Women's Movement in Canada*, OUP, Toronto.

Alexander, D. (1977), *The Decay of Trade: an Economic History of the Salt Fish Trade*, ISER, St. John's.

Alexander, D. (1983), *Atlantic Canada and Confederation*, University of Toronto Press, Toronto.

Allatt, P., et al. (eds.) (1987), *Women and the Life Cycle*, Macmillan, London.

Andersen, R. (1978), 'The 'count' and the 'share': Offshore fishermen and changing incentives', in Preston, R.J. (ed.), *Canadian Ethnology*, 40, Ottawa.

Andersen, R. (ed.) (1979), *North Atlantic Maritime Cultures*, Mouton, The Hague.

Andersen, R. and Wadel, C. (eds.) (1972), *North Atlantic Fishermen*, ISER, St. John's.

Anderson, J. (1987), *Communication Research: Issues and Methods*, McGraw Hill, New York.

Anger, D., McGrath, C. and Pottle, S. (1986), *Women and Work in Newfoundland*, Background Report, Royal Commission on Employment and Unemployment, St. John's.

Antler, E. (1977), 'Women's Work in Newfoundland Fishing Families', *Atlantis*, 2 (2):106-113.

Antler, E. (1977b), 'Maritime Mode of Production, Domestic Mode of Production or Labour Process: An Examination of the Newfoundland and Labrador Inshore Fishery', Paper to NE Anthropological Association.

Antler, E. (1982), *Fisherman, Fisherwoman, Rural Proletariat: Capitalist Commodity Production in Newfoundland Fishery*, Ph.D. Thesis, Connecticut.

Apostle, R. and Barrett, G. (1992), *Emptying Their Nets*, University of Toronto Press, Toronto.

Armstrong, P. (1984), *Labour Pains: Women's Work in Crisis*, The Women's Press, Toronto.

Armstrong, P. (1988), 'Where have all the Nurses gone', *Healthsharing*, Summer.

Armstrong, P. and Armstrong, H. (1982), 'Beyond numbers: problems with quantitative data', in Kinnear and Mason (eds.), *Women and Work*, Proceedings of a Conference on Data Requirements, Ottawa.

Armstrong, P. and Armstrong, H. (1983), 'Beyond sexless class and classless sex: towards feminist Marxism', *Studies in Political Economy*, Vol. 10, Winter.

Armstrong, P. and Armstrong, H. (1984), *The Double Ghetto*, McClelland and Stewart, Toronto.

Armstrong, P. and Armstrong, H. (1990), *Theorizing Women's Work*, Garamond Press, Toronto.

Atkinson, P. (1990), *The Ethnographic Imagination*, Routledge, London.

Baker, M. (1988), *Aging in Canadian Society: A Survey*, McGraw-Hill Ryerson, Toronto.

Bannerji, M., et al. (eds.) (1991), *Unsettling Relations: The University as a Site of Feminist Struggles*, Women's Press, Toronto.

Barron, R.D. and Norris, B. (1976), 'Sexual Division and the Dual Labour Market', in Barker and Allen (eds.), *Dependence and Exploitation in Work and Marriage*, Longman, London.

Bauman, Z. (1991), 'A Sociological Theory of Postmodernity', *Thesis Eleven*, No. 29.

Beckett, E. (n.d.), 'Union and Bank Workers: Will the twain ever meet', *Labour Canada*, Women's Bureau, Ottawa.

Beechey, V. (1977), 'Some notes on female wage labour in capitalist production', *Capital and Class*, No. 3, Autumn.

Beechey, V. (1979), 'On Patriarchy', *Feminist Review*, No. 3.

Beechey, V. (1983), 'What's so special about women's employment? A review of some recent studies of women's paid work', *Feminist Review*, 15.

Beechey, V. (1985), 'Conceptualising part-time work', in Roberts, B., et al. (eds.), *New Approaches to Economic Life*.

185

Beechey, V. and Perkins, T. (1986), *A Matter of Hours: An Investigation of Women's Part-time Employment*, Polity Press, Cambridge.

Begin, M. (1988), *Medicare: Canada's Right to Health*, Optimum Publishing International, Ottawa.

Bennholdt-Thomsen, V. (1981), 'Subsistence Production and Extended Reproduction', in Young, K., et al. (eds.), *Of Marriage and the Market*.

Benoit, C. (1989), 'Traditional midwifery practice: the limits of occupational autonomy', *Canadian Review of Sociology and Anthropology*, 26:4.

Benoit, C. (1990), 'Mothering in a Newfoundland Community: 1900-1940', in Arnup, K., Levesque, E. and Roach-Pearson, R. (eds.), *Delivering Motherhood*.

Benoit, C. (1991), *Midwives in Passage: The Modernisation of Maternity Care*, ISER, St. John's.

Bertaux, D. (ed.) (1982), *Biography and Society*, Sage Publications, London.

Boserup, E. (1970), *Women's Role in Economic Development*, Allen and Unwin, London.

Boyne, R. and Rattansi, A. (eds.) (1990), *Postmodernism and Society*, Macmillan, London.

Bradbrook, P. (1980), 'The Telegraph and Female Telegraphists in Newfoundland', unpublished paper in Centre for Newfoundland Studies, St. John's.

Brox, O. (1969), *The Maintenance of Economic Dualism in Newfoundland*, ISER, St. John's.

Brox, O. (1972), *Newfoundland Fisheries in the Age of Industry*, ISER, St. John's.

Bruegel, I. (1979), 'Women as a reserve army of labour: a note on recent British experience', *Feminist Review*, No. 3.

Bruegel, I. (1983), 'Women's employment, legislation and the labour market', in Lewis, J. (ed.), *Women's Welfare: Women's Rights*, Croom Helm.

Brym, R.J. and Sacouman, R.J. (eds.) (1979), *Underdevelopment and Social Movements in Atlantic Canada*, New Hogtown Press, Toronto.

Bryman, A., Bytheway, B., Allatt, P. and Keil, T. (1988), *Rethinking the Life Cycle*, Macmillan, London.

Bulbrook, M.J.T. (1987), *Documentation of the Nature of Occupational Stress among Newfoundland and Labrador, Nurses' Union Membership*, Newfoundland and Labrador Nurse's Union, St. John's.

Bulmer, M. (ed.) (1977), *Sociological Research Methods*, Macmillan, London.

186

Butler, J. (1990), *Gender Trouble: Feminism and The Subversion of Identity*, Routledge, London.

Cain, M. and Finch, J. (1981),. 'Towards a rehabilitation of data', in Abrams, P., et al. (eds.), *Practice and Progress: British Sociology, 1950-1980*, Allen and Unwin, London.

Callincos, A. (1990), 'Reactionary Postmodernism', in Boyne, R. and Rattansi, A. (eds.).

Campbell, M. (1988), 'Management as 'Ruling': a class phenomenon in Nursing', *Studies in Political Economy*, 27, Autumn.

Canadian Advisory Council on the Status of Women. (1987), *Integration and Participation: Women's Work in the Home and in the Labour Force*, Ottawa: Canadian Advisory Council on the Status of Women.

Caplain, P. and Bujra, J. (1978), *Women United: Women Divided*, Tavistock, London.

Cell, G.T. (1972), *Newfoundland Discovered: English Attempts at Colonization, 1610-1630*, London.

Chiaramonte, L. (1970), *Craftsman-Client Contracts, Interpersonal Values in a Newfoundland Fishing Community*, ISER, St. John's.

Christiansen-Ruffman, L. (1982) 'Women's political culture and feminist political culture', paper presented to 10th World Congress of Sociology, Mexico.

Christiansen-Ruffman, L. (1984), 'Participation theory and the methodological construction of invisible women: Feminism's call for an appropriate methodology', unpublished paper.

Christiansen-Ruffman, L. (1985), 'Exploratory Research as Appropriate Methology', paper presented at CSAA meetings.

Christiansen-Ruffman, L. (1985b), "'Wealth re-examined'. Toward a feminist analysis of women's development projects: Canada and the Third World", paper presented to the Association of Women in Development, Washington.

Clifford, J. and Marcus, G. (eds.) (1980), *Writing Culture*, University of California Press, Berkeley.

Committee on Young Women's Issues. (1986), *Growing Up Female: A Study of Adolescent Women in Newfoundland and Labrador*, St. John's.

Community Resource Service (1984) Ltd. (1984), *Scoping Study of Family Life in Newfoundland and Labrador*, Family Life Institute, St. John's.

Connelly, P. (1983), 'On Marxism and Feminism', *Studies in Political Economy*, No. 12, Fall.

Connelly, P. and MacDonald, M. (1983), 'Women's work: domestic and wage labour in a Nova Scotia Community', *Studies in Political Economy*, 10, Winter.

Connelly, P. and MacDonald, M. (1985), 'Women and development: the more things change, the more they stay the same', paper presented to the Conference on Women and Offshore Oil, St. John's.

Courtney, G. (1982), *Isle of Sheppey Study. Technical Report*, Social and Community Planning Research, London.

Coward, R. (1985), *Female Desires*, Grove Press, New York.

CRIAW/ICREF. (1986), *Women's Involvement in Political Life*, CRIAW Papers 16/17, Ottawa.

Croll, E. (1978), *Feminism in China*, Routledge, London.

Crook, S. (1990), 'The End of Radical Social Theory? Notes on Radicalism, Modernism and Postmodernisn', in Boyne and Rattansi.

Cullum, L. (1993), '"Home-making Help-meet or Woman Wage Earner": The work of two women's Voluntary Organizations in Newfoundland ⅆ Labrador', paper presented at AASA Meetings, Antigonish, NS.

Dalley, G. (1988), *Ideologies of Caring*, London: Macmillan.

Davis, A. (1991), *Dire Straits: The Dilemmas of a Fishery*, ISER, St. John's.

Davis, D. (1980), *Women's Experiences of the Menopause in a Newfoundland Fishing Village*. Ph.D. Thesis, University of North Carolina.

Davis, D. (1983a), *Blood and Nerves: an Ethnographic Focus on Menopause*, ISER, St. John's.

Davis, D. (1983b), 'The family and social change in a Newfoundland outport', *Culture*, 3(1):19-32.

Davis, D. (1983c), 'Woman the Worrier: confronting feminist and biomedical archetypes of stress', *Women's Studies*, 10 (2):135-246.

Davis, D. (1990), 'The sexual division of leisure in a Southwest coast Newfoundland fishing village', paper presented at CSAA meetings, Victoria.

Davis, D. (1990b), 'Dependable to dangerous: changing gender ideologies in rural Newfoundland', paper prsented to C.A.S. Meetings, Calgary.

Davis, D. (1990c), 'There's nothing here for young folks, no more', paper presented to Future of Adult Life Conference, Netherlands.

Davis, D. (1992), 'Changing self-image: studying menopausal women in a Newfoundland fishing village', in Whitehead and Conaway (eds.), *Sex and Gender in Fieldwork*, University of Illinois Press, Urbana.

Davis, D.L. (1979), 'Social Structure, Sex Roles and Female Associations in a Newfoundland Fishing Village", CESCE Meetings, Banff, Alberta, February.

De Beauvoir, S. (1953), *The Second Sex*, Jonathan Cape, London.

de Vreis, P.J. and G. Macnab. (1983), 'Occupational multiplicity and the organization of petty commodity production in Cape Breton: a retrospect', paper presented to AASA meetings, Halifax.

Deere, C. (1976), 'Rural women's subsistence production in the capitalist periphery', *Review of Radical Political Economics*, 8:1, Spring.

Delphy, C. (1984), *Close to Home*, Hutchinson, London.

Denzin, N. (1970), *The Research Act*, Aldine, Chicago.

Derrida, J. (1978), *Eperons: Les Styles de Nietzche*, Flammarion, Paris.

Diack, L. (1964), *Labrador Nurse*, Victor Gollancz, London.

Dulude, L. (1988), 'Getting old: men in couples and women alone', in McLaren Tigar, A. (ed.), *Gender and Society*, Copp, Clark, Pitman, Toronto.

Edholm, F., et al. (1977), 'Conceptualizing Women', *Critique of Anthropology*, Vol. 3, Nos. 9 and 10.

Eichler, M. (1980), *The Double Standard: A Feminist Critique of Feminist Social Science*, Croom Helm, London.

Eichler, M. (1988), 'The relationship between sexist, non-sexist, woman-centred and feminist research', in McLaren, A. (ed.), *Gender and Society: Creating a Canadian Women's Sociology*, Copp, Clark, Pitman, Toronto.

Estelle-Smith, M. (ed.) (1977), *Those Who Live From the Sea: A Study in Maritime Anthropology*, West Publishing Co., St. Paul.

Evers, M. (1983), 'Elderly women and disadvantage: perceptions of daily life and support relationships' in Jerome, D. (ed.), *Aging in Modern Society*, Croom Helm, London.

Evers, M. (1985), 'The frail elderly woman: emergent questions in aging and women's health', in Lewin and Olesen (eds.), *Women, Health and Healing*.

Fairley, B. (1985), The struggle for capitalism in the fishing industry in Newfoundland', *Studies in Political Economy*, No. 17, Summer.

Fairley, B., Leys, C. and Sacouman, J. (eds.) (1990), *Restructuring and Resistance: Perspectives from Atlantic Canada*, Garamond, Toronto.

Faris, J.C. (1972), *Cat Harbour: A Newfoundland Fishing Settlement*, ISER, St. John's.

Felt, L. and Sinclair, P. (1992), 'Everyone does it: Unpaid work in a rural peripheral region', *Work, Employment and Society*, Vol. 6, No. 1.

Ferguson, A. (1989), *Blood at the Root*, Pandora Press, London.

Finch, J. (1983), *Married to the Job: Wives Incorporation in Men's Work*, Allen and Unwin, London.

Finch, J. (1988), 'Family obligations and the life course', in Bryman, A., Bytheway, B., Allatt, P. and Keil, T. (eds.), *Rethinking the Life Cycle*, Macmillan, London.

Finch, J. and Groves, D. (eds.) (1983), *A Labour of Love: Women, Work and Caring*, Routledge and Kegan Paul, London.

Firestone, M.M. (1978), *Brothers and Rivals: Patrilocality in Savage Cove*, ISER, St. John's.

Fonow, M. and Cook, J. (eds.) (1991), *Beyond Methodology: Feminist Scholarship as Lived Research*, Indiana University Press, Indianapolis.

Forestell, N. (1989), 'Times were Hard: the pattern of women's paid labour in St. John's between the two World Wars', *Labour/Le Travail*, 24.

Fox, B. (1988), 'Conceptualizing Patriarchy', *Canadian Review of Sociology and Anthropology*, 25:2, May.

Fox, B. (ed.) (1980), *Hidden in the Household: Women's Domestic Labour under Capitalism*, Women's Press, Toronto.

Frankenberg, R. (1966), *Communities in Britain*, Harmondsworth: Penguin.

Fraser, R. (1984), *In Search of a Past*, Verso, London.

Gallie, D. *The Social Change and Economic Life Initiative: An Overview*, ESRC, Working Paper 1.

Garmarnikow, E. (1978), 'Sexual division of labour: the case of nursing', in Kuhm, A. and Wolpe, A.M. (eds.), *Feminism and Materialism*, Routledge and Kegan Paul, London.

Gersuny, J. (1979), 'The Informal Economy', *Futures 1979*.

Government of Canada. (1980), *Women, Care and Caring*, CACSW, Ottawa.

Government of Canada. (1987), *Health and Social Support 1985*, Department of Housing, Family and Social Statistics Division, Ottawa.

Government of Canada. (1988), *Profiles on Home Care/Home Support Programme*, Department of Health and Welfare. Ottawa.

Government of Newfoundland and Labrador: Department of Health. (1988), *Report of the Advisory Committee on Nursing Workforce*, St. John's.

Graham, H. (1983), 'Caring: A labour of love', in Finch, J. and Groves, D. (eds.), *A Labour of Love*.

Graham, H. (1985), 'Providers, Negotiators and Mediators: Women as Hidden Carers', in Lewin and Olesen (eds.), *Women, Health and Healing*, Tavistock, London.

Grant-Head, C. (1976), *Eighteenth Century Newfoundland*, Toronto University Press, Toronto.

Greene, G. and Kalin, C. (eds.) (1985), *Making a Difference: Feminist Literary Criticism*, Methuen, London.

Guberman, N. (1989), 'The family, women and caring: who cares for the carers', *RFR*, Vol. 17, No. 2.

Gunderson, M. and Muszynski, L. (1990), *Women and Labour Market Poverty*, Canadian Advisory Council on the Status of Women, Ottawa.

Hanrahan, M. (1988), 'Living with the dead: Fishermen's licensing and unemployment programmes in Newfoundland', ISER Research Policy Paper No. 8.

Harevan, T. (1982), *Family time and industrial time*, Cambridge University Press, Cambridge.

Harvey, D. (1989), *The Condition of Postmodernity*, Blackwells, Oxford.

Heller, A.F. (1986), *Health and Home: Women as Health Guardians*, CACSW, Ottawa.

Hersom, N. and Smith, D. (1982), *Women and the Canadian Work Force*, SSHRC.

Hill, R. (1983), *The Meaning of Work and the Reality of Unemployment in the Newfoundland Context*, Community Services Council, St. John's.

Hiller, J. and Neary, P. (eds.) (1980), *Newfoundland in 19th and 20th century*, University of Toronto Press, Toronto.

House, D. (1986), *Building on Our Strengths*, Final Report of the Loyal Commission on Employment and Unemployment, St. John's.

Humphries, J. (1977), 'Class struggle and the persistence of the working class family', *Cambridge Journal of Economics*, 1:3.

Hussey, G. (1987), *Our Life on Lear's Room: Labrador*, Newfoundland Centre.

Ilcan, S. (1985), 'The social organization of the Nova Scotia secondary fishing industry', MA Thesis, Dalhousie University.

Iverson, N. and Matthews, R. (1968), *Communities in Decline*, ISER, St. John's.

Jones, A. (1985), 'Inscribing Femininity: French theories of the feminisive', in Green and Kahn (eds.), *Making a Difference: Feminist Literary Criticism*, Methuen, London.

Kaden, J. and McDaniel, S. (1988), 'Caregiving and care-receiving: a double bind for women in Canada's aging society', paper presented at CSAA, Windsor.

Kaluzynska, E. (1980), 'Wiping the floor with theory: a survey of writings in housework', *Feminist Review*, No. 6.

Kaplan, A. (ed.) (1988), *Postmodernism and its Discontents*, Verso, London.

Kealey, L. (1986), *Factors Affecting Women's Labour Force Participation*, background report, Royal Commission on Employment and Unemployment, St. John's.

Kinnear, M. and Mason, G. (1982), *Women and Work*, proceedings of a Conference on Data Requirements to Support Research into Women and the Canadian Economy.

Kirby, M. (1982), *Navigating Troubled Waters: A New Policy for the Atlantic Fisheries*, Report of the Task Force on Atlantic Fisheries, Ottawa.

Kirby, S. and McKenna, K. (1989), *Experience, Research, Social Change: Methods from the Margins*, Garamond Press, Toronto.

Kleiber, N. and Light L. (1978), *Caring for Ourselves*, University of British Columbia Press, Vancouver.

Klein, D. (1983), 'How to do what we want to do: thoughts about feminist methodology', in Bowles, G. and Klein, D. (eds.), *Theories of Women's Studies*, Routledge, London.

Lench, C. (1919), *The Story of Methodism in Bonavista and of the Settlements Visited by the Early Preachers*, Robinson and Co., St. John's.

Lewin, E. and Olesen, V. (eds.) (1985), *Women, Health and Healing*, Tavistock, London.

Lewis, J. and Meredith, B. (1988), *Daughters who Care: Daughters Caring for Mothers at Home*, Routledge and Kegan Paul, London.

Lovibond, S. (1990), 'Feminism and Postmodernism', in Boyne and Rattansi.

Luxton, M. (1980), *More Than a Labour of Love*, Women's Press.

MacInnes, D., Jentoft, S. and Davis, A. (eds.) (1991).

Mackintosh. (1977), 'Reproduction and Patriarchy', *Capital and Class*, No. 2, Summer.

Malos, E. (ed.) (1980), *The Politics of Housework*, Allison and Busby, London.

Mannion, J. (ed.) (1977), *The Peopling of Newfoundland*, ISER. St. John's.

Matthews, A. (1980), 'The Newfoundland migrant wife', in Murielgarb and Richardson (eds.), *People, Power and Process*.

McAllister, P. (ed.) (1982), *Reweaving the Web of Life: Feminism and Non-Violence*, New Society Publisher, Philadelphia.

McCall, G. and Simmons, J.L. (1969), *Issues in Participant Observation*, Addison-Wesley.

McCay, B. (1987), 'Old People and Social Relations in a Newfoundland 'Outport'', in Strange and Teitebaun (eds.), *Aging and Cultural Diversity*, South Hodley. Massachusetts.

McCay, B. (1988), 'Fish guts, hair nets and unemployment stamps: Women and work in cooperative fish plants', in Sinclair, P. (ed.), *A Question of Survival*.

Meillassaux, C. (1975), *Maidens, Meal and Money*, Cambridge University Press, Cambridge.

Miles, A. (1984), 'Feminism and women's community action: Antigonish town and country, 1970-83', unpublished.

Molyneux, M. (1979), 'Beyond the housework debate', *New Left Review*, No. 116.

Murray, H. (1979), *More than 50%: A Woman's Life in a Newfoundland Outport, 1900-1950*, Breakwater Books, St. John's.

Nadel-Klein, J. and Davis, D. (eds.) (1988), *To Work and to Weep: Women in Fishing Economies*, St. John's: ISER.

Neis, B. (1988), 'Doin' time on the protest line: Women's political culture, politics and collective action', in Sinclair, P. (ed.), *A Question of Survival*.

Neis, B. (1991), "'It's the patriarchy': women in the Newfoundland and Labrador fisheries", paper presented to CSAA, Charlottetown, PEI.

Neis, B. (1991), 'Flexible specialization: What's that got to do with the price of fish?', *Studies in Political Economy*, No. 36, Autumn.

Neis, B. (with Fisheries Research Group) (1986), *The Social Impact of Technological Change in Newfoundland Deepsea Fishery*, Report, Labour Canada, St. John's.

Neis, B. (with Williams, S.) (1992), *Occupational Stress and Repetitive Strain Injuries: Report*, ISER, St. John's.

Neis, B.L. (1984), 'Gus! It's time to surrender: women and resistance in Burin', paper presented to AASA meetings, Fredericton.

Nemec, T. (1971), 'I Fish with My Brother', in Andersen, R. (ed.), *North Atlantic Maritime Cultures*, Mouton, The Hague.

Nevitt, J. (1978), *White Caps and Black Bands*, Jesperson Press, St. John's.

Noel, S.J.R. (1971), *Politics in Newfoundland*, University of Toronto Press, Toronto.

NORDCO. (1981), *It Were Well to Live Mainly Off Fish*, Report, St. John's.

Norris, C. (1991), *Deconstruction Theory and Practice*, Routhledge, London.

Oakley, A. (1981), 'Interviewing women: a contradiction in terms', in Roberts, H. (ed.), *Doing Feminist Research*, Routledge, London.

Oldfield, S. (1984), *Spinsters of this Parish*, Virago, London.

Orbach, M (1977), *Hunters, Seamen and Entrepreneurs*, University of California Press, Berkeley.

Overton, J. (1979), *Towards a Critical Analysis of Neo-Nationalism in Newfoundland* in Bryce and Sacouman.

Pahl, R. (1984), *Divisions of Labour*, Blackwell, Oxford.

Panitch, L. (ed.) (1977), *The Canadian State: Political Economy and Political Power*, University of Toronto Press, Toronto.

Phillips, D. (1972), *'Knowledge from What?'*, Rand McNally, Chicago.

Pocius, G. (1979), 'Hooked rugs in Newfoundland', *Journal of American Folklore*, Vol. 92.

Pocius, G.L. (1979), *Textile Traditions of Eastern Newfoundland*, Canadian Centre for Folk Culture Studies Paper No. 29, National Museums of Canada, Ottawa.

Poland, F. and Stanley, L. (1988), 'Feminist Ethnography in Rochdale', *SSP*, No. 22, Manchester.

Porter, H. (1979), *Below the Bridge*, Harry Cuff, St. John's.

Porter, M.B. (1983), *Home, Work and Class Consciousness*, Manchester: Manchester University Press.

Porter, M.B. (1985), 'Women and old boats: The sexual division of labour in a Newfoundland outport', in Garmarnikow, E., et al. (ed.), *Public and Private: Gender and Society*, Heinemann and BSA, London.

Porter, M.B. (1985b), "'The Tangly Bunch': outport women of the Avalon Peninsula", *Newfoundland Studies*, No. 1.

Porter, M.B. (1986), 'She was skipper of the shore-crew': Notes on the history of the sexual division of labour in Newfoundland, *Labour/Le Travail*, 15.

Porter, M.B. (1987), 'Gender, the labour market and restructuring of household economic strategies in rural Newfoundland', in Byron, R. (ed.), *Public Policy and the Periphery: Problems and Perspectives in Marginal Regions*, ISSMR, Proceedings of the 9th International Seminar, Skye.

Porter, M.B. (1987), 'Peripheral Women: Towards a feminist analysis of the Atlantic region', *Studies in Political Economy*, No. 23, May.

Porter, M.B. (1987b), 'Patriarchal figures: getting to work on women and the economy in Newfoundland', paper presented at the 5th Social Sciences Conference, Havana.

Porter, M.B. (1988), 'Mothers and Daughters: Linking Women's Life Stories in Grand Bank, Newfoundland', *Women's Studies International Forum*, Vol. 11, No. 6.

Porter, M.B. (1988b), 'When the Margins Meet: Thoughts arising from women's economic lives in Newfoundland', paper presented to the conference on Political Economy of Margins, Toronto.

Porter, M.B. (1989), *Gender and Social Theory, Course Manual*, MUN, St. John's.

Porter, M.B. (1991), 'Time, the Life Course and Work in Women's Lives: Reflections from Newfoundland', *Women's Studies International Forum*.

Porter, M.B. (1992), 'Secondhand Ethnography: Some problems in analyzing a feminist project', in Burgess, R. and Bryman, A. (eds.), *Analyzing Qualitative Data*, Routledge, London.

Porter, M.B. (with Brown, B., Dettmar, E. and McGrath, C.) (1990), *Women's Economic Lives in Newfoundland: Three Case Studies: Final Report to SSHRC*, SSHRC, Ottawa.

Porter, M.B. and Pottle, S. (1987), *Women and the Economy in Newfoundland: A Cast Study of Catalina, Final Report*, Department of Career Development, Government of Newfoundland and Labrador, St. John's.

Radway, A. (1984), *Reading the Romance*, Verso, London.

Randall, V. (1982), *Women and Politics*, Macmillan, London.

Redclift, N. and Mingione, E. (1985), *Beyond Employment: Household Gender and Subsistence*, Blackwell, Oxford.

Roberts, Finnigan and Gallie (eds.) (1988), *New Approaches to Economic Life*, Manchester University Press.

Rogers, B. (1980), *The Domestication of Women*, Kogan Sage, London.

Rogers, S.C. (1978), 'Woman's Place: A Critical Review of Anthropological Theory', *Comparative Studies in Society and History*, 20, 123-62.

Rowbothan, S. (1972), *Women, Resistance and Revolution*, Allen Lane, London.

Rowe, A. (with Neis, B. and Williams, S.) (1991), *The Effect of the Crisis in the Newfoundland Fishery on Women who Work in the Industry*, Report to Women's Policy Office, St. John's.

Rowe, F.W. (1980), *A History of Newfoundland and Labrador*, McGraw-Hill, Toronto.

Rubery, J. (1978), 'Structured labour markets, order, organization and low pay', in *Cambridge Journal of Economics*, Vol. 2, 17-36.

Sacouman, R.J. (1980), 'Semi-proletarianization and rural underdevelopment in the Maritimes', *Canadian Review of Sociology and Anthropology*, 17:3.

Sinclair, P. (1985), *From Traps to Draggers*, ISER, St. John's.

Sinclair, P. (1991), 'Coping with scarcity: A critical analysis of fisheries management in the North Atlantic', in MacInnes, D., Jentoft, S. and Davis, A. (eds.), *Social Research and Public Policy Formation in the Fisheries*, Ocean Institute of Canada, Halifax.

Sinclair, P. (ed.) (1988), *A Question of Survival: The Fisheries and Newfoundland Society*, ISER, St. John's.

Sinclair, P. and Felt, L. (1989), 'Gender, Work and Household Reproduction: Married men and women in an isolated fishing region', paper presented to Canadian Association of Rural Studies, Quebec.

Sinclair, P. and Felt, L. (1991), 'Home Sweet Home!': Dimensions and determinants of life satisfaction in a marginal region', *Canadian Journal of Sociology*, Vol. 16, No. 1.

Sinclair, P. and Felt, L. (1992), 'Separate Worlds: Gender and domestic labour in an isolated fishing region', *Canadian Review of Sociology and Anthropology*, Vol. 29, pp. 55-71.

Sinclair, P. and Felt, L. (forthcoming), *Living on the Edge: The Great Northern Peninsula of Newfoundland*, ISER, St. John's.

Smith, D. (1987), *The Everyday World as Problematic: A Feminist Sociology*, Northeastern University Press, Boston.

Smith, D. (1990), *Texts, Fact and Femininity: Exploring the Relations of Ruling*, Routledge, London.

Smith, J., et al. (eds.) (1984), *Households and the World-Economy*, Sage, London.

Smith, M.E. (1977), *Those Who Live from the Sea*, New York.

Stacey, J. (1988), 'Can there be a feminist ethnography?', *Women's Studies International Forum*, Vol. 11, No. 1.

Stacey, M. (1988), *The Sociology of Health and Healing*, Unwin Hyman, London.

Stacey, M. and Price, M. (1981), *Women, Power and Politics*, Tavistock, London.

Stanley, L. (1990), *Feminist Praxis: Research, Theory and Epistemology in Feminist Sociology*, Routledge, London.

Stanley, L. and Wise, S. (1983), *Breaking Out: Feminist Consciousness and Feminist Research*, Routledge and Kegan Paul, London.

Steedman, C. (1986), *Landscape for a Good Woman*, Virago, London.

Strauss, A. and Corbin, T. (1990), *Basis of Qualitative Research: Grounded Theory Procedures and Techniques*, Sage, New York.

Straw, P. and Elliott, B. (1986), 'Hidden rhythms: Hidden powers. Women and time in working class culture', *Life Stories*, 2.

Summerfield, P. (1982), *Women Workers in the Second World War*, Croon Helm, London.

Szala, K.K. (1978), 'Clean women and quiet men: Courtship and marriage in a Newfoundland fishing village', MA Thesis, Memorial University of Newfoundland.

Szwed, J.F. (1966), *Private Cultures and Public Imagery; Interpersonal Relations in a Newfoundland Peasant Society*, ISER, St. John's.

Taylor, B. (1983), *Eve and the New Jerusalem*, Virago, London.

Thompson, D. (ed.) (1983), *Over our Dead Bodies: Women Against the Bomb*, Virago, London.

Thompson, E.P. (1967), 'Time, work-discipline and industrial capitalism, *Past and Present*, 38.

Thompson, P. (1978), *The Voice of the Past: Oral History*, Oxford University Press, Oxford.

Thompson, P. (1981), 'Life histories and the analysis of social change, in Bertaux, D. (ed.), *Biography and Society*, Sage Publications, London.

Thompson, P. (1983), *Living the fishing*, Routledge and Kegan Paul, London.

Tilly, L.T. and Scott, J.W. (1978), *Women, Work and Family*, Holt, Rinehart and Winston, New York.

Tunstan, J. (1962), *The Fishermen*, MacGibbon and Kee, London.

Turner, D. (1986), 'The Wages of Virtue', *New Left Review*, No. 189, September/October.

Ungerson, C. (1983), 'Why do Women Care?', in Finch and Groves (eds.), *A Labour of Love*, Routledge and Kegan Paul, London.

Vanek, J. (1973), 'Keeping busy: Time spent in housework, USA, 1920-1970', unpublished doctoral dissertation, University of Michigan.

Veltmeyer, H. (1979), 'The Capitalist Underdevelopment of Atlantic Canada', in Byron and Sacouman (eds.).

Wadel, C. (1969), *Marginal Adaptation and Modernization in Newfoundland*, ISER, St. John's.

Wadel, C. (1973), *Now Whose Fault is That*, ISER, St. John's.

Walby, S. (1986), *Patriarchy at Work*, Polity Press. Cambridge.

Walby, S. (1989), *Theorizing Patriarchy*, Polity Press, Cambridge.

Waring, M. (1988), *If Women Counted*, Harper Collins, San Francisco.

Weedon, C. (1987), *Feminist Practice and Post-structuralist Theory*, Blackwell, London.

West, J. (1978), 'Women, Sex and Class', in Kuhn, A. and Wolpe, A.M. (eds.), *Feminism and Materialism*, Tavistock, London.

White, J. (1983), *Women and Part-Time Work*, Canadian Advisory Council on the Status of Women.

Williams, R. (1976), *Keywords*, Fontana, London.

Williams, W. (1988), *Women's Health Issues*, Women's Policy Office. St. John's.

Willis, J. (1991), *A Place in the Sun: Shetland and Oil, Rights and Realities*, ISER, St. John's.

Wilson, E. (1985), *Adorned in Dreams*, Virago, London.

Wilson, E. (1990), 'These New Components of the Spectacle: Fashion and Postmodernism', in Boyne and Rattansi.

Wilson, E. (1991), *The Sphinx in the City*, Virago, London.

Wilson, W. (1966), *Newfoundland and its Missionaries*, Massachusetts: Dakin and Metcalfe, Cambridge.

Wright, G. (1984), *Sons and Seals*, ISER, St. John's.

Zulaika, J. (1981), *Terra Nova: The Ethos and Luck of Deepsea Fishermen*, ISER, St. John's.